"How can there still be things to learn about Jackie Kennedy, one of the world's most scrutinized women? Paul Brandus manages to do that by exploring the five years between the death of John F. Kennedy and her marriage to Aristotle Onassis, an event that shocked many who revered her. This dishy, insidery account explains what was happening behind the scenes."

—SUSAN PAGE, Washington Bureau Chief
of *USA Today*, and author of *The Matriarch:
Barbara Bush and the Making of an American Dynasty*

"Jackie Kennedy was the most private of public figures, yet Paul Brandus has managed to paint a full portrait of his fascinating subject through her most painful years, 1963 to 1968. Widowed at age thirty-four by an assassin's bullets, Jacqueline Bouvier Kennedy helped a nation mourn the loss of its popular young president with enormous strength and class. But Jackie was now alone and shattered; she had to make a new life for herself and her children when Americans and the rest of the world wanted her to hold onto the past. Beautifully written, powerful, and deeply moving, this book traces Jackie's evolution from a grief-stricken First Lady to the wife of one of the world's wealthiest men, Aristotle Onassis. It's a wrenching journey you will understand much better after reading this marvelous volume."

—LARRY SABATO, Director of University of
Virginia's Center for Politics, and author of the
New York Times bestseller *The Kennedy Half-Century*

Jackie

HER TRANSFORMATION FROM FIRST LADY TO JACKIE O

PAUL BRANDUS

Post Hill
PRESS

A POST HILL PRESS BOOK

Jackie:
Her Transformation from First Lady to Jackie O
© 2020 by Paul Brandus
All Rights Reserved

ISBN: 978-1-64293-345-1
ISBN (eBook): 978-1-64293-346-8

Cover art by Cody Corcoran
Interior design and composition by Greg Johnson, Textbook Perfect

Post Hill Press
New York • Nashville
posthillpress.com

Published in the United States of America

To Kathryn, Julia, Rosemary, and Eugene.
Love always and forever.

Contents

Prologue

When Jacqueline Kennedy married Aristotle Onassis on Skorpios, his tiny island retreat in the Ionian Sea off the western coast of Greece, the world was stunned. The headlines were vicious and full of betrayal:

"The Reaction Here Is Anger, Shock and Dismay," said the *New York Times*.

"Jackie Sells Out!" cried the *Los Angeles Times*.

"Jackie, How Could You?" asked a Stockholm paper.

"Jackie Weds Blank Check," sneered a Fleet Street tabloid.

And, perhaps worst of all, Rome's *Il Messaggero*: "JFK Dies a Second Time."

It was October 1968. Not five years since the assassination of her first husband, President John F. Kennedy, and barely four months since her brother-in-law Robert F. Kennedy was himself gunned down in Los Angeles, moments after winning California's Democratic presidential primary.

Both murders shocked America and devastated Jackie to the core. The first robbed her of one husband; the second drove her into the arms of another. This book examines Jackie's life during the five-year period in between, bookended by her marriages to two of the richest and most powerful men in the world.

Jackie

To the casual observer, John F. Kennedy and Aristotle Onassis were polar opposites. The former was tall, sophisticated, and charming. His movie star looks and quick wit made women swoon. The latter was short and squat, "had the face of a gangster,"[1] and sometimes came off as greedy and abrasive. Such generalizations were not without merit, yet beneath the surface both men were, in key respects, more similar than different. They were wealthy, hypercompetitive, power-hungry womanizers who stopped at nothing to get whatever—and whomever—they desired. Kennedy, the Pulitzer Prize-winning author who delivered some of the twentieth century's most soaring speeches, could be—and often was—crude and vulgar in private. Onassis was often seen as having almost thuggish characteristics, as a selfish and narcissistic interloper who didn't belong. Yet the Greek tycoon was also—and critically, was seen by Jackie as—charming and gregarious, and not just in his native Greek and English, but in French and Spanish, languages in which she was also fluent. And friends, particularly women, considered him the perfect listener. Thus, where some saw a rough, unpolished, and physically unattractive man, Jackie saw a man of culture, a lover of music and poetry. Aristotle Onassis may have been a sharp-elbowed, corner-cutting wheeler-dealer, but Jackie—whose father and father-in-law had harbored similar traits—was used to, and tolerant of, such behavior. Onassis also afforded her something she desperately sought in the wake of Robert Kennedy's murder: security.

Despite all this, the news that Jackie would wed Ari was still a great shock. In retrospect, it should not have been. After all, she had known him almost as long as she had known John F. Kennedy himself. They first met not in the 1960s, as is often believed, but at a Georgetown neighborhood dinner party in the 1950s, when JFK was merely the junior senator from Massachusetts. They spoke briefly and casually, but it was enough, and a year later, when the Kennedys were visiting Jack's parents on the French Riviera, Onassis—who by then owned much of Monaco—learned of their presence and invited them aboard the *Christina*, his ostentatious 325-foot yacht that he kept docked at Monte Carlo.[2]

JFK was thrilled to meet another Onassis guest that day: Winston Churchill, a personal hero. As the two of them reminisced—JFK's father, Joseph P. Kennedy, had been ambassador to the Court of Saint James from 1937 to 1941, as World War II was beginning and Churchill became prime minister—Ari gave Jackie a private tour of his ship. Jackie found parts of it, such as the murals of naked women that had been painted on the walls of the dining salon, to be gaudy, even vulgar. Yet wanting to be diplomatic to her host, she held back. "Mr. Onassis, I have fallen in love with your ship," she gushed. As for any personal attraction, she gave "no outward signs" of it at the time,[3] though it seems hardly unreasonable to surmise that the *Christina's* sheer opulence, the world-famous company onboard, and the glittery port they were in gave Jackie a warm impression of her host. What is undeniable, however, is that beyond conversing in French, Jackie, clad in a simple yet elegant above-the-knee white A-line dress, made a very good impression upon Ari. "There's something damned willful about her," he later told his friend and aide Costa Gratsos. "There's something provocative about that lady. She's got a carnal soul."[4]

Ari was also there for Jackie when it counted most: in her *annus horribilis* (horrible year), 1963, when she lost, in the space of three and a half months, a son and her husband—the father of her two surviving children.

The son who died, Patrick Bouvier Kennedy, was born on August 7, five weeks early, with what today is known as respiratory distress syndrome. The infant lived just thirty-nine hours. His death—the second child the Kennedys had lost in their decade-long marriage—shattered JFK and Jackie, drawing them closer, observers said, than they had been in years. Terribly depressed, Jackie retreated from public view, recuperating at Hyannis (on Massachusetts's Cape Cod) and nearby Squaw Island, where she was joined by her sister Lee Radziwill.

It was Lee who opened the door to a renewed, and deeper, connection between Jackie and Ari. Here, the story grows tangled and somewhat soap opera-ish.

Nearly four years younger than Jackie, Lee was living a scandalous life. Married to a Polish prince, Stanislaw ("Stas") Albrecht Radziwill, she nevertheless began dating Onassis after they met at a London party in 1961. Onassis, meanwhile, was involved with the famed opera singer Maria Callas. Naturally, Lee and Ari's gallivanting about town, and cruises on the *Christina*, were fodder for the Fleet Street gossip columnists.

Two years later, they were still an item, and when Lee joined Jackie on Squaw Island she passed along an invitation from Onassis: Why not come to Greece? A pleasure cruise would, the tycoon suggested, help Jackie recover from the loss of her son. He said the *Christina* and its crew would be at her full disposal, and that he and Lee would keep her company.[5]

Jackie was intrigued. She had visited Greece for the first time in June 1961, at the end of President Kennedy's trip to Paris, Vienna, and London. She'd spent eight days there, sailing, shopping, and sightseeing; she fell in love with Greece—its history, architecture, and lively culture—and vowed to return.

But an invitation from Onassis? That might be problematic. Not because of Jackie, but because of her husband. Just before the Kennedys were to leave on their 1961 trip, the president had called Clint Hill, Jackie's principal Secret Service agent, into the Oval Office. Hill had never been summoned to the Oval before, and when he entered, found Attorney General Robert Kennedy there as well.

It was a short conversation. Kennedy said he had learned that Hill would be doing the advance work for his wife's trip. He looked at his brother and then back at Hill.

"The attorney general and I want to make one thing clear…and that is, whatever you do in Greece, do not let Mrs. Kennedy cross paths with Aristotle Onassis."

"Yes, sir, Mr. President."

"Okay then," JFK replied. "Have a great trip."[6]

The Kennedys were leery of Onassis, who had been on the federal government's radar for years. In the 1950s, he was indicted on fraud and conspiracy charges in connection with the purchase of surplus ships from World War II. The charges were eventually dropped, but Onassis was fined seven million dollars.[7] Hill knew none of this at the time, but he and Jackie's other agents on the Greek trip made sure that Onassis didn't come anywhere near the First Lady.

Now, in the fall of 1963, Onassis's invitation presented President Kennedy with a dilemma. He was concerned about Jackie's health, and wanted her to get some rest. But his antipathy toward the shadowy Onassis had hardly dissipated, and with what he expected would be a tough reelection fight coming up in 1964, he fretted about the political imagery of his wife's taking a ritzy European cruise with Onassis. Robert Kennedy and the president's top political lieutenant, Kenny O'Donnell, warned it might become an election issue. In the end, the president decided to allow it, saying it would be "good for her."[8] Any political consequences, should they arise, could be dealt with later.

Jackie was certainly aware of her husband's reservations. "I don't want a lot of publicity," she told Hill, "but I suppose everyone will find out."

"Yes," Hill replied, "I'm sure the word will get out and there will be a great deal of interest."[9] On October 1, skipping a state dinner for Ethiopian emperor Haile Selassie, Jackie quietly departed.

Remembering President Kennedy's 1961 admonition about Onassis, Hill cringed as the "oily" Greek tycoon welcomed Jackie aboard the *Christina* with a kiss on each cheek. *This is the man President Kennedy had told me—in no uncertain terms—to make sure Mrs. Kennedy did not meet in 1961,* he thought. *Now, here she is being greeted by* him *on his yacht as* his *guest. Did I misunderstand something?*[10]

Just like everyone whom Onassis invited onto his floating palace— an antisubmarine frigate bought for scrap at a 1952 auction—Jackie was dazzled by the ship, which had been painstakingly turned into a glittering reflection of its new owner's self-indulgence. The actor Richard Burton, who on another occasion stayed on the ship with Elizabeth Taylor, summarized the experience in one sentence: "I don't think there is a man or woman on earth," he said, "who would not be seduced by the pure narcissism shamelessly flaunted on this boat."[11]

Fears the Kennedy brothers and O'Donnell had were quickly justified. Even though the First Lady was recuperating from a terrible blow, criticism of her Greek jaunt was intense. Newspapers played up the "brilliantly lighted luxury yacht," "gay with guests, good food and drinks," "lavish shipboard dinners," "dancing music," "a crew of sixty, two coiffeurs and a dance band." Photos of Jackie strolling down the streets of Smyrna (now Izmir), Turkey, with a solicitous Onassis weren't helpful either. President Kennedy had sent undersecretary of commerce Franklin D. Roosevelt Jr. and his wife, Suzanne, along as escorts, but this only led to further attacks about Onassis's trying to influence Roosevelt to smooth out legal problems the shipping magnate was having with the U.S. Marine Commission and Robert Kennedy's Justice Department.[12] One Republican congressman from Ohio, Oliver Bolton, even took to the House floor to attack the First Lady, saying the trip reflected poorly on the judgment of the president. President Kennedy was so concerned that he telephoned Jackie "on a number of occasions" in an attempt to persuade her to cut the trip short. Jackie, having a marvelous time, declined.[13]

Much has been written over the years about a rivalry between Lee and her older sister for Onassis's attention, including allegations that the tycoon and the First Lady slept together on the trip, but Suzanne Roosevelt insists they did not. "He [Onassis] wasn't especially paying attention [to Jackie]. He was a very good host, he wasn't courting her." She adds that, to her knowledge, the two had never gone off together privately: "The only time that Ari went off with anybody that I knew was with me and Franklin."[14]

Even so, it seems clear that Onassis and Jackie, seeing each other for the first time in years, began to develop feelings for each other. Their initial formality melted away under the Greek sun, as they began conversing in English, Spanish, and French, sometimes sitting on the deck of the ship talking until dawn. Jackie was fascinated by Onassis's gregariousness and zest for life, his "energy, his charisma in a ruthless pursuit of her, his earthiness, his intelligent attention to detail and most of all, his ostentatious romancing."[15] As for Onassis, this was certainly not the Jackie he remembered from the 1950s, when she was the mere wife of a boyish politician. The influence she now possessed and her fame—which exceeded his own—were powerful lures. She seemed even more striking, more mature, possessing a regal bearing. She was engaging yet enigmatic, interested yet ever so imperious. And the fact that she was ostensibly unavailable only added to her allure. For a man used to having anything and anyone he wanted, Onassis felt an attraction to her that was, at its most basic level, quite carnal. "I'm going to get her," he was overheard saying. At the end of the weeklong trip, all of the women on the trip were given gifts, with Jackie getting the most extravagant present: a ruby choker.[16] Jackie would later send Onassis an engraved silver cigarette box from Tiffany's.[17]

By the time Jackie returned to the White House on October 17 (after a stop in Morocco to visit King Hassan), President Kennedy had paid a political price in acquiescing to her lavish vacation. His journalist friend and former Georgetown neighbor Ben Bradlee wrote in 1975's *Conversations with Kennedy* (a book that severed his friendship with Jackie) that the president had decided that Onassis should not visit the United States until after the 1964 election.[18]

In fact, the president now felt emboldened to ask his wife for a favor: would she accompany him on a campaign swing through Texas in late November? Even with Texan Lyndon Johnson as his running mate, Kennedy had barely carried the Lone Star State in 1960—the winning margin was a mere 46,257 votes—and its twenty-five electoral votes would be crucial in 1964. Jackie's presence, JFK judged, would be helpful.

"I'll campaign with you anywhere you want," Jackie said. She opened her red leather appointment book and scribbled "Texas" across November 21, 22, and 23.[19]

The announcement that Jackie would make the trip was big news. Jackie had never been to Texas before; in fact, she hadn't ventured west of the Kennedys' Middleburg, Virginia, home since the 1960 election. Now, for the first time, she would make a whirlwind trip through

San Antonio, Houston, and—on Friday, November 22—Fort Worth, Dallas, and Austin.

And so, the fact that Jacqueline Kennedy was beside her husband in Dallas, on Elm Street, in the back of that Lincoln Continental on November 22 when he was assassinated can be linked to her vacation, the month before, with Aristotle Onassis. She was there because of what the president called "Jackie's guilt feelings," and the fact that he could occasionally work them to his advantage.[20]

Yet even as Kennedy pressed his wife to join him in Texas, he was jittery about it, and feared that she would later regret going.[21] The one leg of the trip that concerned him most was Dallas, a city that disliked him intensely. He had lost "Big D" by sixty thousand votes in 1960; "Dallas just murdered us," Texas governor John Connally told him in a November 7, 1962, call, a year before both of them were shot there. Kennedy's reply: "I don't know why we do anything for Dallas."[22]

When Kennedy was killed, Onassis was in Hamburg, Germany, overseeing construction of a new tanker for his shipping fleet. Deeply shaken, he called Lee Radziwiłł, who asked him to accompany her and Prince Radziwiłł to Washington for the funeral. He soon got a call from Angier Biddle Duke, the State Department's chief of protocol, inviting him to stay at the White House.[23]

Thus Aristotle Onassis, who so worried John F. Kennedy that Kennedy wanted him barred from the United States until after the 1964 election, slept in the president's own home during the weekend of his murder—the special guest of the widow. It instantly elevated Onassis, making it abundantly clear that the ruthless tycoon had succeeded in positioning himself right where he wanted to be—close to Jackie. He indulged her that weekend as he had the month before on the *Christina*, listening to her, empathizing in her hour of maximum need. And he made sure to get along with the rest of the Kennedy family. This excerpt is from William Manchester's book *The Death of a President*:

Rose Kennedy dined upstairs with Stas Radziwill; Jacqueline Kennedy, her sister, and Robert Kennedy were served in their sitting room. The rest of the Kennedys ate in the family dining room with their house guests, McNamara, Phyllis Dillon, David Powers and Aristotle Socrates Onassis, the shipowner who provided comic relief, of sorts. They badgered him mercilessly about his yacht and his Man of Mystery aura. During coffee, the Attorney General (Bobby) came down and drew up a formal document stipulating that Onassis give half his wealth to help the poor in Latin America. It was preposterous (and obviously unenforceable) and the Greek millionaire signed it in Greek.[24]

Onassis's presence in the White House, in that darkest of moments, can be seen as a foreshadowing of what was to come. Over the next five years, there would be numerous other men in Jackie's life. Most were mere social escorts. However, there would be romances, some more serious than others. But always lurking in the shadows was Aristotle Onassis. He kept such a low profile as he bided his time that he referred to himself as "the invisible man."[25] But to Jackie, he was anything but. Years before they wed, she defined him perfectly: "A strange man," she observed. "Such a rogue, but also so understanding. I was fascinated by him from the beginning."

Chapter One

November 1963 to June 1964:
The Long, Dark Winter

Barely one hundred hours a widow, and twenty-four since she had buried her husband before the eyes of a disbelieving world. Yet here she was, smiling and gracious, serving tea to her successor. And Jacqueline Kennedy, said the new First Lady of the United States, Lady Bird Johnson, was "orderly, composed, and radiating her particular sort of aliveness and warmth." But Lady Bird also got a close-up view of what the world had just seen: "an element of steel and stamina somewhere within her to keep her going on as she is."[1]

As they sat in the West Sitting Hall, beneath the elegant half-moon window that overlooks the West Wing, Jackie asked a favor. Would it be alright, she asked in her soft voice, if Caroline's kindergarten and first-grade schoolmates could continue to hold class on the third floor? Just until Christmas, she quickly added. In 1964 she would make other plans, but disrupting everyone during the holidays might be too unsettling. "The way she asked this," Lady Bird says, "if it had been a request to chop off one's right hand one would have said 'Sure,' just that minute." It was "an easy, most delightful thing to say 'Yes' to."[2]

Occasionally, there were small signs that Jackie hadn't quite come to grips with the cruel reality that her husband was gone. "Jack never likes those rich things that René does," she said—using the present tense as she described the creations of White House chef René Verdon.[3]

Lady Bird didn't know if Jackie's use of the wrong tense was just a slip of the tongue or, perhaps, some sort of defense mechanism. She did know, as Jackie escorted her into the Yellow Room, that the widow was more than cognizant of the past. There, on a table, stood two glaring reminders of it: the black boots that had been placed in the riderless horse's stirrups during the prior day's funeral procession, and the neatly folded flag that had covered the slain president's coffin.[4]

Thanksgiving, Jackie's first holiday as a widow, was two days later. It was also the first time since Friday's horror that she was without her rock—Robert—to lean on. He had taken his family to Florida instead, deciding that Hyannis and all its memories were too much to bear.

Jackie had intended to fly to the Cape on the *Caroline*, the family plane, with in-laws Edward Kennedy, Eunice Kennedy Shriver, Jean Kennedy Smith, and Patricia Kennedy Lawford, and their spouses and children. But she decided to visit Arlington again, and flew up later, accompanied by sister Lee and brother-in-law Stas Radziwiłł.

Arriving at the family compound, she went to the famous beachfront home on Marchant Avenue where her in-laws lived. Rose Kennedy had traveled to Washington for her son's funeral, but Joseph P. Kennedy, the seventy-five-year old family patriarch, had suffered a paralyzing stroke in 1961 and was unable to attend. Jackie went upstairs to his bedroom. Perched on a low stool beside his bed and caressing his wrinkled hand, she quietly told him the entire story of the assassination. Jack was the third of old Joe Kennedy's children to die violently; there would be a fourth, and nearly a fifth.

Up until this point, Jackie's telling and retelling of her grisly story had been for a small audience of family and friends. But on Friday, one week to the day after Dallas, she decided that the nation had to hear as well. She summoned *Life* magazine's Theodore White, chosen not so much because of his immense journalistic talent but because he was a "friendly," a trusted scribe who had gotten along well with—and, more important, had written well of—the Kennedys in the past. In a monstrous storm—"either an old fashioned northeaster or a full-fledged hurricane"—that made flying impossible, White hired a car and driver and raced from New York to the Cape. He went to Jackie despite the fact that his mother had just suffered a heart attack.

As White shook off the cold rain upon entering, his first observation of Jackie echoed Lady Bird Johnson's earlier in the week. He was struck by her remarkable demeanor: "…composure…beautiful…dressed in black trim slacks, beige pullover sweater…eyes wider than pools…calm voice." Family and friends who had been with Jackie left the room at her request so she and White could be alone.[5]

On the chaotic afternoon of the killing, White had dashed down from New York, eventually making his way that evening to Bethesda Naval Hospital, where he saw Jackie "for a moment, still bloodstained, and so numb of expression I could not bring myself to speak to her."[6] Now, as the storm lashed Hyannis, rain pounding ceaselessly on the roof, he spoke with her—or mostly listened—as she again told the tale. The killing in the bright noon sun, "his blood, his brains are all over me." The frantic race to Parkland Memorial Hospital. Placing her bloody wedding ring on his pinkie, the body placed in what she called the "long, long, coffin."[7] Scribbling furiously on a yellow pad, White was struck by how the widow remained "without tears; drained, white of face." He was stunned by her total recall and clarity, as she had what would, years later, be dubbed "an involuntary rush of agonized flashbacks."[8] He strained to listen as she spoke "so softly in the particular whispering intimacy of Jacqueline Kennedy's voice." The rain continued to pour.

White had a tape recorder with him but curiously chose not to use it. It was a lapse that would bedevil future historians. The following spring, William Manchester would record his lengthy interviews with Jackie for *The Death of a President*—arguably still the definitive book on the assassination—but those tapes are sealed until 2067. But a recording of Jackie, exactly a week after the shooting, would have been priceless. "A talk with Mary Todd Lincoln a week after Lincoln's assassination would not have been nearly as compelling, for Jacqueline Kennedy was a superior wife, a superior person and wise."[9],[*]

In her initial call to White, Jackie told him of her displeasure that other journalists were already writing assessments of John F. Kennedy's presidency. Her fear: that Jack would not be seen in what she regarded as the proper light. "She wanted me to rescue Jack from all these 'bitter people,'" White says. She was determined to wrest control of her husband's legacy from them.[10]

In one sense, Jackie's emphasis on using words and writers to shape the counters of her husband's legacy was ironic. His had been a visual presidency after all, the first true one, and the seventy-two hours that elapsed between his murder and burial were a watershed moment in the shifting of American culture to one that forever cemented the dominance of television.

Like radio thirty years before in the Roosevelt era, the television had become the new hearth around which Americans gathered. John F. Kennedy understood this better than most men of his era; it took his own slaying and the coverage that followed to make this abundantly clear to others. When people today think of the Kennedy presidency, they invariably think not so much of the first 1,035 days of his presidency, but the 1,036th and final one—and the overwhelming, indelible imagery that was burned into the national psyche that weekend, choreographed flawlessly and nearly single-handedly by Jackie herself.

The thirty-four-year-old widow was of the television generation herself and knew of its vast power. On February 14, 1962, she had guided CBS reporter Charles Collingwood on a tour of the mansion after her

---

[*] Mary Todd Lincoln, by contrast, was emotionally erratic and prone to hysteria. Ten years after her husband's murder, she was involuntarily institutionalized for psychiatric disorders. Beyond this glaring difference, she had much in common with Jacqueline Kennedy: she was well polished, with particular interests in French, literature, and the arts. Mrs. Lincoln suffered the loss of three children, one while she was First Lady. And, like Jackie, Mrs. Lincoln was by her husband's side when he was assassinated. After killing Lincoln in a theater on a Friday, assassin John Wilkes Booth fled to a warehouse (a barn). Lee Harvey Oswald shot Kennedy from a warehouse and fled to a theater. Both murdered presidents were succeeded by Southerners named Johnson.

yearlong, top-to-bottom restoration of it. A staggering eighty million Americans—about two-fifths of the nation's population—watched that tour.* The three days of nonstop funeral coverage garnered an audience even bigger than that—in fact, far bigger, because it was a global event. Between one p.m. on November 24, when she appeared on the North Portico clutching the hands of her children, and 3:15 p.m. the next day, when she departed Arlington National Cemetery holding the flag from her husband's coffin, more eyes were cast upon her, it can be argued, than on any human being in history up to that time. The poise, class, and composure that she conveyed over that twenty-four-hour period, under the most stressful circumstances imaginable, said as much about the man in the mahogany box as it did about the woman who walked behind it. Which was her implicit objective—to burnish the aura of her dead husband. Find out how Lincoln was buried, she instructed aides hours after the killing.

Through the pageantry of his mourning, Jacqueline Kennedy had already elevated John F. Kennedy, transforming him into an almost mythical figure. And yet here she was, four days later, in a quiet room on a cold, wet night, talking with one man about how the world should remember him. But Jackie, thinking ahead through her grief, was right: words still mattered. Furthermore, by carefully selecting and limiting her words, she could guide and better control perceptions of her husband long into the future. And limit those words she did. In addition to her conversation with White on November 29, 1963, Jackie would speak publicly of John F. Kennedy just three more times in her life: Between March 2 and June 3, 1964, she gave a series of interviews to historian Arthur Schlesinger, another "friendly" who was on the Kennedy payroll as special assistant to the president. Their conversations overlapped with a series of interviews (May 4 to July 20, 1964) that she

---

* It was, CBS executives gushed, "the greatest sight-seeing trip in history," for which was given an honorary Emmy award. But CBS president Blair Clark said, "We had to amplify her voice so people could understand what she was saying." And to put Jackie's 1962 audience in further perspective, the two-fifths of the nation's population that tuned in for her White House tour far exceeded the one-third of Americans who routinely watch the Super Bowl each winter.

gave Manchester.* And on June 5, 1964, she spoke with members of the Warren Commission who were investigating the president's murder. Her testimony, commission records show, lasted about ten minutes. Jackie, who died in 1994, never wrote a memoir, never kept a diary, and—with one exception—remained largely silent about her first husband for the final three decades of her life. "I want to live my life, not record it," she said in 1981.†

The interviews she gave between November 1963 and July 1964 obviously carry tremendous weight—they are, after all, all we have. The Schlesinger conversations dealt with John F. Kennedy's life from childhood to White House: what he was like, what he read as a boy, his rise to power, and such. There is an air of deference in Schlesinger as he sits with Jackie. His adoration of her, particularly when the shock of the assassination was still fresh, is understandable. But the conversations, read more than half a century later, come off as somewhat glossy; uncomfortable and/or embarrassing subjects are avoided. The overall scarcity of material in Jackie's own words means that the Schlesinger chats are useful; they add context to the Kennedy narrative. But tapes and transcripts weren't released to the public until 2011—long after basic impressions about the president had been ingrained in the minds of most Americans.

Manchester had a narrower and far more intense focus: the five days spanning the assassination and related events, from the White House to Texas to Arlington. Jackie's Warren Commission testimony, just ten minutes long, was a subset of Manchester's, dealing with the presence of SS100X—the presidential limousine—on Elm Street and her recollections about the shooting.

---

* Manchester had first met Jackie on April 7, but she was not ready to talk, so he left.

† That one exception was a thirty-five-minute interview she granted Terry L. Birdwhistell on June 13, 1981. Birdwhistell, a scholar and an official at the University of Kentucky, was then the director of the Louie B. Nunn Center for Oral History. It was in this capacity that he found himself sitting nervously with Jackie in her apartment to discuss President Kennedy's friendship with John Sherman Cooper, who served with JFK in the Senate and was later on the Warren Commission. Her "I want to live my life, not record it" comment was made during that interview, but the bulk of her chat with Birdwhistell focused on Cooper and is not relevant here.

Jackie

Therefore, it is the White conversation, for our purposes here, that is most revealing of all. Other than the funeral itself, it was Jackie's first effort to shape her husband's legacy. It also foreshadowed the fierce battles that she would undertake to protect it—notably her ugly row with Manchester himself, which would spill out into the public.

After Jackie "rid herself of the blood scene," as White calls it, she pivoted to what seemed the real objective of her conversation with the *Life* reporter.

"There's this one thing I wanted to say…" she began. "It's been almost an obsession with me, all I keep thinking of is this line from a musical comedy." She repeated how she was obsessed with it.

"At night before we'd go to sleep…we had an old Victrola. Jack liked to play some records. His back hurt, the floor was so cold. I'd get out of bed and play it for him…and the song he loved most came at the very end of this record, the last side of *Camelot*, sad *Camelot*…'Don't let it be forgot, that once there was a spot, for one brief shining moment that was known as Camelot.'"

The lyrics that Jackie found so enchanting were from *Camelot*, the Alan Jay Lerner and Frederick Loewe musical that, not coincidentally, ran on Broadway for much of the Kennedy presidency. Camelot was a mythical twelfth-century castle, home to a heroic figure, King Arthur, who lead a chivalric group of knights who congregated with him around a round table, thus becoming known as the Knights of the Round Table. Jackie of course saw her husband as the king, which would have made her Lady Guinevere.[*]

The lines that Jackie recited to White were from the musical's final number, in which King Arthur knights a young boy and tells him to pass along the story of Camelot—and its brief and shining moment—to future generations. One can imagine that the young boy in her mind was John F. Kennedy Jr., whose saluting of his father's coffin just

---

[*] The Camelot myth has been debunked—even JFK himself would have scoffed at it—but there is certainly a connection: Kennedy and Lerner were classmates at both Choate, the Connecticut boarding school, and Harvard. See: Malnic, "Alan Jay Lerner, Lyricist of 'My Fair Lady,' Dies at 67."

16

four days before provided the most poignant moment of the entire assassination weekend.

"History!" she told White. And that was the subtext of their three-and-a-half-hour talk that stormy evening on the Cape: her husband was a hero and must be remembered as one. "She believed, and John F. Kennedy shared the belief," White writes in his 1978 memoirs, "that history belongs to heroes, and heroes must not be forgotten."

"There'll never be another Camelot again," Jackie told him."

White understood what Jackie was imploring. "What she was saying to me now was: Please, History, be kind to John F. Kennedy. Or, as she said over and over again, don't leave him to the bitter old men to write about." At midnight he withdrew into a servant's room and began to type "in haste and inner turmoil."¹²

In about forty-five minutes he had his story. Jackie went over it with a pencil, substituting words, moving lines around. At two o'clock in the morning—it was now Saturday, November 30—he phoned it in to his editors in New York.

The editors, Ralph Graves and David Maness, thought the whole Camelot theme was over the top. Holding the presses at a cost of thirty thousand dollars per hour, they tried to water it down, but Jackie, overhearing White's end of the phone call, was firm: Camelot—with its heroes and legends—must remain. At one point, Maness, sensing the strain in White's voice, asked, "Hey, is she listening to this now with you?" White muffled the phone, went on dictating, and the story ran just the way Jackie wanted.

And so, the thousand-day administration of John F. Kennedy would forever be cemented to the brave and chivalrous King Arthur and his stately and dignified wife, Lady Guinevere. Of course, Camelot, which had earlier been written about by everyone from Alfred, Lord Tennyson to Mark Twain (*A Connecticut Yankee in King Arthur's Court*), was all a myth, the construction of a larger-than-life figure. That may have been the point, though lost in this wistful romanticism was something that actually *was* reminiscent of the Kennedy era: "how badly the actual Camelot story played out—with infidelities, betrayals, and even the death of King Arthur himself."¹³,* In his memoirs, White writes: "More than any other President since Lincoln, John F. Kennedy has become myth." Perhaps more than anyone save the widow herself, White helped make it so. Years later, one observer, removed from the emotions of 1963, would call it "one of the most significant examples of the power of storytelling to build a brand in modern history."¹⁴

Jackie and her children returned from Hyannis on December 1, to begin their final five days in the White House. President and Mrs. Johnson told Jackie that of course she could move out at her own pace. For Jackie, that meant as soon as possible. She wanted to go no later than December 3, now just a day away, but this was obviously impossible.

Among her unfinished business: sorting through her husband's closets and determining what should be given away. Aides laid out suits on furniture and garment racks. It was draining to look at Jack's clothes, which brought back specific memories of happier times, trips, and triumphs. White House staffers wept, yet Jackie refused to do so. "Now is not the time to cry, Provi," she told her personal assistant, Providencia ("Provi") Paredes. "We will cry later when we're alone."¹⁵

Jackie also had another emotionally wrenching task. Before leaving the mansion for the final time, she wanted the two children she had lost—Arabella and Patrick—reinterred next to their father. The two infants had been buried in the Kennedy family plot at Holyhood Cemetery in Brookline, Massachusetts, and Edward Kennedy had the difficult mission of having their tiny coffins dug up and flown south.

As she was packing, she got a call from Lyndon Johnson, who was in the Oval Office.

"I just wanted you to know you were loved and by so many and so much and—" he began.

"Oh, Mr. President!" she interrupted.

"I'm one of them," LBJ said.

---

* In a January 31, 1964, letter to former British prime minister Harold Macmillan, Jackie acknowledged that the Camelot theme was "overly sentimental—but I know I am right—for one brief shining moment there was Camelot—and it will never be that way again." See: Jacqueline Kennedy, Historic Conversations on Life with John F. Kennedy.

Johnson had written her a letter as well, but Jackie, in her girlish voice, said she didn't want to bother him with a reply. "I was so scared you'd answer!"

"Listen, sweetie," the president said, laying on the LBJ schmaltz. "Now, first thing you've got to learn—you've got some things to learn, and one of them is that you don't bother me. You give me strength." He asked her to "just come on over and put your arm around me. That's all you do. When you haven't got anything else to do, let's take a walk. Let's walk around the backyard and just let me tell you how much you mean to all of us and how we can carry on if you give us a little strength!"

Jackie laughed. "'She ran around with two Presidents.' That's what they'll say about me!" Johnson chuckled.

Jackie: Okay! Anytime!

LBJ: Goodbye, darling.

Jackie: Thank you for calling, Mr. President. Goodbye.

LBJ: Bye, sweetie. Do come by.

Jackie: [warmly] I will.[16]

She never did. Not because she disliked Johnson; she did like him, and Lady Bird. But Jackie had a singular focus: to leave the presidency and White House—a painful reminder of what had been lost—and get on with her life. Her focus now, made clear to White House press secretary Pierre Salinger two days after the assassination, was as narrow as it was clear: "I only have one thing to do now—I have to take care of these kids. I have to make sure they grow up well, they have to get intelligent, they have to move forward to get good jobs, they have to have a whole very important life because if I don't do that for them, they'll spend all their time looking back at their father's death and that's not what they should be doing."[17]

Such sentiments notwithstanding, Jackie did want her kids to look back, so they would know and appreciate who their father was. She was fiercely determined that the world remember John F. Kennedy, and Caroline and John were the rightful extension of his legacy. "She was firmly of the opinion that having had such a wonderful father, they should grow up knowing all about him," nanny Maud Shaw writes. "It was Mrs. Kennedy's aim to make her children proud of their father, so that they were always aware of what he was and who he was."[18]

Jackie's last full day in the White House—Thursday, December 5—coincided with her first public appearance since the funeral. It was an awkward occasion: an award ceremony for Secret Service agents Rufus Youngblood and Clint Hill for their actions in Dallas. As Oswald rained bullets down on the presidential limousine, Youngblood threw Lyndon Johnson to the floor of his car—two vehicles behind—and shielded his body. LBJ personally pinned the award on his agent, praising him as "one of the most noble and able public servants I have ever known."

Jackie had insisted that Hill also be awarded, and Treasury Secretary C. Douglas Dillon, whose department oversaw the Secret Service, did the honors. As Dillon read the citation noting Hill's "extraordinary courage in the face of maximum danger," Hill looked glum and felt embarrassed. *I don't deserve an award*, he thought. *The president is dead.* As the room applauded, Jackie stood feet away, wearing a black two-piece suit and a blank look on her face.[19]

She also fulfilled an important obligation to her children. She had promised them a birthday party. John had turned three on November 25—the day of his father's funeral; Caroline had turned six two days after that.

In the second-floor dining room that Jackie had earlier converted from a bedroom, friends and family gathered.* Adults guests included longtime Kennedy aide Dave Powers, Air Force general Godfrey McHugh, Navy captain Tazewell Shepard, and Jackie's lifelong friend Nancy Tuckerman. They sang "Happy Birthday," had ice cream and cake, then went into the West Sitting Hall for games and the unwrapping of presents. Caroline got a cardboard dollhouse with punch-out

* The former bedroom has a deeply morbid history. The first president to die in office—William Henry Harrison—passed away there in 1841. William "Willie" Lincoln, the third son of Abraham Lincoln and Mary Todd Lincoln, died there in 1862, and after President Lincoln's assassination in 1865, the autopsy and embalming of his body were performed in the room.

figures and a giant stuffed bear; John, who was crazy about anything that flew, was thrilled to get a model of Air Force One.[20]

But the gift the boy had wanted more than anything—other than to see his daddy—had been inspired by a Veterans Day visit with JFK to Arlington National Cemetery just twenty-four days before. John, enthralled by the crisp, colorful military uniforms he saw that day, declared that he, too, wanted a uniform. Jackie passed this anecdote on to Powers, who worked his magic and came up with a blue jacket with brass buttons, white pants, and a naval officer's hat—not unlike the real one his father had worn so proudly. John put the uniform on immediately. He then raised his right hand to his temple and saluted. The adults who had been trying to make the children happy found themselves fighting back tears.

Meanwhile, the remains of Patrick and Arabella had arrived at Arlington. In contrast to the arrangements for her husband, who had gone to his rest ten days earlier before a worldwide audience, Jackie arranged for her first and fourth children to be buried quietly at night after the cemetery had closed. She invited just three family members to join her: brothers-in-law Robert and Edward, and sister Lee.[21]

Making her way across the darkened Potomac and into the cemetery's quiet grounds, Jackie approached the flickering orange and yellow flame that danced atop her husband's grave. On each side lay a white coffin, heartbreakingly tiny. It was clearly an ordeal. Seeing the distress she was in, Bishop Philip Hannan, who was presiding over the service, opted for a brief prayer and nothing more. When he finished, Jackie let out a loud and audible sigh, and the coffins were deposited into the cold earth next to their father, his own plot still bearing the scars of the gravedigger.

As Hannan escorted Jackie back to her limousine, she began to talk about Dallas, how senseless it was, how she just couldn't come to grips with the dimensions of the tragedy. Hannan, surprised that Jackie was revealing such thoughts in public, suggested that perhaps it would be better to talk in private—at his rectory or the White House. Jackie, abandoning discretion, continued to talk. How could this have happened? she demanded to know. Why had God taken her husband in such a monstrous way? It was evident to the others that these matters, obviously indecipherable, gnawed at Jackie; she seemed obsessed with them.[22]

Her first night in the White House, not three years before, had been one of joy and the promise of all that lay ahead. Her final one was spent burying two children next to their murdered father. She made her way back to the mansion, where she stayed up until four thirty in the morning writing letters to Soviet premier Nikita Khrushchev, urging him to work for peace; to Marie Tippit, the wife of police officer J. D. Tippit—who was also murdered by Lee Harvey Oswald on November 22; and to all 114 permanent White House staffers, thanking them for their condolences.[23]

The night of President Kennedy's assassination, while the autopsy and embalming were being hastily conducted in the basement morgue of Bethesda Naval Hospital, Jackie waited seventeen floors above in a drab navy suite. Still wearing her pink suit stained with her husband's blood and brains, she wondered aloud, "Where am I going to live?"[24] The Kennedys had sold their Georgetown home—a red-brick Federal-style row house at 3307 N Street NW—after the 1960 election, and now, the world's most famous woman had nowhere to go.*

"I'll buy it back for you," Defense Secretary Robert McNamara offered. A simpler solution was devised: W. Averell Harriman, a wealthy sixty-eight-year old advisor to the president—known as one of Washington's "wise men" for his service to Presidents Franklin D. Roosevelt and Harry S. Truman—offered his seven-bedroom home at 3038 N Street NW for as long as Jackie needed it. He and wife Marie would move to a nearby hotel.

Now, two weeks later, it was moving day. The second floor, once so alive with music parties and the laughter of children, was quiet and

---

* The Kennedys had bought the house in 1957 for seventy-eight thousand dollars and sold it in 1960 to Mr. and Mrs. Perry Ausbrook for $105,000. It was later bought, ironically, by an aide to President Richard Nixon.

empty. The moving trucks had come and gone. Around noon, President Johnson presided over an Alliance for Progress ceremony in the State Dining Room. It had been launched by JFK in 1961 to mend ties with Latin America.

Chief Usher J. B. West was watching from an adjoining room when he heard Jackie's soft voice. "May I watch?" she asked. And unseen by anyone, she stood behind a screen, listening as the new president carried on with her husband's agenda. Before it ended, she slipped away.

Perhaps her final gesture was to her successor. "I wish you a happy arrival in your new house, Lady Bird," she scribbled in a note to the new first lady. "Remember—you will be happy here. Love, Jackie." The note was placed next to a small vase of flowers on a mantel.[25]

She also made a more permanent final gesture. Just as she had tried to link her martyred husband to Lincoln in the hours after he was gunned down, Jackie oversaw the installation of a small plaque in the presidential bedroom on the second floor. It read: "In this room lived John Fitzgerald Kennedy with his wife, Jacqueline, during the two years, ten months and two days he was President of the United States."*

She made sure that it was placed directly below an older inscription that read: "In this room Abraham Lincoln slept during his occupancy of the White House March 4, 1861–April 13, 1865."† Just as the memory

---

* It is often reported that Richard Nixon ordered the plaque removed after he became president in 1969. Not true. In 1968, during the final months of the Johnson presidency, the Committee for the Preservation of the White House recommended replacing the mantel on which the plaque was mounted (the mantel itself dated to only 1951, when it was installed during the rebuilding of the White House during the Truman era). It should be replaced, the committee decided, by a mantel dating back to 1816 that had come on the market. It had been removed from a Washington home designed by Benjamin Latrobe, the architect of the White House under Presidents Thomas Jefferson and James Madison. Lady Bird Johnson, the outgoing First Lady, agreed with the committee's recommendation, and the 1816 mantel was installed in 1969, when the Nixons were in the White House. They had nothing to do with it.

And in yet another twist, there is another plaque honoring JFK that is still in the White House today. In 1963, Jackie had a second plaque, this one made of Plexiglas, mounted on the side of a white marble mantel in the room that her husband actually slept in. (Prior to the presidency of Gerald Ford, presidents and First Ladies officially had separate bedrooms.)

† What people believe today to be the Lincoln Bedroom on the second floor of the White House was actually Lincoln's office, which he called "the shop." It was turned into a bedroom by Harry and Bess Truman during the White House renovation of 1948–1952 to honor the sixteenth president. Lincoln slept down the hall in the southwest-corner bedroom, as do all U.S. presidents.

of Abraham Lincoln lived on in the great mansion, so, she was determined, would John F. Kennedy's.

But Jackie left behind much more than a plaque. The White House itself had been restored to its glorious, original authenticity on her watch, thanks to a diligent effort she undertook shortly after moving in nearly three years earlier.

The restoration had its roots in 1941, when Jackie first visited the White House with her mother and Lee during Easter vacation. It was about two-thirds into the long administration of Franklin D. Roosevelt. She was just eleven. Years later she recalled feeling "strangely let down. It seemed rather bleak; there was nothing in the way of a booklet to take away, nothing to teach one more about that great house and the presidents who had lived there."[26] Little did she know that two decades later, she would call the great mansion home and would be the third-youngest First Lady to grace its halls.*

In her mind, the mansion she moved into in 1961 was largely as she remembered it from twenty years before: dowdy, unsophisticated, not sufficiently reflecting the history and heritage of the nation it represented. "Oh, God. It's the worst place in the world," she told a friend. "So cold and dreary. A dungeon…. I've never seen anything like it. I can't bear the thought of moving in. I hate it, I hate it, hate it." Obviously an exaggeration, it said more about Jackie—a sophisticated habitué of Paris and Park Avenue—than about the mansion itself, which had been torn down and completely rebuilt less than a decade earlier, when Truman was president.

Yet she had been right about one thing: many of the furnishings and decor pieces of the Truman and Eisenhower eras were reproductions of period pieces that had been selected for financial reasons—unacceptable to a woman for whom the word "budget" was anathema. "It looks

---

* On that same trip, Jackie had another memorable experience: she visited the National Gallery of Art. "My love of art was born there," she said. "It was then that I first discovered one of my greatest delights—the deep pleasure experienced in looking at masterpieces of painting and sculpture." See: Spoto, 41

like it's been furnished by discount stores," Jackie complained.[27], * "It looks like a house where nothing has ever taken place. There is no trace of the past."[28] This, she thought, was unsuitable for a building that represented the American people and their nation's rich cultural heritage.

The White House, Jackie felt, should not just *appear* grand; it must be authentically so. She vowed not to redecorate it but to restore it.[29] Armed with the fifty thousand dollars given by Congress to new first families, Jackie began with the living quarters on the second floor. Rooms were brightened up. Art borrowed from museums was hung. She sent for furnishings from the Kennedys' Georgetown home. She ended the tradition of first families' taking all their meals in a dining room on the ground floor, creating one on the second floor, where they actually lived. A small room in the northwest corner was converted into a kitchen. Aside from the convenience of having a kitchen within their living quarters, it gave Jackie what she craved: additional privacy for her family.[30]

As for her desire to restore authenticity to the White House, Jackie formed a Fine Arts Committee to advise her on the acquisition of genuine furnishings from America's past. She asked for citizens in possession of any authentic antique furnishings to donate them to the White House—and they did. Paintings, sculptures, and historic prints, many associated with George Washington, James Madison, and Abraham Lincoln, soon arrived,[31] as did three original chairs that had stood in James Monroe's Oval Room in 1818, when the president's house reopened following the British attack of 1814. She left just one room untouched: the Lincoln Bedroom—where the sixteenth president had his office. It was, she felt, "the one room in the house with a link to the past."[32]

The committee found donors to pay for these treasures, and by the end of 1961, much of the mansion's original authenticity had been restored. It was a stunning achievement. "I hope you can realize what

---

* Actually, most of the furnishings she encountered in 1961 had come from B. Altman & Company, an upscale New York department store. See: Whitcomb and Whitcomb, 348.

this means to us…" Jackie wrote to donors. "I do hope you will come this fall to the White House—then together we will see what a difference your things have made."[33]

But all that was behind her now as she and the children prepared to move out. West had the staff line up for a final goodbye. Many were crying. Gripping the hands of Caroline and John, Jackie asked him: "My children, they're good children, aren't they Mr. West?"

"They certainly are."

"They're not spoiled?"

"No indeed."

West, who had grown close to them, was subdued. "It was very sad, of course," he said.*

The group quietly proceeded to an elevator. "There was a lump in my throat," Maud Shaw recalled, "knowing that we would never retrace these footsteps." At the door, she turned for one final look at their rooms; they were now silent and empty. "A pall of sadness hung like a dust sheet over everything," she said.[34]

As they rode down, Jackie was silent. She wore the same black dress, simple and elegant, that she had worn exactly a fortnight earlier when her husband was laid to rest. Caroline and John wore the same powder-blue coats, though Caroline also wore red tights.

They were all she had now, her kids, and as they left their home of nearly three years, she gripped their hands tightly. They walked out of the Palm Room into a brisk, bright day, and climbed into the gleaming black Chrysler Imperial limousine that waited on the South Lawn. Nanny Maud Shaw also sat in back; Clint Hill sat in the front passenger seat next to the driver, Army sergeant Irv Watkins.

They proceeded slowly down the curved driveway, passing the Rose Garden Jackie and her husband had designed and the oval-shaped office where he had toiled—the office where his very presence had offered, for millions around the globe, inspiration and hope. The car exited

---

* At one point, sitting alone with West in the Cabinet Room, Jackie said, in her quiet voice, "Mr. West, will you be my friend for life?" He nodded yes.

through the southwest gate, passed West Executive Avenue and the Old Executive Office Building, and headed west through the city.

She never looked back and never said a word. The pain was such, the memory of happy times so ravaged, that from that moment on, drivers were told to avoid routes that offered even the remotest glimpse of the residence she had just vacated. After a brief visit to Caroline's school later that month, Jackie would return to the mansion just once over the final three decades of her life.

The car headed into Georgetown. Christmas was nineteen days away. Shops were all lit up with bright holiday lights; holly wreaths hung from doors on the village's quaint cobblestone streets. But inside the car were silence and gloom. "I never felt less festive in my life," Shaw says.[35]

As they headed north on 31st Street and turned right onto N, onlookers—alerted by the sudden bustle of police officers and photographers—gazed from a respectful distance. The car glided to a halt. Hill climbed out and opened the door. John Jr. emerged first, clutching an American flag that was half as big as he was. He clambered up the three broad steps and disappeared inside. Jackie followed, sporting a tight-lipped smile and still clutching Caroline's right hand. Aides lugged suitcases and boxes. There was a model sailing ship. A bicycle. The sad caravan from the White House included Robert and Ethel Kennedy; they went inside and spent half an hour trying to cheer Jackie up, a hopeless task. After they left to the glare of flashbulbs, the widow was alone with her children and the small household staff left by the Harrimans.

"There was just a heavy sadness for all of us," Hill remembers. "A very difficult day."[36] Night was worse, a precursor of what was to come for Jackie. The strange surroundings, the small rooms, and the overwhelming sense of loss and despair enveloped her. She quickly learned that her nightmares had accompanied her to Georgetown.

Amid the uncertainty and gloom that first weekend out of the White House, Jackie was sure of one thing: she had left the president's house in the rearview mirror, both literally and figuratively, and was determined to keep it that way. Of the Harriman home, she told Caroline, "We will stay here until we can find a house of our own. But it has to be just right for us."

But Lyndon Johnson wasn't about to let Jackie go. Before leaving the mansion, she had gotten numerous calls from the new president, always respectful, always asking her to visit. Knowing she would never go back, never could go back, she rebuffed him. She hadn't been in the Harriman home more than a day when the phone rang. It was LBJ calling to see how her move had gone. The first part of this Saturday, December 7 call—it was also LBJ's first full day in his new home—doesn't exist because Johnson turned on the recorder after the call started—but the rest clearly reveals Johnson's diligent effort to flatter her:

Jackie: Tonight, will it be in the news?

LBJ: It might be. I don't know…. I just had them come in the office, and they just sat around while I was drinking coffee. I don't know whether they even took TV of it, or not. I guess they did have some shining stuff in my eyes, but I don't imagine it's worth being on.

Jackie: Oh, listen. Oh, good, because I thought it might have been one of those things that went on while you were doing it.

LBJ: Did it keep you busy all day?

Jackie: Oh, listen, I'm just collapsed. I haven't gotten out of bed.

LBJ: Your picture was gorgeous. Now you had that chin up and that chest out and you looked so pretty marching in the front page of the *New York Daily News* today, and I think they had the same picture in Washington. Little John-John and Caroline, they were wonderful, too. Have you seen the *Daily News*? The *New York Daily News*?

Jackie: No, but I haven't seen anything today except the [*Washington*] *Post* 'cause I just sort of collapsed, but they're all downstairs.

LBJ: Well, you look at the *New York Daily News*. I'm looking at it now, and I just came, sat in my desk and started signing a lot of long things, and I decided I wanted to flirt with you a little bit.

Jackie: How sweet! And I read—Will you sleep in the White House tonight?

LBJ: [Laughs.] I guess so. I'm paid to.

Jackie: Oh!… You all three sleep in the same room, because it's the worst time, your first night.

LBJ: Darling, you know what I said to the Congress—I'd give anything in the world if I wasn't here today. [Laughs.]

Jackie: Well, listen, oh, it's going to be funny because the rooms are all so big. You'll all get lost, but anyway—

LBJ: You going to come back and see me?

Jackie: [Chuckles.]

LBJ: Hmm?

Jackie: Someday I will.

LBJ: Someday?

Jackie: But anyway, take a big sleeping pill.

LBJ: Aren't you going to bring—You know what they do with me, they just keep my—they're just like taking a hypo; they just stimulate me and I just get every idea out of every head in my life comes back and I start thinking new things and new roads to conquer.

Jackie: Yeah? Great.

LBJ: So I can't. Sleeping pill won't put me to sleep. It just wakes me up.

Jackie: Oh.

LBJ: But if I know that you are going to come back to see me some morning when you are bringing your—

Jackie: I will.

LBJ: —kid to school, and first time you do, please come and walk and let me walk down to the seesaw with you like old times.

Jackie: I will, Mr. President.

LBJ: Okay. Give Caroline and John-John a hug for me.

Jackie: I will.

LBJ: Tell them I'd like to be their daddy!

Jackie: I will.

LBJ: Goodbye.
Jackie: Goodbye.[37]

Jackie was "gorgeous," Johnson said. He "wanted to flirt with" her. And, to the grieving woman who'd just lost the father of her children: "I'd like to be their daddy!" Jackie was often both touched and repelled by Lyndon Johnson, a man capable of warmth and charm—but also of thoughtless insensitivity. She was deeply moved by something he had done on his first night as president, sending handwritten notes to Caroline and John Jr., telling them what a great man their father had been, how proud they could always be of him. But then two weeks later, telling Jackie he wanted to their dad. That was just good ole LBJ. But to Jackie, adrift in her new world, it seemed a bit much.

HER WHITE HOUSE YEARS BEHIND HER, Jackie settled in at the Harriman home. The handsome red-brick Federal-style house had seven bedrooms, a cavernous dining room, multiple fireplaces, and a swimming pool. Harriman, a serious art collector, also had an extensive collection of Impressionist paintings. It was comfortable, but it wasn't the White House.

No longer a First Lady, Jackie needed no reminders that the glorious accoutrement of power and privilege she once had at her beck and call—an army of servants, aides, limos, and helicopters—was no more. "I guess we'll have to drive," she told Clint Hill when she wanted to visit Atoka, near Middleburg, Virginia, where she and JFK had built a home that year.[38, *]

Preparing to move out of the White House had kept her occupied, but alone now in a strange house, she was quickly engulfed by self-pity. "I'm dried up," she said. "I have nothing more to give, and some

---

* She also told Hill that she would be calling the home Wexford, in honor of the president's ancestral home in County Wexford, Ireland.

days I can't even get out of bed. I cry all day and all night until I'm so exhausted I can't function. Then I drink."[39]

Friends tried to help. She spent a few awkward weekends at the country house with Ben Bradlee and his wife, Antoinette (Tony), "trying with no success to talk about something else or someone else," as Bradlee wrote years later. "Too soon and too emotional for healing, we proved only that the three of us had very little in common without the essential fourth."

On December 20, Jackie wrote them a sad note:

Dear Tony and Ben:

Something that you said in the country stunned me so—that you hoped I would marry again.

You were close to us so many times. There is one thing that you must know. I consider that my life is over and I will spend the rest of it waiting for it really to be over.

With my love,

Jackie[40]

She had no title, wasn't a government official, and wasn't related to one. That she had access to a government car and a cook derived not from not from any position, but from Lyndon Johnson's largesse.

The realization that she was cut off, just a private citizen—albeit hardly a normal one—added to her sense of isolation. This, combined with unending grief and nightmares that invaded even her futile attempts to sleep, sent her on a downward spiral. She obsessed, absolutely obsessed, over those few seconds in the limo. She was convinced that had she only understood what was happening sooner, she could have saved her husband's life. "I would have been able to pull him down," she told visitors, "or throw myself in front of him, or do something. If only I had known."[41]

Few saw the widow more during this period than Mary Gallagher, Jackie's personal secretary, who described visiting Jackie on Monday, December 9 for her usual jobs of taking dictation and performing other duties as needed. "At 11 a.m., I was in her [second-floor] bedroom in the Harriman home and found her in a lonely, depressed mood. We chatted for about twenty minutes. She wept, saying how utterly lonely she was."

"Why did Jack have to die so young?" Jackie asked. "Even when you're sixty, you like to know your husband is there. It's so hard for the children," she observed, as tears rolled down her cheeks. "Please, Mary, don't ever leave. Get yourself fixed for salary on my Government appropriation—just don't leave me!"[42]

Two Jackies emerged as fall gave way to winter: there was the "angry" Jackie, who was "so bitter" about what had happened, the Jackie who frequently lashed out at others. There was also the "guilty" Jackie, who was despondent, alone, afraid—the Jackie who remained in her second-floor bedroom much of the day, crying, fearing for her children. As she ricocheted between these debilitating personas, there was one constant: alcohol. She drowned her sorrows in vodka, occasionally switching to scotch even though she hated it.*

"I was constantly aware of her suffering," Gallagher said.[43]

Jackie's overwhelming despair certainly wasn't lost on Caroline. She knew what had happened, and at six was just old enough to comprehend its dimension. Her most basic awareness, however, was the terrible impact it was having on her mom.

Sitting with her classmates one day while their teacher, Sister Joanne Frey, read a story of a woman who washed the feet of Jesus with her tears, Caroline suddenly blurted out, almost in a stage whisper, "My mummy cries all the time."

Frey chose to ignore the comment and continued reading aloud. Caroline said it again.

"Caroline, we'll talk about that later; yes we will."

---

* Jackie's penchant for scotch was contradictory. On the sad flight home from Texas, JFK aide Ken O'Donnell offered to make her one. "I've never had scotch in my life," Jackie said, but "now is as good a time as any to start." She disliked its taste and never learned to like it. But it soon became the only whiskey she would drink, William Manchester writes, because "it always reminded her of that trip back from Dallas, of the hours she wouldn't permit herself to forget." And yet she was also trying desperately to put those terrible hours behind her. See: Manchester, *The Death of a President*, 349.

After class was over and the other students had left, Frey sat with her. Caroline, clearly upset by her mother's condition, and seemingly with no one to confide in about it, told Frey, "Every morning when I go and get in bed with Mummy, she's crying."[44]

At night, Caroline would often climb into bed with her mother, giving her a reassuring hug and stroking her hair until both of them, exhausted, fell asleep.

But the six-year-old couldn't be strong all the time. One evening at dinner, Caroline held one end of a wishbone while Janet Auchincloss, Jackie's teenage half-sister, held the other. "Can I have any wish I want?" Caroline asked.

"*Any one*," Janet answered, not sensing what was coming.

"I want to see my daddy," Caroline said.[45]

While lacking his sister's comprehension, John Jr. certainly was aware of his father's absence and sensed that something was wrong. On the weekend of the assassination, he complained that he didn't have anybody to play with and that "a bad man shot my daddy."[46] On the day the family left the White House, Secret Service agent Bob Foster took John on a final stroll around the grounds of the only home he had ever known. A White House photographer appeared and started to take a photo. "What are you taking my picture for?" John asked. "My daddy's dead." The photographer and Foster broke down in tears.[47]

Yet John also expected his daddy to return at any moment. After moving into the Harriman home, he and Caroline, with the help of Shaw or Gallagher, often phoned Evelyn Lincoln in the Old Executive Building, where she worked each day organizing the late president's papers for the Kennedy library. Such calls were treats for Lincoln, until the day John said, after a little playful chitchat, that he was coming over to see her. He then asked, "Is Daddy there?"[48]

Well-meaning efforts by others only added to Jackie's pain. Shortly after the move into the Harrimans' house, she got a delivery from McNamara and his wife, Margaret (Marg): two beautiful paintings of President Kennedy. Jackie knew she could never accept them; she simply couldn't bear to look at such striking images of her husband. In anticipation of returning them, she placed them on the floor outside her bedroom, leaning against the wall. John Jr. saw them and kissed his father's face, saying, "Goodnight, Daddy." Such an innocent and heartfelt expression of love was surely among Jackie's more difficult moments.[49]

In these first weeks when the wound was so fresh, the grief so overpowering, there were unexpected moments that fueled the pain: Jackie's eyes spotting a magazine cover, a headline, a photo. For Robert Kennedy, one happened at the most innocuous of events—a Christmas party at a Washington orphanage, just a month after the assassination. A friend, the journalist Peter Maas, accompanied him.

"The moment he walked into the room all these little children—screaming and playing—there was just suddenly silence," Maas says. "Bob stepped into the middle of the room, and just then, a little black boy," six or seven years old, "suddenly darted forward and stopped in front of him and said, 'Your brother's dead! Your brother's dead!'"

For the adults, it was a brutal moment; some turned away. "There wasn't anyplace in the world any of us wouldn't have rather been than in that room," Maas recalls. "The little boy knew he had done something wrong, but didn't know *what*, so he started to cry."

Kennedy scooped up the boy and hugged him. "That's all right. I have another brother," he said quietly.[50]

The approach of Christmas accentuated Jackie's despair. Were it not for the children, she would have been content to let the holidays slide by unnoticed. The crying, the drinking, the nightmares—it was an endless loop, and yet it was Christmas, with a six-year-old girl and three-year-old boy excited that Santa would soon be coming. Their excitement and anticipation buoyed the widow.

Preparations for Christmas had been well underway before JFK and Jackie left for Texas. The Christmas cards had arrived, much to the president and First Lady's delight. They depicted a crèche—a model representing the scene of Jesus Christ's birth—with men, women, angels, animals, kings, and cherubs, all arranged in the shape of an evergreen tree. The inspiration had come from a stunning 1961 exhibit in the East Room put together by Loretta Hines Howard, a noted collector of religious icons.

Inside, the left side of the card was blank. On the right, below a golden imprint of the presidential seal, were the words:

WITH OUR WISHES

FOR A

BLESSED CHRISTMAS

AND A

HAPPY NEW YEAR

The card was typical Jackie: elegant in its simplicity. The Kennedys had each signed about thirty of the cards, intending to sign hundreds more when they returned to Washington.

Now alone, Jackie took the kids to Palm Beach, Florida, where they stayed at C. Michael Paul's estate on North County Road, the same house they stayed at in 1962—President Kennedy's final Christmas.* Jackie was determined, as Maud Shaw says, to "make it a good time" for them. For their benefit, she maintained the traditions they had enjoyed when their father was alive: there was a tree, of course, beautifully decorated. Stockings were hung on a fireplace mantel. There were carols and treats and visions of Santa, Rudolph, and all the rest. The forced jollity masked her deep pain, and after the kids were tucked in each night, Jackie would retreat to her own room to weep and drink. It was "exceptionally difficult," Clint Hill says.[5]

President Johnson continued reaching out to Jackie. Typical Johnsonian behavior—solicitous, manipulative, charming, and cunning, all seemingly at the same time—reinforced preexisting suspicions about him among Kennedy loyalists. After a December 21 call to wish her a merry Christmas (he threatened to spank her if she didn't come visit

---

* In their pre-White House years, the Kennedys spent Christmas at Joseph P. Kennedy's estate at 1095 North Ocean Boulevard. But it wasn't big enough for the entire Kennedy family and JFK's presidential entourage. Colonel C. Michael Paul was a wealthy financier and retired Army officer. The home had eight bedrooms, museum-quality art on the walls, sweeping views of the ocean, a grand marble staircase, and a heated swimming pool. It was surrounded by tall hedges that provided privacy and security, which enabled Caroline and John Jr. to play outside without being observed.

him), Johnson called her again two days later—only this time and without telling Jackie, he invited four female reporters to eavesdrop on the call. With the newswomen listening, he gave her the LBJ treatment. An excerpt:

LBJ: You know how much we love you?

Jackie: Oh, well, you're awfully nice.

LBJ: You don't know?

Jackie: [embarrassed] Well, no, I don't—well, yes, I do—you know.

LBJ: You better know! All the 180 million love you, dear.

Jackie: Oh, thanks, Mr. President.

LBJ: And all the world, and I'll see you after Christmas, I hope. And if you ever come back here again and don't come to see me, why, there's going to be trouble.

Jackie: All right.

LBJ: You don't realize I have the FBI at my disposal, do you?

Jackie: [Laughs.] No, I promise I will.

LBJ: I'm going to send for you if you don't come by.

Jackie: Good.[52]

Historian Michael Beschloss notes that Jackie's responses seem guarded here, a sign perhaps that she recognized that Johnson might have been up to something. There's no indication that Jackie was aware that four reporters were listening in, but she found out soon enough when one of them, Frances Lewine of the Associated Press, asked Jackie, through her assistant Nancy Tuckerman, for a comment.

"You must be joking," Jackie told Tuckerman. "But how did they even know that the president called me?" Upon learning that the reporters had listened to what she thought was a private conversation with LBJ, Jackie understandably hit the roof. "I think that's going just a bit far. I don't like it at all. I think you should talk to Pierre [White House press secretary Pierre Salinger] about this. Tell him I'm very angry."

Salinger had already heard from a livid Robert Kennedy. "He's using Jackie," RFK said. "Tell him we know it, and we want him to fucking stop it."[53]

Salinger called the president and, treading carefully with his boss, asked if any reporters had been present during the December 23 call. Johnson admitted that there had been, before quickly adding—as if this would somehow make it okay—that the reporters were told to mention only that there had been a call and nothing more, "because I didn't want a private conversation to be recorded." As Johnson told Salinger this, he was recording their private conversation as well.

Johnson, who saw everything through the lens of his own political ambitions, didn't see how he was using anyone. He was running in 1964, of course, and wanted Jackie's help—he even hoped she would campaign for him. Thus the calls, the flattery, the Texas schmaltz. The day before Jackie moved out of the White House, he had taken Salinger aside. "I want to do something nice for Jackie," he said. "I'll name her ambassador to France." Salinger told Jackie, who immediately rejected it. He later offered Mexico and Great Britain; the answer was the same.

"President Johnson said I could have anything I wanted," Jackie told Charlie Bartlett, who, with his wife Martha, had introduced Jackie to John F. Kennedy in 1951. "But I'm just not interested."[54]

She wasn't interested in social invitations, either. "They asked me to every state dinner automatically," she said. "Then Mrs. Johnson kept the [White House] restoration committee going and I'd always be asked to that, but I explained to her in writing and on the telephone that it was really difficult for me and I didn't really ever want to go back. I think she understood, but out of courtesy they kept sending the invitations."[55]

What Jackie did want was something that no one could give, of course. Days were spent telling and retelling to any visitor what had happened. The long, dark nights, when she was alone with her thoughts, were worse. Over and over again, she was pulled back to Elm Street. If only she hadn't confused gunfire for the sound of a motorcycle backfiring. If only she had turned to her right sooner. If only she had pulled him down even a fraction of a second sooner. And then, when it was too late, if she had only managed to keep her husband's brains in during the six-minute race to Parkland. *If, if, if.* The nightmares, so vivid and vicious that she awoke screaming, continued.

On Christmas morning, Caroline and John were disciplined enough to sit down for breakfast before ripping open their presents. It wasn't long though, before the living room was strewn with wrapping paper, ribbons, and boxes as they opened their gifts: dolls and stuffed animals for Caroline; airplanes and cars for John. For both there were clothes, games, and candy. They squealed with delight, hugging and kissing their mother; their joy "so infectious the grown-ups temporarily forgot the grief of a month before," Shaw said.

Yet the absence of their father on Christmas Day could hardly go unnoticed by the children. Just before dinner, Caroline asked Shaw if God was keeping her father busy. Shaw said yes.

"What do you think he is doing, then?"

"Well…" Shaw wondered how to handle such a poignant question. "I should think God has made him guardian angel over you and John and Mummy, so that he can watch over you all."

Looking into her nanny's eyes, Caroline asked if her brother Patrick, who had gone to heaven that August, could help their father.

"Yes, he will. They'll keep each other company."

That night, Shaw told Jackie about the exchange. If Caroline was asking about how her father was doing in heaven, it meant, Jackie reasoned, that the six-year-old girl had come to accept the fact of her father's passing. Her mother seemed relieved.[56]

Eager to turn the page on 1963, Jackie turned in early on New Year's Eve, lulled to sleep by the gentle ocean surf outside her window. It was the year she lost a son and her husband, the father of her two surviving children, within the space of 105 days. One can only imagine the thoughts running through her mind as her head touched her cool pillow. If the night of December 31 was like all the other nights since November 22, she wouldn't make it to morning without a nightmare—the same one that assaulted her slumber over and over again, jolting her awake with a scream.

"I've heard that gun go off ten thousand times," she told her sister-in-law Joan Kennedy at one point. "I picture my own head splattering. I'd give my own life gladly, if I could just get back Jack." Then, as she did with everyone, she would tell the tale of his gruesome murder. "My God, his brains were all over me," she would say. "All over my dress. Just brains. And blood. So much blood." By now, some had heard the story countless times.[57]

She slept in as 1964 began, waking to a rainy, windy, and chilly morning. Had she glanced at the front page of the local paper, the *Palm Beach Post*, she might have been encouraged by the thumbnail editorial in the upper-left corner:

> *Looking back at 1963 gives a feeling of confidence*
> *that 1964 will be better.*

If only that were so for Jackie. A new year did nothing to alleviate her pain; the pain seemed, in fact, to intensify. The more she tried to put November 22 behind her, she kept getting dragged right back. One of the biggest sources of her despair was her knowledge that the assassination was about to become the subject of countless books. Everyone naturally wanted to interview Jackie.

The president's coffin had barely been lowered into the ground on November 25 when writers began thinking about chronicling his murder. Jackie would have preferred that no book be written about the assassination—obviously an untenable position. She was besieged with interview requests. Given that she rarely granted interviews even in better times, it seemed inconceivable—beyond her hagiographic Camelot talk with Theodore White in Hyannis Port on November 29—that she would speak with anyone about the gruesome events in Dallas. Though she was, as she would later acknowledge, "not in any condition to make much sense of anything," she decided, after several conversations with Robert Kennedy, that the best way to tell the story was to select one writer and extend their full cooperation to him—and no one else.[58]

In particular, Jackie wanted to thwart Jim Bishop. A syndicated columnist who specialized in chronicling the twenty-four hours surrounding historic events—his 1955 book *The Day Lincoln Was Shot* was a huge bestseller—he had also finished, just ten days before Kennedy's death, a short book called *A Day in the Life of President Kennedy*. JFK himself had approved it without revisions.[59,*] But Jackie had asked for sixty "small changes," which Bishop made. It, too, was a bestseller when published in 1964. Despite Bishop's commercial success, however, Jackie considered him a hack, unqualified to write about her husband's death.

Jackie and Robert's first two choices said no. One was Theodore White, whose deference at Hyannis the week after the assassination showed him—the Kennedys thought—to be malleable. But White, objecting to their demand to have the final say about the manuscript, turned them down. For the same reason, so did Walter Lord, whose riveting accounts of the sinking of the *Titanic* and the attack on Pearl Harbor were bestsellers in the 1950s.[60,†]

They then approached William Manchester. A Marine who had been badly wounded on Okinawa, Japan, in 1945, he had joined the *Baltimore Sun* as a reporter in 1947 before becoming an editor and an adjunct history professor at Connecticut's Wesleyan University.

Jackie had never met Manchester but had read his 1962 book *Portrait of a President*, which examined a twelve-month period—April 1961 to April 1962—of the Kennedy presidency. One of the more

---

* Bishop recalled the last conversation he'd had with President Kennedy, a month before his assassination. The president told Bishop that he had read Bishop's book *The Day Lincoln Was Shot* and had enjoyed it. Kennedy then discussed the possibility of his own assassination. "My feelings about assassination are identical with Mr. Lincoln's," he said. "Anyone who wants to exchange his life for mine can take it." See: Bishop, *The Day Kennedy Was Shot*, xi.

† At least that's the version presented by Sam Kashner in *Vanity Fair* in 2009. But William Manchester said he asked Theodore White about this and that White said he had no memory of being asked to write the story. An aide to Robert Kennedy did reach out to Lord, who was interested, Manchester acknowledged—but before talks had progressed, "Jacqueline Kennedy decided that she preferred me," he said. See: Manchester, *Controversy*, 5.

famous photos of the First Couple, taken while they sailed aboard the *Manitou* off Newport, Rhode Island, that September, shows JFK peering over Jackie's shoulder as she read it.* She found his prose graceful, dignified—and flattering.

That *Portrait* would be favorable was almost preordained. Manchester—who was granted four interviews with the president—admired his subject from the beginning, and Kennedy appeared to enjoy his company in return. The two had enough in common, after all: both were war heroes, earning Purple Hearts in the Pacific, and shared Massachusetts roots. At the end of their sessions, which were usually the last thing on the president's schedule that day, "We'd have a daiquiri and sit on the Truman Balcony. He'd smoke a cigar and I'd have a Heineken," Manchester later said.[61]

On February 5, Manchester got a call from Pierre Salinger, the cigar-chomping press secretary to the late president. Mrs. Kennedy wants you to write the official, authorized book on the assassination, Salinger told him. Manchester—who had never even met the widow—was floored and at first reluctant to take on such a massive, emotionally fraught undertaking. "How can I say no to Mrs. Kennedy?" he asked his secretary.

"You can't," was the reply.[62]

And so began a three-year saga that would make a physical and emotional wreck of the writer, dent Jacqueline Kennedy's seemingly untouchable image—and result in a seven-hundred-page blockbuster that half a century later remains widely regarded as the definitive account of what happened between November 20 and 25, 1963. It would be, Manchester wrote in 1976, "the longest presidential obituary in history, and, in the end, the most controversial."[63]

---

* Someone else who read *Portrait of a President: Lee Harvey Oswald*. Records from the New Orleans public library show he checked it out just months before the assassination.

KNOWING THAT SHE COULDN'T STAY in the Harriman home forever, Jackie was determined to find a new home. When she could drag herself out of bed, she went house hunting with Robert, determined to find something suitable. She didn't have to look far: it was at 3017 N Street, a mere fifty yards away, across the street. Purchased in December for $170,000, the fourteen-room Colonial, built in 1794, was believed to be Georgetown's second-oldest home. After making some renovations—including the removal of a shotgun that had been mounted above a library fireplace—Jackie began moving in on January 27. She had never owned a home of her own before, and was "flushed with happiness" at her achievement.

"Welcome home," she told Shaw, as the nanny walked Caroline and John up the steps.

"Oh, this is a lovely house, Mrs. Kennedy. It feels like home. I am sure you and the children are going to be happy here."

"Yes," Jackie replied. "I hope so, anyway."[64]

Jackie's room was on the second floor, overlooking N Street. Across the hall was the library, and next to that a guest bedroom and bath. Caroline, John, and Shaw had the expansive third floor all to themselves. Jackie made sure that their rooms were decorated as their rooms in the White House had been—blue for John, pink for Caroline. The top of the house had a cupola with a skylight; this quickly became their favorite hangout.[65]

But Jackie soon—that very first day—got an uncomfortable glimpse of what this new chapter in her life would involve: minimal privacy, the prying eyes of strangers, and increased security concerns for her children. It was untenable from the beginning.

Tour buses began showing up almost immediately, belching both exhaust and camera-toting tourists eager for a glimpse of the world's most famous woman, John, or Caroline. "Jack-eee," they would call from the street. "Jack-eee..." There was no let-up. Sidewalks on both sides of the street were typically clogged. Some spectators made a day of it, setting up small tables and spreading out food. Others climbed trees and peered into the home, which stood atop a modest hill, with binoculars. Someone even stole the "3017" next to the front door. Others tried to knock on the door itself, hoping for an autograph or a photo, before being told to leave by Secret Service agents.

It became a round-the-clock circus, forcing Jackie to keep the curtains drawn tight. Any hope the anguished widow had of finding happiness or security—or pushing the nightmare of Dallas into the rearview mirror—disintegrated quickly.

"I do wish they would go away," Jackie told Shaw. "I know they mean well, but I can't stand being stared at like that every time I go out on the street."[66]

Even three-year-old John was bothered by the stares and flashbulbs that greeted him daily. "What are these silly people taking my picture for?" he would ask.[67]

"I'm a freak now," Jackie told Robert McNamara when he visited one day. "I'll always be a freak. I can't take it anymore. They're like locusts; they're everywhere…. I can't even change my clothes in private, because they can look into my bedroom window."[68]

Even in the White House—with its fifty-five thousand square feet, 132 rooms, sixteen bedrooms, and thirty-five bathrooms, sitting on an expansive eighteen-acre plot—Jackie had never felt like she had any privacy. "I'm sick and tired of starring in everybody's home movies," she'd complained at one point, and asked for a "solid wall" of trees or bushes to be planted in front of the mansion's fence. She was particularly anxious to keep tourists and news photographers from taking pictures of Caroline and John playing. So if that's how she felt about the president's house, she must have felt like a caged animal on N Street. It didn't take long to realize that buying 3017 had been a horrible mistake.

But it wasn't just 3017. It was Georgetown itself. The charming cobblestone streets, cozy restaurants, and homes of so many friends—there wasn't a street that didn't evoke ghostly memories that she was now trying to purge from her troubled mind.

"Can anyone understand how it is to have lived in the White House and then, suddenly, to be living alone as the president's widow?" she told her interior decorator, Billy Baldwin. "There's something so final about it. And the children. The world is pouring terrible adoration at the feet of my children and I fear for them. How can I bring them up normally? We would never even have named John after his father if we had known…"[69]

Indeed, no one could understand. Slowly, it dawned on Jackie that the nation's capital was simply uninhabitable. She would soon decide that she needed to make a clean break. She began to let old friends drift away: Ben and Tony Bradlee, and even (or particularly) Charles and Martha Bartlett, who had thrown the 1951 dinner party where John F. Kennedy and Jacqueline Bouvier first met.*

On the night of January 31, 1964, Jackie, unable to sleep as usual, wrote a letter to Harold Macmillan. Macmillan had been the British prime minister for the entire Kennedy presidency until October 1963.†

Jackie had intended to tell "Supermac," one of Macmillan's nicknames, how much he had meant to Jack. But overwhelmed by grief and self-pity, she veered off and scribbled how bitter she was about her husband's murder, how meaningless it was and how life was unfair.

Three weeks later she received a fifteen-page reply. It was no ordinary letter. It proved to be a salve for Jackie; it was, she said, "the rock that I went back to over and over" in 1964. Of all the letters and telegrams she received in the weeks and months after the assassination, nothing "could ever have been" what Macmillan's letter was for her. Even years later, passages would come "crashing back" into her head that would comfort her.[70]

Macmillan, who dated his letter February 18, had turned seventy the week before, meaning he had been born in 1894—and was thus old enough to have served during the first World War. It was through this

---

* At a September 12, 1963, party to celebrate their tenth anniversary, Jackie thanked the Bartletts for making the introduction that had helped change American history. "Without Jack," she told them, her life would have "all been a wasteland, and I would have known it every step of the way." See: Smith, *Grace and Power*, 90.

† Macmillan retired for health reasons, but this was perhaps a face-saving excuse, given the fact that his government had been badly weakened by an explosive sex scandal involving his defense minister, a "model," and a Soviet naval officer. The lurid details no doubt fascinated President Kennedy, who, it was later learned, had an affair with an alleged East German spy. Robert Kennedy had the woman, Ellen Rometsch, deported.

terrible lens of his experience—the incalculable amount of bloodshed, the suffering, the horror—that he framed his response to her.

The old warrior had been wounded three times, being hit once by a bomb and getting shot on two occasions. The first time he was shot, during 1915's Battle of Loos, a bullet ripped through his hand; months later, a bullet tore through his thigh and he lay wounded and in agony for hours before someone could get to him. In one battle, sixty thousand fellow soldiers were slaughtered, many by poison gas that the Germans used. Death was ubiquitous.

Yet Macmillan was lucky: he lived. But he would forever be haunted by his experience, and as he wrote Jackie—his battered right hand made his penmanship difficult to read—he told her that he, too, had been bitter; that he, too, kept asking, "Why—oh, why"; that he, too, suffered from depression and survivor's guilt. "How can we accept it?" he asked. "Why did God allow it[?] I am sure you say this to yourself (as I do) over & over. Such waste!" And then: "Can there really be a God, who makes & guides the world?"[7]

Finally, Jackie felt, finally there was someone who truly understood what she had been through, who felt as she did, who grieved and questioned as only she could. "You have shown the most wonderful courage to the outer world," the wise old man counseled. "The hard thing is really to feel it, inside."

Having found this comrade-in-arms, Jackie tried to respond but could not. She began numerous letters to Macmillan only to throw them away; she found the process cathartic. She would thank him in person more than a year later.

JACKIE'S GRIEF WAS SO DEEP, so shattering, that it could truly be understood by only one other person: Robert Kennedy. From the moment RFK ran up the stairs of Air Force One after it landed at Andrews Air Force Base on November 22—"I want to see Jackie," he had said, brushing past President Johnson—to middle-of-the-night visits to Arlington and quiet talks before her crackling fireplace in Georgetown, the two had leaned on each other for comfort as they tried, and failed, to make sense of the tragedy.

The hours they kept and the inordinate amount of time they spent together sparked questions about the nature of their relationship. RFK biographer Evan Thomas notes that "there can be no doubt that they shared a deep affection and emotional bond" and wonders whether "in their grief and yearning for solace, they may have shared more."[72]

Some Jackie biographers, perhaps predisposed to salaciousness, are sure that Jackie and Bobby had an affair, as are some officials who knew them both well. "Everybody knew about the affair. The two of them carried on like a pair of lovesick teenagers," claims Franklin D. Roosevelt Jr., son of the 32nd president and undersecretary of commerce during the Kennedy administration.[73] There very well may have been a romantic relationship. And yet, if "everybody knew," it must be asked why Robert's FBI file—eagerly kept updated by Director J. Edgar Hoover at the behest of RFK's number-one political enemy, Lyndon Johnson—contained "not even the rumor of an affair" between him and Jackie.[74]

There were rumors about other men as well. Given the state Jackie was in—a widowed wreck, flooded with nightmares, crying her eyes out, drowning in vodka, fearful for her life and those of her two children—it seems wildly out of place to even imagine her with anyone just weeks after the death of her husband. And yet, on January 27, she enjoyed a two-hour dinner with Marlon Brando, the sexually ravenous Hollywood heartthrob. Joining them at Washington's chic Jockey Club were her sister Lee and Brando's friend George Englund. The dinner, reports said, was to plan a charity function.

One account of the public portion of the evening says Jackie appeared "smitten" by the smoldering actor and found him "irresistible."[75] Another says that "he and Jackie seemed to have instant rapport." According to the restaurant's manager, Jackie and Lee left first, making their way through a gauntlet of photographers ("Those goddamn parasites!" Jackie cried), followed minutes later by Brando and Englund.

Back at Jackie's house, the four danced to a Wayne Newton record. At one point, Brando kissed her; she "froze in his arms. The look in her eyes said it all: The dance was over and he should leave."[76]

Brando fled—and quickly denied that the dinner had even taken place. "It's all a gross error,"[77] he said, adding that he had never met Jackie.

Clint Hill, Jackie's Secret Service agent during this period, stood watch outside her Georgetown home the night of the dinner and guarded her in New York until after the 1964 election. He says simply, "There was no relationship between the two."[78]

There may have been one later, though accounts written by others vary wildly. Biographer J. Randy Taraborrelli, in his 2000 book *Jackie, Ethel, Joan*, claims that Jackie and Brando "never saw one another again—at least not that anyone close to them can remember." But Christopher Andersen, in *Jackie After Jack*, claims that months later, the two went to bed in Jackie's suite at the Carlyle. Brando himself is said to have written about it in an original draft of his memoirs, but was persuaded by his Random House editor, Joe Fox—who counted Jackie among his acquaintances—to remove it. The 1994 book *Brando: Songs My Mother Never Taught Me*—disingenuously makes no mention of Jackie at all.

The broader significance of whether Jackie did—or did not—have a relationship with Brando is that she was taking what appear to be her first tentative steps toward socializing and trying to enjoy herself again. That she could go out at all during this period—again, one dominated by nightmares, drinking, and a deep depression—is remarkable in and of itself. It also shows that the press's obsession with Jackie—following her everywhere, documenting her every move, publishing every scrap of detail that could be found—was well established, and it would not let up until a later stage of her life. The Jackie who was generally portrayed prior to November 22 as an elite, snobbish clotheshorse seemingly floating above it all, was now seen as the martyr's widow, regarded as being above reproach. Both characterizations were flawed at their essence, but the one trait that defined Jackie, both before and after Dallas—her deep desire for privacy—meant that she would live her life as best she could without bothering to correct either one.

On March 2, Schlesinger made his way through the tourists loitering in front of 3017 and climbed the steps to Jackie's home, where she guided him into the living room. It was a half library, half mini-museum: shelves groaned under the weight of books and numerous artifacts from ancient Egypt, Rome, and Greece that John F. Kennedy had given to her over the years. Jackie sat on a crushed-velvet sofa; Schlesinger on a pale yellow chair that had been in the family's private quarters at the White House. In between them, on a black Oriental table, he placed his tape recorder.[79]

As had been the case with White in November, Jackie's implicit goal was to use Schlesinger in the burnishing of her husband's reputation. She wanted, Caroline Kennedy wrote in 2011, "to make sure that the record of his administration was preserved. She had confidence that his decisions would stand the test of time and wanted future generations to know what an extraordinary man he was."[80] Schlesinger was obviously a "friendly," having joined JFK's campaign in 1960 and the White House staff the following year, where he was, as the president saw him, an in-house historian, and in Robert's eyes a "sort of roving reporter and troubleshooter."[81]

Jackie imposed two conditions on Schlesinger. First, the tapes would remain sealed until after her death. Second, she had the right to delete anything she wished from the transcript. There seemed no question that despite Schlesinger's scholarly reputation, his deference to Jackie would supersede any pretense of objectivity.

Over the next three months, they would talk seven times. If, during the interviews, she ventured into territory she would rather avoid, she would ask Schlesinger to stop recording and ask, "Should I say this on the record?" Reminding her of the conditions that he had agreed to, he would urge her to go ahead, because "you have control over the manuscript."[82]

Although anything from Jackie is valuable to historians, her control over Schlesinger meant that a great deal of material on John F. Kennedy and their marriage would remain hidden. Her goal of putting her late husband on a pedestal, of building on the Camelot theme that she had foisted upon Theodore White, precluded any discussion of the seamier side of JFK. Questions of that nature were never asked to begin with.

The Jackie/Schlesinger interviews are ostensibly about JFK's life and career. But the subtext—the way in which Jackie dealt with these conversations—reveals much about her as well. The "why?" question that had overwhelmed her for months was more than evident. "I think God's unjust now," she told Schlesinger on March 4.[83]

Caroline Kennedy says, "As her child, it has sometimes been hard for me to reconcile that most people can identify my mother instantly, but they really don't know her at all. They may have a sense of her style and her dignified persona, but they don't always appreciate her intellectual curiosity, her sense of the ridiculous, her sense of adventure, or her unerring sense of what was right." She adds: "Even though most of her answers are about my father, by listening to the audio, people will learn a great deal about the person that she was. Much is revealed by tone, and by her pauses as well as by her statements."[84]

That Jackie even sat down with Schlesinger for seven long interviews might strike some as odd. She was, after all, an intensely private woman who rarely had granted interviews during her marriage. She was in deep grief. Depression held such a grip on her that she was contemplating suicide—you'll hear about this shortly—so for her to open up about her marriage to John F. Kennedy and their brief time in the White House (she called 1961 to 1963 "our happiest years") seems incongruous.

Jackie got five of her seven interviews with Schlesinger out of the way and then spent Easter weekend skiing in Vermont with Bobby, Ethel, and both sets of kids. From there it was off to Mill Reef, the sparkling Antigua home of her dear friend Rachel ("Bunny") Lambert Mellon, where they were joined by Lee, Stas, and Chuck Spaulding, an old buddy of JFK's who had served as an usher at Jack and Jackie's wedding.

Dallas had shaken Jackie's and Bobby's faith to the core. Now, drawn closer in their shared grief, they struggled together that winter, wiling away many an afternoon before the fire trying to comprehend God's ways. "The innocent suffer—how can that be possible and God be just[?]" RFK scribbled at one point. And: "All things are to be examined & called into question—There are no limits set to thought." If anything, Jackie's faith was more even tenuous.[85]

Jackie's exploration into—and skepticism of—religion began long before her husband's assassination. In the 1950s, she discussed it with Benedictine priests; she also delved into the poetry and philosophy of the ancient Greeks.[86] Now, in the sad winter of 1963–1964, this infatuation was revived when she turned to a book, *The Greek Way*, by Edith Hamilton.

Written in 1930, Hamilton's essays on Greece in the fifth century BC—about philosophers, the supremacy of reason and spiritual power, and, perhaps most of all, the mystery of death—made an indelible impact on Jackie. In one passage that surely got the widow's attention, Hamilton writes of the announcement by Clytemnestra (in ancient Greek legend, the wife of Agamemnon, ruler of the Ancient kingdom of Mycenae, or Argos) that Troy had fallen:

"The women have flung themselves on lifeless bodies, husbands... "[87]

Hamilton also writes of Greek poets; these "poets who were able to sound the depths of human agony were able also to recognize and reveal it as tragedy. The mystery of evil, they said, curtains that of which 'every man whose soul is not a clod hath visions.' Pain could exalt and in tragedy for a moment men could have sight of a meaning beyond their grasp."[88]

The next paragraph also conveys a tragic relevance:

Why is the death of the ordinary man a wretched, chilling thing which we turn from, while the death of the hero, always tragic, warms us with a sense of quickened life?... So the end of a tragedy challenges us. The great soul in pain and in death transforms pain and death.[89]

Fifth century BC to 1964: two and a half millennia. Jackie's attempt to comprehend the incomprehensible took her far into the dusty crevices of history. But ultimately there were no answers; there was no way to rationalize what had happened in Dallas. The nightmares continued.

But Jackie's despair went deeper than questioning the judiciousness of her maker. As winter gave way to spring, nothing save her two children could keep her from spiraling further into her own abyss, or provided her with a "reaffirmation of the will to live in the face of death," as Hamilton, quoting a more recent philosopher, Friedrich Nietzsche, says.[90] Her will to live—more tenuous than is commonly known—led her to consider ending her life that spring.

William Manchester interviewed 266 people for *The Death of a President*, most just once. It was a grueling experience. "Half the people I interviewed displayed deep emotional distress while trying to answer my questions," he later wrote. But "none of the other sessions were as affecting as those with Jackie." She was the seventh person to speak with him.[91]

Their interviews—they met five times—extended over a three-month period, all at Jackie's home on N Street. The first was at noon on April 7, and as Manchester lugged his bulky Wollensak reel-to-reel tape recorder up the stairs to her front porch, he wasn't quite sure what to expect. He was shown to the living room.

"Mr. *Man*chester!" she said in that famous breathy voice as she entered. She "closed the sliding doors behind her with a sweeping movement and bowed slightly from the waist." Alone with the world's most famous woman, he was struck by her beauty. "She was wearing a black jersey and yellow stretch pants, she was beaming at me, and I thought how, at thirty-four, with her camellia beauty, she might have been taken for a woman in her mid-twenties. My first impression—and it never changed—was that I was in the presence of a very great tragic actress. I mean that in the finest sense of the word."[92]

That Jackie anticipated her conversations with Manchester as a dreadful necessity cannot be doubted. Other than her brief session with Theodore White in Hyannis on November 29, she had not spoken on the record with anyone outside her family about Dallas—nor, at the conclusion of her final talk with Manchester on July 20, would she do so ever again.

Her trepidation was such, in fact, that just minutes after welcoming Manchester into her home, she changed her mind. "She told him," Barbara Leaming writes, "that her emotional state made it impossible for her to be interviewed just now," and that Manchester—who makes no mention of this vignette in his own memoir—"had no choice, really, but to be patient." It was the right thing to do; Jackie indeed was in no position to talk to the writer.[93]

Three weeks later, she went to Hickory Hill—Robert and Ethel Kennedy's home in McLean, Virginia—to play tennis with a family friend, Father Richard McSorley. It would improve her game, Bobby offered. It was the thinnest of pretexts: Bobby, deeply worried about Jackie's mental state, wanted the priest (who was also a Georgetown University professor) to counsel the grief-stricken widow.

McSorley was a colorful character. Born into a large Catholic family—he had fourteen siblings—he was teaching at a Jesuit school in the Philippines when World War II broke out. Captured by the Japanese in December 1941, he survived three years in a prison camp, and upon returning to the United States, was assigned to a Maryland church that was segregated. Offended, he became a civil rights activist. This drew him into the Kennedy orbit, and after meeting Robert and Ethel at Georgetown in 1961, he began giving their kids tennis lessons. This evolved into tutoring sessions for two of them, Joseph and Robert F. Kennedy Jr.

Jackie and McSorley swatted balls around for a while, but their game soon turned into a counseling session. Jackie, confiding in the priest, acknowledged her struggles and her questioning of her Catholic faith. McSorley captured her deeply personal thoughts in his diary. "I don't know how God could take him away," Jackie said. "It's so hard to believe."[94]

The horrifying vignette that Jackie played in her mind over and over and over again consumed her. The very next day, April 28, she met McSorley again. This time Jackie went further: she was contemplating suicide. The priest noted the conversation in his diary: "Do you think God would separate me from my husband if I killed myself?" she asked. "It is so hard to bear. I feel as though I am going out of my mind at times." She asked the priest to pray—for her death. The priest, keeping his composure, said yes, he would pray for her death—"if you want that. It's not wrong to pray to die."[95]

Wallowing in self-pity, Jackie said that Caroline and John would be better off living with Robert and Ethel in Hickory Hill. "I'm no good for them," she said. "I'm so bleeding inside." Here, the priest pushed back, pointing out that Robert and Ethel, with seven children, could not possibly give Jackie's kids the time and attention they needed. Ethel "has so much pressure from public life and so many children," Father McSorley said. "Nobody can do for them except you."[96]

McSorley's counsel got through. His typewritten diary entry about a month later notes that Jackie, in a subsequent letter, came to the realization that suicide was "wrong. It's just a way out." He also notes her sadness and regret at not being able to say goodbye to her husband, and the struggle to deal with his sudden, brutal death while still coping with the August 1963 passing of their infant son, Patrick. "I know now I won't ever get over [the assassination]," she wrote to McSorley. "But I am getting better at hiding it from my children."*

As she contemplating doing away with herself, Jackie finally sat down again with Manchester in her living room for their first of four excruciating interviews. It was May 4, a sticky spring day. "I had carefully

---

* Perhaps the darkest secret of Jacqueline Kennedy's life is that she never shared her thoughts of suicide with the one person she was closer to than anyone—Robert Kennedy. But the president's brother, struggling with his own guilt and agony, perhaps sensed the depths of his sister-in-law's despair. It might have remained a secret were it not for McSorley's diary. After his 2002 death, his papers were inadvertently released by Georgetown University, leading to posthumous criticism of the priest's ethics for recording Jackie's private thoughts. See: McSorley, "Kennedy Letters to McSorley Released."

put the Wollensak recorder where I could see it and she wouldn't," he wrote. He switched it on. The reels began to turn.[97]

Seeking to get it over with, Jackie sat with the writer for long sessions on May 4, 7, and 8. By now, it had been nearly half a year since Dallas. Talking about it, in all its gruesome detail, seemed almost cathartic for her.*

Manchester couldn't get enough. His appetite for detail and color was voracious; his style was to probe and prod and mine the most minute details. He wanted to know every word spoken, everything seen, felt, heard, touched. His goal was to bring the reader to the scene of the crime, to the assassin's lair, to the back of the bloody car, to the frantic emergency room, the autopsy, everything—everything Jackie wanted to forget.

As mentioned previously, the tapes, kept at the Kennedy library in Boston, are off limits until 2067. But when future historians peruse them, they'll hear some "odd clunking noises." They were ice cubes. "The only way we could get through those long evenings was with the aid of great containers of daiquiris," Manchester later said.[98]

Barely a week before, she had confessed to Father McSorley that she wanted to kill herself; the pain was just too much. Now she was being asked to focus like never before on the very source of that pain. To go deep into detail, to not leave anything out. "I just talked about the private things," she later said. The sessions were agonizing.[99]

But if Jackie had hoped that talking and talking would help get Dallas out of her system, she was wrong. Seeing McSorley again, her suicidal thoughts intensified; she told the priest that "death is great," and that people should be allowed to "get out of their misery."[100]

McSorley kept trying to talk her down. It would be wrong to kill yourself, he insisted. He was relieved when she told him that she

---

* During the ride from Andrews Air Force Base to Bethesda Naval Hospital on the evening of November 22, Robert Kennedy sat with Jackie in a Navy ambulance with the president's casket. "It was so obvious that she wanted to tell me about it that whether or not I wanted to hear it wasn't a factor," he recalls. "I didn't think about whether I wanted to hear it or not. So she went through all that...." See: Manchester, *The Death of a President*, 392.

wouldn't really try to do herself in. But that such thoughts lurked so closely to the surface, and occasionally escaped, were a sign that six months after her husband's murder, Jackie had made little to no improvement.[101]

May 29 would have been JFK's forty-seventh birthday.* Although Jackie's preference was to remember the day of his birth, not his death, she nevertheless found herself tracing steps she had taken at his funeral six months before. With Caroline and John, who wore bright cream-colored coats, she began with a memorial service at Saint Matthews's Cathedral. Bishop Philip Hannan, who had eulogized the president in November, delivered the requiem sermon. The widow, dressed in black as usual, broke down and cried openly. It was, said David Ormsby-Gore, the British ambassador who had been particularly close to the Kennedys, "an agony to her. She now feels she is no nearer to being reconciled to what's happened than she was last November."[102] Little did he know that Jackie, just days before, had discussed taking her life.

The Kennedys then made their way to Arlington, where they knelt in prayer before the grave. The eternal flame, surrounded by pine boughs, burned in the midday sun. Jackie placed a sprig of lilies of the valley on them; John left the gold PT-109 tie clasp that had been on his coat. Ever since the president's burial, his gravesite had been overrun with tourists; on this day some fifty thousand paid their respects. Those on hand when the Kennedys arrived stood behind ropes and watched the scene reverently, while snapping photos. Other than birds chirping and the occasional plane overhead, all was quiet. The flag at nearby Arlington House, the Robert E. Lee Memorial, flapped at half-staff. It would be Jackie's last public appearance in Washington.[103]

Next, they flew to Hyannis, where a TV program about the late president—and a plug for the Kennedy library—was broadcast.

"His office will be there," Jackie said. "You can hear every speech he made. You can see all the manuscripts of his speeches and how he changed them."

---

* JFK thought he wouldn't live beyond age forty-five; he made it to forty-six years and five months.

Jackie also used the attention being lavished on her late husband to write, for the May 29 issue of *Life*, a one-page essay on his favorite mementos. She had selected them, with input from Robert, for a traveling exhibit that would raise money for the Kennedy library. She was deeply involved in the fundraising and wrote a personal thank-you note to anyone who donated more than a thousand dollars.

If the interview she had given to *Life* six months before was overblown in how it elevated the Kennedy aura by embellishing it with an association with Camelot—John F. Kennedy himself would have scoffed—Jackie's contribution now was far more honest in how it portrayed the late president. Not as some mythical, larger-than-life figure but, in her own words, "how he really was."

In fact, the 790-word article makes no mention of Camelot at all. Jackie notes well-known Kennedy artifacts that were in the exhibit, like the famous Resolute desk* and his rocking chair. There was also a model of the Patrol Torpedo boat (PT-109) on which JFK served in World War II. Other items included drafts of speeches and pages of doodles that he made during meetings, notably during meetings about the Cuban Missile Crisis.

Written during the depths of despair, the *Life* article was likely an ordeal for Jackie, as she described JFK's childhood and how "he wrote the most touching letters as a little boy," and his lifelong love of history and literature, including poetry. She recalled how Kennedy had taught Caroline short poems of Shakespeare and Edna St. Vincent Millay, and how proud he had been when his daughter could recite them by heart. "I just hope that everyone who visits the exhibit will come away feeling that they now know him a little bit better," she wrote.

---

* That the Resolute desk is even associated with the modern presidency today is because of Jackie. The Oval Office was built in 1909, yet the desk—an 1879 gift from Queen Victoria to President Rutherford B. Hayes—wasn't installed there until Jackie did so in 1961. The desk has since been used by six presidents—Jimmy Carter, Ronald Reagan, Bill Clinton, George W. Bush, Barack Obama, and Donald Trump. But four others—Lyndon Johnson, Richard Nixon, Gerald Ford, and George H. W. Bush—opted for different desks. It is today regarded as the most famous piece of furniture in the White House.

Over the next year, the JFK exhibit traveled to twenty-two cities throughout the United States (Dallas was pointedly excluded) and fifteen cities in Europe.*

Besides her children, there was something else that kept Jackie hanging on. Through her darkness and self-pity, she recognized a higher calling: her husband, who had planned to write a record of his presidency, had been denied the opportunity to define his legacy on his terms. Historian Beschloss notes that "Mrs. Kennedy feared that reminiscing at length about life with her husband would make her 'start to cry again,' but she was determined to win Jack a fair hearing from historians." He continues: "She felt an overwhelming obligation to do whatever she could."[104]

That meant sanitizing the details of her husband's sordid private life. While common knowledge today, they weren't in 1964. Jackie, knowing that she was speaking for posterity, tread carefully with Schlesinger whenever family matters came up. There are pauses in the tapes, and one imagine the wheels in Jackie's mind turning as she contemplated how to discuss certain matters. For history's sake, it certainly would have been valuable if Schlesinger, who was hardly unaware of JFK's extramarital adventures, hadn't censored himself. At one point, it did come up when he asked her about Kennedy's friendship with Florida senator George Smathers. Smathers and JFK had been notorious skirtchasers during the 1950s, but Jackie said their friendship was before she and Jack were married in September 1953. She says Smathers "was really a friend of one side of Jack—a rather, I always thought, sort of crude side," before quickly adding "I mean not that Jack had a crude side."[105] Of course she knew otherwise and moved on.

After her final conversation with Schlesinger on June 3, Jackie described the ordeal as "excruciating." As difficult as those conversations

---

* The exhibit was all very sanitized, of course. Any true description today of John F. Kennedy "as he really was" certainly cannot omit the constant philandering that nearly wrecked his marriage to Jackie; prior to Kennedy's run for the presidency, his father reportedly offered Jackie a cool $1 million not to dump him. Such messiness, quite inconvenient in the spring of 1964, would remain hidden from the public view for years.

unquestionably were, they presumably were nowhere near as painful as the overlapping Manchester sessions. The Schlesinger conversations began on March 2 and ended three months later. Manchester, who was also trooping up the stairs to 3017 with a tape recorder, dealt with her from April 4 through July 20. Knowing that Manchester was focusing exclusively on the murder, Schlesinger did not ask about it—an unquestionable blessing to the widow. In speaking with both men at the same time, Jackie was accelerating her efforts to put her marriage, her White House years, and Dallas behind her; after the last Manchester chat, she retreated Garbo-like into a three-decade silence on this period of her life.

Chapter Two

July 1964 to December 1964:
Farewell to All That

On November 18, 1963, four days before the Kennedys settled into the back seat of their Lincoln Continental in Dallas, a band from Liverpool, England, made their first appearance on American television. They called themselves the Beatles. President Kennedy, in a motorcade through Tampa in the Lincoln, with the top down and Secret Service agents relegated to a follow-up vehicle as he preferred, missed their debut. Had he watched, he would have gotten a glimpse of the changes that would begin sweeping across the nation after his death.

In fact, if 1968 was the worst year of the 1960s—the year everything exploded—then the most pivotal year, it could be argued, was 1964. Even as Americans grieved for their martyred president and his beautiful young widow, they began to change. Societal cracks emerged between young and old, rich and poor, liberal and conservative. Authority began to be questioned. The Vietnam War truly began, the sexual revolution was picking up steam, and the bestselling nonfiction book that year—*The Feminine Mystique*, by Betty Friedan—told women that there was more to life than being a housewife and mother. Twenty-three-year-old Robert Zimmerman—better known as Bob Dylan—released "The Times, They Are a-Changin'."

Jackie, too, felt the need to change. She felt like a prisoner. Not just in her own home, and not just in Washington. She was also a prisoner of the past.

"You can't imagine how I felt," she told a friend that first summer, "when I was going through Jack's things in the White House and found a set of cuff links in his drawer, emblazoned with the map of Texas. Oh, God—it's awful. I try not to be bitter, but I know I am."[1]

Her desire to flee was evident when she spent one weekend at the suburban New York home of Jim and Mary Fosburgh. Jim Fosburgh, an art collector and a historian, had advised Jackie during her restoration of the White House. Another guest, the entertainer Kitty Carlisle Hart, recalls that everyone was sitting around the pool and the conversation lagged. Hart said, "Let's all tell what our Walter Mitty [our fantasy] is. We all have a Walter Mitty." When it was Jackie's turn, she said quietly: "I'd like to be a bird."[2]

She flew away whenever she could. On the evening of July 2, Lyndon Johnson signed the Civil Rights Act, arguably the twentieth century's most important piece of legislation. It ended legal segregation in public places and banned employment discrimination on the basis of race, color, religion, sex, or national origin. It was a stunning achievement. It was the fulfillment of John F. Kennedy's dream, but it took the shock of his assassination and Johnson's parliamentary skills to make it happen. Had she wanted to attend the ceremony in the East Room, Jackie certainly could have; instead she was hundreds of miles away on the Cape as her husband's successor basked in triumph.

Disappointed—at times angry—at Jackie's refusal to visit him in the White House, Johnson continued to obsess about her. Calling to wish her a happy Fourth of July, he was laughing and cheerful, as if he weren't bothered at all. But he was, and he let others know it.

The Democratic convention was coming up—it would be held in Atlantic City—and Johnson, paranoid and insecure, worried about the role "Miz Kennedy" would play. His nightmare was that his mortal enemy—Attorney General Robert Kennedy—would seek the vice presidency, and that Jackie would make a dramatic appearance to place his name in nomination. This, the president fretted, would cause an emotional outpouring that would overshadow his own carefully choreographed moment in the spotlight.[3]

The idea of Robert Kennedy serving as Johnson's running mate emerged as early as December 1963, and the notion—referred to in the West Wing as "the Bobby problem," horrified LBJ. "I don't want history to say I was elected to this office because I had Bobby on the ticket with me," he told Kenneth (Ken) O'Donnell, the late president's top lieutenant, some three weeks after Dallas. "But I'll take him if I need him."[4]

But that was then. Now, in early July 1964, the president's Gallup approval rating stood at 74 percent,* while other surveys indicated that he would crush the likely Republican nominee, Arizona senator Barry Goldwater, in November. Johnson changed his tune. "I don't need that little runt to win," he told his brother, Sam.[5] But now the president had a new dilemma: how to cut his nemesis loose. LBJ, always scheming, wanted him out of the picture but worried about the deep reservoir of goodwill the American people had toward the Kennedys—and particularly toward Jackie.

A joke circulating around Washington reflected Johnson's disdain for Robert: if the choice for VP came down to him or Ho Chi Minh, the leader of communist North Vietnam, why of course, the president would do the right thing and take Ho. The president came up with a solution. He announced that "it would be inadvisable for me to recommend to the convention any member of the Cabinet" to join him on the ticket. In throwing everyone overboard, LBJ was fooling no one,

---

* Johnson's Gallup approval rating would never be that high again. It would gradually decline to 36 percent in March 1968, just before he decided not to seek reelection. It rebounded in his final months, but when he left office in January 1969, it was slightly underwater at 49 percent.

least of all his attorney general, but it gave him the political cover he desired.[6],*

Some Americans even wanted Jackie herself on the ticket. "Johnson and Jackie in '64—Her Plan to Run for Vice-President," blared the cover of the gossipy *Ladies Home Companion.* Magazine publishers in 1964 seemed to have a two-step marketing plan to boost circulation: find a photo of Jackie and/or her kids, splash it across the cover with a giant headline, and then concoct a story around it. In this case, the story was preposterous—as if a shy, soft-spoken woman who never cared much for the profession she had married into would for a second consider such a thing—but that wasn't the point. "The former First Lady has not stepped forward to encourage or discourage the rumor that she might become the Vice-Presidential candidate," the article, which had no byline attached to it, said tantalizingly. In this case, and others like it, "the rumor" may have been started by the magazine itself because its editors knew it would sell.

Not only did Jackie want nothing to do with politics; she wanted nothing to do with Washington, period. She decided to return to New York, where she had spent her early childhood, hoping it would provide the privacy and security she craved. On some level, she hoped that teeming Manhattan would also provide something else: anonymity, though this was hardly feasible for someone ubiquitous like Jackie.

The news broke on July 6. The announcement, made through her press secretary, Pamela Turnure, acknowledged that Jackie wished to leave the nation's capital and its now tragic memories behind and start fresh in Manhattan. It was to be a clean sweep: she would sell not only 3017 N Street but Wexford, too.

"While she will always maintain her close ties in Washington," the statement said, "Mrs. Kennedy feels that the change of environment in New York, from Georgetown and its many memories, will be beneficial to her and the children."[7]

---

* Johnson was so paranoid about Bobby that he ordered J. Edgar Hoover to wiretap him during the convention. See: Thomas, 295

The news that Jackie was coming to Manhattan set off immediate speculation among status-conscious New Yorkers about where she would live and what elite schools Caroline and John would attend. "Although thus far the word from Mrs. Kennedy's office is 'no comment,'" reported the *New York Times* a few days later, "the most likely prospects for Caroline seem to be the Convent of the Sacred Heart, 1 East 91st Street, and the Chapin School, 100 East End Avenue, with St. David's School, 12 East 89th Street, in the lead for John." Of course, Jackie had attended Chapin herself, the paper noted, adding that the Kennedys were expected to settle "somewhere in the 60's or 70's." It wasn't necessary to say "East" Sixties or Seventies, of course.

The prospect of rubbing elbows with Jacqueline Kennedy—of having her as a neighbor and follow school mother—was the talk of the town that summer. Social climbers were agog.

The clean sweep involved more than real estate. Mary Gallagher, who learned of the move like everyone else—in the paper—got a call from Jackie.

"I suppose by now you've read the newspapers about my move to New York," Jackie began.

"Yes, Jackie," Gallagher replied, "I have, but—"

"Well," Jackie interrupted, "since my life is all changed now and my staff will be located in New York, I guess I really won't be needing you anymore after September first."

Gallagher, weak and in a state of shock, struggled to answer.

"Well, Jackie, if that's your decision..." Her voice dropped off.

"Oh now, Mary," Jackie responded, "Don't get huffy..." Gallagher realized that Jackie couldn't tell the difference between huffy and hurt.

Jackie continued, "I know it's all very sad. But it would be just too impractical to try to operate between New York and Washington, dictating over long distance. And the New York office can handle my bills and bookkeeping, since they do it for all the other Kennedys."[8,] *

---

* Years later, Gallagher, by then in her late eighties, said she was tired of talking about Jackie and the Kennedys, and politely ended my call.

Jackie's first summer as a widow was split largely between the Kennedy family's suite at the Carlyle hotel, her Manhattan base while she hunted for an apartment, and Hyannis, where she stayed as usual in her husband's cottage on Irving Avenue. A small army of Kennedy kids was usually around, providing Caroline and John with more than enough playmates each day.

After six months on N Street with the daily hordes of tourists who had been not only an irritant but a security concern, the Hyannis compound provided both privacy and a safety buffer. Other than her visit to Bunny Mellon's estate in Antigua, it was really the first time since the assassination that Jackie could let her guard down. There were no sidewalk catcalls, no photographers or reporters lurking about.

Yet despite her antipathy toward the press, Jackie was shrewd enough to recognize the power she had over it, and how she could leverage it to her own ends. Anticipating a barrage of coverage on the approaching first anniversary of the assassination, she was determined to focus—as she had with her White and Schlesinger interviews—not on her husband's death but on his life and legacy. And as she had with Manchester and his book on the assassination, she would cooperate with one outlet, she decided, and no other.

Look was preparing a special issue to coincide with November 22, and Stanley Tretick, who had photographed the Kennedys in the White House, had written to Jackie in mid-May asking for her cooperation. She hadn't been interested. Now he tried again. Tretick had been moved by a memorial issue that rival *Life* had run on JFK's birthday, particularly by Jackie's tribute to her slain husband. He wrote her on July 12:

> My feeling is that in the context of the Memorial Issue, it would not be harmful to show that [JFK's] children…are getting along fine with the help of his brother and some of the rest of the family. And that Mrs. John F. Kennedy (even though the scar will never heal) is not in the depths of deep despair, that she is working hard to preserve the fine image of President Kennedy and that she is building a new life for her and her children.[9]

Jackie still might have said no were it not for Robert Kennedy. Johnson hadn't taken his cabinet, and thus the attorney general, out of the "veepstakes" yet; Bobby also had his eye on a Senate seat from New York. Either possibility meant the need to "play nice" with the press, and Bobby had been cooperating with *Look* for some time. The magazine had done a spread of Kennedy at his Virginia home—the famous Hickory Hill—and written that RFK was stepping out of his late brother's shadow while also looking after Jackie, Caroline, and John in their hour of need. Perhaps you should cooperate with *Look*, RFK told his sister-in-law.*

She did, albeit reluctantly. Describing herself that summer as "a living wound"[10]—it had been only a few weeks since her suicide chats with Father McSorley—Jackie was wistful and preoccupied in Tretick's photos. It was a beach setting, and she was dressed casually: tight white capri pants that hugged her hips, and an untucked yellow T-shirt. It was a bright summer day, and Tretick had her walk with her back to the sea. As she strolled barefoot across the lawn holding her shoes, the wind tousled her brunette hair just so. The overall effect was stunning. Her thirty-fifth birthday was days away.

And yet she could barely smile, even in the photos with her children. In one shot, she looked on as Caroline hugged her cocker spaniel, Shannon. Another shows Caroline and John sporting serious looks as their mother looks on. The overall effect conveyed the accurate mood: deep sadness.

THE ANTICIPATION NEW YORKERS HAD at the prospect of Jackie's moving to Gotham was offset by some Washingtonians, who accused her of abandoning her husband's world. It was a selfish thought, one that often defined public expectations of Jackie in the mid-sixties.

---

* *Look's* December 3, 1963, issue was regrettable. It featured President Kennedy and a playful John on the cover. The headline: "The President and His Son." It had been too late to stop the issue, which hit newsstands shortly after the assassination.

The martyred president's widow was, some felt, supposed to live and behave in a certain way. But Jackie wanted to live her way, on her terms, regardless of whether this satisfied the expectations of others. In the end, the healthiest thing that anyone could do for her was to let her be that bird flying away.

But where would she live? And how would the most famous, most recognizable woman in the world discreetly find a home? After her disastrous and short-lived experience at 3017 N Street, Jackie was determined that this next move would succeed. She and her friend Nancy Tuckerman cooked up a scheme to keep her apartment hunt a secret. To avoid publicity, Tuckerman pretended to be the buyer, while Jackie, in disguise, played the role of nanny. Somehow, they pulled it off.

She learned from another close friend, Jayne Wrightsman, that an apartment on the fifteenth floor at 1040 Fifth Avenue, on the corner of Fifth Avenue and Eighty-Fifth Street, was for sale. Wrightsman, the wealthy widow of an Oklahoma oilman, had helped Jackie redecorate the White House, and passed word that Beverly Weicker, the owner of the unit and partial heiress to the Squibb pharmaceutical empire, was looking to sell. Jackie looked at it and felt at home immediately.

Then, as now, one of the taller apartment buildings along Fifth Avenue, 1040, was designed by Rosario Candela, a Sicilian immigrant who had earned his mark as an architect during the Roaring Twenties and early thirties. It was constructed in 1930 and was immediately branded as a haven of luxury for the discerning buyer. It went co-op in 1951, meaning a prospective buyer had to pass muster with an often-snooty group of busybodies who approved or rejected applications.

But who wouldn't want to have Jacqueline Kennedy as a neighbor? Actually, Robert Kennedy, who liked 1040 for its location and security, worried that the co-op board might be turned off by her fame and the unwanted attention her presence would undoubtedly bring. It was an old-money building, a building of quiet wealth, and although the board unquestionably would be sympathetic to the beautiful young widow, it still might prefer that she settle down elsewhere.

Such concerns proved unfounded. Jackie's application sailed through, and she began planning for the move. She was so eager to flee Washington that she left before renovations to her new home were even finished. In less than a year, she had lived in the White House, a borrowed home on N Street, and then a home of her own on the same block. But 1040 Fifth Avenue would stick. Here, in her fifteenth-floor aerie, she would remain for the final three decades of her life. She would never refer to it as her "building"; it was always "ten forty."

"FOUR MORE YEARS" should have been the chant in Atlantic City, New Jersey, where the Democratic convention was held in 1964. Instead, the thundering cheers that echoed through Boardwalk Hall were for an accidental chief executive. A Texas murder had made a Texan president, and Lyndon Johnson was hungry to win the presidency in his own right.

Behind the rostrum in the cavernous convention hall, huge photos of past Democratic heroes had been hung: Roosevelt, Truman, and in between, John F. Kennedy. But an even bigger photo of Johnson, in fact two of them, were also featured, under the slogan "Let Us Continue."

This was to be Johnson's coronation, but he knew that the Kennedy shadow loomed large. Having taken his mortal enemy Robert Kennedy out of consideration for a running mate on the flimsiest of pretexts, the president now maneuvered to minimize Bobby's presence in Atlantic City. Minimizing Jackie's, however, was a far more delicate task. On the final night of the convention, August 27, there would be a tribute to John F. Kennedy—it was unavoidable—and a short documentary about the slain president would be shown. The last thing LBJ wanted was for Jackie to speak before or after the screening. He feared that the presence of the widow would unleash a torrent of emotion and diminish not only his glory but the legitimacy he craved. He sought to prevent this by inviting her to sit next to him in the presidential box during the screening, so the two of them could be seen together.

Jackie

There was no need for such Johnsonian paranoia. Jackie was in no condition, nor did she even desire, to speak at the convention, and minimized her presence on her own. She let it be known that she would fly into Atlantic City on the twenty-seventh for one event—a reception hosted by Averell Harriman, who of course had loaned Jackie his Georgetown home the previous winter—and then depart immediately, skipping the convention hall and tribute to her husband altogether.

But Johnson had been right about the emotional impact of her presence. At the reception, she, along with Robert and Ethel Kennedy, greeted delegates in three shifts, many of whom wept at the mere sight of her. The actor Fredric March and his wife, Florence Eldridge, read parts of JFK's favorite poems, including his favorite—the now eerie "I Have a Rendezvous with Death," by Alan Seeger. "It may be he shall take my hand," they intoned, "and lead me into his dark land…" Later, introduced by Harriman, Jackie spoke in a velvet-soft voice that could barely be heard: "Thank you all for coming, all of you who helped President Kennedy in 1960," she said. "May his light always shine in all parts of the world." Tears also flowed when she twice stepped onto a balcony to wave to crowds on the boardwalk below. And with that, she scurried away to the seclusion and tranquility of Newport."

But after successfully fleeing an emotionally charged Atlantic City, Jackie erred in watching the tribute to her husband that night on TV. There was no politically feasible way for Johnson to keep Bobby from introducing the film, and before he even said a word, there was a sixteen-minute ovation. Delegates were seen dabbing their eyes; RFK's glistened as well, and Jackie, three hundred miles to the north, was overcome. When the crowd finally hushed, Bobby quoted lines from Shakespeare's *Romeo and Juliet*, one of which was: "…and when he shall die, take him and cut him out into stars and he shall make the face of heaven so fine…"[12]

And then the film was shown, and as Jackie's television screen filled with images of her husband with Caroline and John Jr., she was devastated anew. The next day, she wrote a Georgetown friend, the columnist Joseph Alsop, and said it had been a mistake to watch.

THE CONVENTION OVER, JACKIE RETURNED to N Street briefly to pack, then left Washington for good. She had arrived in 1950, an obscure twenty-one-year-old transfer student at George Washington University. Fourteen years later, she was arguably the most famous woman in the world. But now she was done. Done with the city, done with her interviews—with Schlesinger and, most painful of all, with Manchester. Arriving in Manhattan, she plunged in immediately, walking Caroline to her first day of school on September 15 at the exclusive Convent of the Sacred Heart on East Ninety-First Street. Caroline loved her school uniform, which consisted of a gray jumper, white blouse, and gray jacket, topped by a red beret and camel topcoat. She was proud of her new look, and it gave her mother pride as well. Caroline already knew two classmates, her cousins Sydney and Victoria, who lived nearby. Their mother, Patricia Kennedy Lawford (Jackie's sister-in-law), joined the family contingent that morning.

But no sooner had Jackie left Washington and, she had hoped, her painful past, when she was dragged right back.

Writer Jim Bishop, undeterred by Jackie's rejection earlier in the year, had pressed on with his book *The Day Kennedy Was Shot*, and had written again to request an interview. On her distinctive black-bordered stationery, with the letterhead "Mrs. John F. Kennedy," she wrote a four-page letter and got right to the point.

> I write to appeal to you to please not go ahead with your intended book *The Day Kennedy Was Shot,*" [underline original].
>
> The idea of it is so distressing to me. I cannot bear to think of seeing—or of seeing advertised—a book with that name and subject—or that my children might see it or someone might mention it to them. This whole year has been a struggle and it seems you can never escape from reminders. You try so hard to avoid them—then you take the children to the news shop—and there is a picture of Oswald on it staring up at you.

Scribbling on, Jackie told Bishop that it was her intention to avoid as much coverage of her husband's death as possible, including the soon-to-be released Warren Report: "I will try not to read the papers until it is over with."

The problem, of course, is that it would never be over with. Manchester's and Bishop's books were merely the first two of what would be a steady stream of works concerning the assassination. Deep down, she knew this. Her letter continued:

> It was my fear as long ago as December [1963]—that all sorts of different and never ending conflicting, and sometimes sensational things would be written about President Kennedy's death. So I hired William Manchester—to protect President Kennedy and the truth.

Jackie told Bishop that Manchester would:

> …interrogate everyone who had any connection with those days— and if I decide the book should never be published—then Mr. Manchester will be reimbursed for his time. Or if I decide it should be known—I will decide when it should be published—sometime in the future when the pain is not so fresh. I suppose I must let it appear—for I have no right to suppress history, which people have a right to know, for reasons of private pain.[13]

She ended with an emotional appeal:

> I beg you not to go ahead with your book…. You were most sensitive to my feelings the one time I met you—I fervently hope you will be again."[14],*

In the prologue to his book, Bishop said he politely wrote back to Jackie, telling her that whether she cooperated or not, he would press forward. Her response was immediate and stiff. "None of the people connected with November 22nd will speak to anyone but Mr.

---

* Her plea fell on deaf ears. *The Day Kennedy Was Shot* was published on November 22, 1968— the fifth anniversary of the assassination—to good reviews despite the fact that, as one reviewer notes, "the Manchester book (among many others) raises further doubts of its necessity." See: Kirkus review of *The Day Kennedy Was Shot*.

70

Manchester…the Manchester book will be published with no censorship from myself or from anyone else." The Kennedys, Bishop writes, "were trying to copyright the assassination."[15]

On September 24, Chief Justice Earl Warren presented President Johnson with a mammoth 888-page report on the assassination. The report, Jackie knew, would generate an avalanche of TV reports, blaring headlines, and magazine covers. Coming just four months after her talk of suicide with Father McSorley, she feared it would breathe new life into the nightmare that hadn't gone away.

Released to the public three days later, the central finding of the Warren Commission was that Lee Harvey Oswald, acting alone and with the assistance of no one, killed John F. Kennedy. It says Oswald fired three shots, one of which missed, though the report says the evidence was inconclusive as to which one. But, it claims, this much is clear: one bullet struck Kennedy in the back, exited through his throat, and punched through Texas governor John Connally's back and chest before hitting his right wrist and left thigh.* A third and final shot then entered the right rear of the president's head, shattering his skull and brain—the fatal shot. The report also said that Jack Ruby, the organized crime-linked nightclub owner who killed Oswald forty-eight hours after the president's murder, also acted alone.

The news coverage was, as Jackie expected, enormous. On September 28 alone, the *New York Times* overwhelmed readers with a forty-eight-page insert that summarized the commission's findings. "Few who loved John Kennedy, or this country, will be able to read it without emotion," wrote the paper's Anthony Lewis.[16]

Unfortunately, Jackie had been planning to cancel her newspapers ahead of the report's publication but forgot to do so. She immediately

---

* Critics soon began questioning how one bullet could pass through Kennedy's neck, somehow change direction in midair, and strike Connally, who was sitting right in front of the president. It must be "magic," they said, and thus the "magic bullet" theory was born. What these critics never realized was that Connally wasn't sitting right in front of Kennedy. His seat was in front but slightly to the left of Kennedy's, around the eleven o'clock position; it was also lower than Kennedy's. The governor had also been twisting around in that seat when he was struck—meaning the bodies of the two men were aligned in such a way that one bullet could have done exactly what the report said it did.

cancelled them for the rest of the week. She probably watched little television that week, and if she ventured outside, she probably avoided looking at newsstands. But she couldn't wall herself off from coverage completely. When she went into Kenneth's, her hair salon on East Fifty-Fourth Street, she saw the October 2 issue of *Life*. Of all the newspapers and magazines to catch her eye, this was surely the most painful. Editors put four frames, in full color, on the cover, taken after President Kennedy was first hit but before the final shot that killed him. Even a brief, unintentional glance immediately transported Jackie back to the scene: the bright Texas sun, the midnight-blue Lincoln, and the First Lady, in her final moment as First Lady, reaching over to help her stricken husband. For nearly a year, Jackie had relived the assassination countless times in her mind; now she was looking at actual pictures. "It was terrible," she said.[17]

As far as the United States government was concerned, the Warren Commission settled it. The Kennedy assassination was history. It had been solved; it was time to move on. But the commission failed to answer the one question that haunted Americans: why? As Lewis noted, the report "suggested that Oswald had no rational purpose, no motive adequate 'if judged by the standards of reasonable men.'"[18]

None of this mattered to the widow. After the assassination, upon learning of Oswald's background, which included a stint living the Soviet Union, Jackie bitterly remarked that her husband "didn't even have the satisfaction of being killed for civil rights. It had to be some silly little Communist."[19] As for questions of any conspiracy: "What difference does it make whether he was killed by the CIA, the FBI, the Mafia, or simply some half-crazed misanthrope?" she told Theodore White. "It won't change anything. It won't bring him back."[20] Indeed it wouldn't. Abraham Lincoln had been martyred after waging a war in which ending slavery was paramount. But John F. Kennedy's slaying seemed as random as it was meaningless.

Needless to say, Jackie didn't read the report. She had no need to. She had lived it, and continued to live it, each day. And there was no chance of a respite: the first anniversary of the assassination itself loomed.

The Warren Report also revived Jackie's security fears—not just for herself but for Caroline and John. And yet, on October 8, she allowed the protective cloak over them to be briefly lifted to give Bobby's campaign a boost. In an effort to remind voters that he wasn't a carpetbagger, as even some Democrats charged, Jackie allowed him to take John Jr. to Riverdale—the swanky part of the Bronx where the Kennedy family had lived from 1927 to 1929—for a photo op. As they stood in front of the house—a sprawling twenty-room mansion at 5040 Independence Avenue—photographers snapped away at Bobby and his famous nephew, who wore short red pants and a white sweater and had chocolate all over his face. It was adorable, but this merely fueled critics who said it was just another example of Bobby's ruthlessness, that he was a man who would do anything to win.

Looking for good press, RFK also got Jackie to meet, against her better instincts, with Dorothy Schiff, the influential owner and publisher of the *New York Post*. Schiff, twenty-six years older, was deferential as they met in Jackie's suite at the Carlyle. Schiff wanted to do a story on Jackie but also had a misguided idea about signing her up as a columnist.

Jackie exhibited vulnerability to Schiff, saying that for all her eagerness to flee Georgetown, she was apprehensive about New York, too. She told Schiff of her error in not cancelling the newspapers before their blizzard of coverage of the Warren Report.

And she made it clear that she remained stricken. "People tell me that time will heal," she told Schiff quietly. "How much time?"[21]

Election night fell on November 3. President Johnson won a crushing victory over Goldwater, winning 61.1 percent of the vote and 486—90 percent—of 538 electoral votes. For nearly a year, since Johnson had taken the oath of office in a cramped, sweltering cabin on Air Force One, the "accidental president" moniker had gnawed at him. "For millions of Americans I was still illegitimate, a naked man with no presidential covering, an illegal usurper," he said years later.[22] Those insecurities were largely erased by his 22.58 percent winning margin, the fourth biggest in history.* Derided as "Landslide Lyndon" for stealing the 1948 Senate election in Texas by a mere eighty-seven votes—and that's exactly what he did, "he stole it,"[23] asserts LBJ's master biographer Robert Caro—Lyndon Johnson, in the final election of his life, finally, and legitimately, was just that. It was an overwhelming triumph.

But Johnson's 43,127,041 tally was missing the one vote he prized perhaps above all others: Jackie's. He had heard that she hadn't voted on Election Day and was hurt by it. It had nothing to do with him. Jackie admired the president but simply couldn't cast a ballot for anyone. She explained to Joe Frantz of the LBJ Library in 1974:

> I'd never voted until I was married to Jack. I guess my first vote was probably for him for senator.... Then this vote would have been—he would have been alive for that vote. And I thought, I'm not going to vote for any[one] because this vote would have been his. Of course I would have voted for President Johnson. It wasn't that at all. It was some emotional thing, that [JFK] would have been alive.[24]

Johnson's coattails stretched all the way to New York, where Robert Kennedy defeated incumbent senator Kenneth Keating by ten percentage points. In Massachusetts, where no one named Kennedy could have been defeated in 1964, Edward, who had won a special election to his late brother's old seat in 1962, was elected by a three-to-one margin—an even bigger landslide than Johnson's.

The double triumph for the Kennedy family marked the first time that two brothers had ever been elected to the Senate simultaneously, and talk began immediately that Bobby's win was the first step in what followers hoped, dreamed, assumed would result in the eventual return of the Kennedys to "Crown," the Secret Service's code word for the White House.

---

* Johnson's 22.58 percent winning margin has been exceeded only by Richard Nixon (23.15 percent over George McGovern in 1972), Franklin D. Roosevelt (24.26 percent over Alf Landon in 1936), Calvin Coolidge (25.22 percent over John Davis in 1924)—and the granddaddy of all landslides: Warren Harding's 26.17 percent margin over James Cox in 1920.

But to Jackie, as she attended an election night party at Delmonico's, a midtown Manhattan steakhouse, her thoughts were of Jack and what might have been. It should have been *his* night. *His* celebration.

❧

THE *LOOK* ISSUE MARKING THE FIRST ANNIVERSARY of the assassination hit newsstands on November 17. In the upper-right-hand corner was a picture of President Kennedy's coffin, perched atop his grave, its five-hundred-year-old African mahogany gleaming in the buttery afternoon light. But the main image, from many taken that summer by *Look* editor Laura Bergquist, showed an unsmiling Jackie, cuddled up with John, who seemed to be staring off into space.

The president's son, now approaching his fourth birthday, often recalled the "big white house" but seemed confused by it. Whenever he saw a picture of it, he would ask his mother or Maud Shaw: "That's where we live, isn't it?"

"No, John, we don't live there anymore," Shaw would say. Eventually, he figured it out: "That's where we *used* to live, Caroline," he told his sister one day.

As for Caroline, "she is almost seven now," Bergquist writes. "Withdrawn at times, shy, quiet, marked. As her mother leafs through the family album, she remembers: the lost days, the summer sun at Hyannis Port, the excitement of the helicopter awhirl over the compound, cruises at sea and storytelling, Daddy." She continued: "Caroline, once the bubbling White House sprite, was already growing into a reserved young lady last November, but in this difficult year since, she has been a changed child," she added. "Caroline remembers, and she feels her father's loss deeply." A photo shows a pensive-looking Jackie sitting next to Caroline as the girl clings to Shannon, her cocker spaniel.[25]

The entire issue is one long, melancholic tribute to the late president and those he left behind. It is exactly the sort of thing that Jackie had tried so hard to avoid seeing, and yet she had forced herself to cooperate in its preparation. It was another example of the dueling forces pulling at her: her need to forget the pain, to move on—while honoring her late husband.

"A lonely summer for Jacqueline," Bergquist writes, noting that the past year had revealed a side of Jackie previously unknown to the American people. "In her own style," she says, "Jacqueline Kennedy is as complex a human as her husband ever was: gentle, feminine, elusive, witty, ironic, disciplined, stubborn, tough." She quoted an unnamed friend: "That look of fragility is deceptive."[26]

As for Jackie herself, she told Bergquist, "I try not to be bitter." She asked to write her own tribute to Jack. She wrote and wrote, going through numerous revisions, until she was satisfied with these 391 words:

> It is nearly a year since he has been gone.
>
> On so many days—his birthday, an anniversary, watching his children running to the sea—I have thought, "But this day last year was his last to see that." He was so full of love and life on all those days. He seems so vulnerable now, when you think that each one was a last time.
>
> Soon the final day will come around again—as inexorably as it did last year. But expected this time.
>
> It will find some of us different people than we were a year ago. Learning to accept what was unthinkable when he was alive, changes you. I don't think there is any consolation. What was lost cannot be replaced.
>
> Someone who loved President Kennedy, but who had never known him, wrote to me this winter: "The hero comes when he is needed. When our belief gets pale and weak, there comes a man out of that need who is shining—and everyone living reflects a little of that light—and stores some up against the time when he is gone."
>
> Now I think that I should have known that he was magic all along. I did know it—but I should have guessed it could not last. I should have known that it was asking too much to dream that I might have grown old with him and see our children grow up together.
>
> So now he is a legend when he would have preferred to be a man. I must believe that he does not share our suffering now. I think for him—at least he will never know whatever sadness might

have lain ahead. He knew such a share of it in his life that it always made you so happy whenever you saw him enjoying himself. But now he will never know more—not age, nor stagnation, nor despair, nor crippling illness, nor loss of any more people he loved. His high noon kept all the freshness of the morning—and he died then, never knowing disillusionment.

She quoted from the English poet John Masefield:

...he has gone
Among the radiant, ever venturing on,
Somewhere, with morning, as such spirits will.

Her conclusion reflected her continued despair:

He is free and we must live. Those who love him most know that "the death you have dealt is more than the death which has swallowed you."

And then, in her distinctive sweeping handwriting:

Jacqueline Kennedy[27]

Parts of Jackie's tribute seem, from the vantage point of nearly six decades past, overwrought in its effusiveness ("his high noon kept all the freshness of the morning"). Yet the overall effect remains touching and eloquent—very much reflective of a woman in pain. And of course there's the irony of a woman so dismissive of the press, so resentful of its constant intrusiveness, now using it to further her ongoing mission—to place her martyred husband on a pedestal—is rather rich; but in 1964 it worked for her, it worked for circulation-minded publishers, and it worked for a mournful public.*

As important as the *Look* project was to Jackie, a far more consequential matter was on her mind: selecting the final design for her husband's

---

* *Look's* November 17 issue marking the first anniversary of the assassination was planned well in advance yet contained an odd insensitivity: a full-page ad of a woman carefully firing a shotgun. Placed adjacent to the end of an article that noted how "President Kennedy is mourned by millions," it was an ad for, all of things, 7UP. "Get Real Action," the ad read. "7-Up Your Thirst Away!"

grave. The Arlington site that had been hastily prepared for John F. Kennedy the year before was never meant to be permanent. Shortly after the funeral, had Jackie hired the architect John Carl Warnecke to design something new.

Ironically, Warnecke and Jackie had first connected because of JFK himself. In March 1962, when Jackie was working to save the historic federal buildings in Lafayette Square across from the White House, Kennedy asked Warnecke to help. The divorced, ex-Stanford University football star was only too happy to oblige. That fall, the night before their first meeting, the architect and the First Lady both happened to be at a dinner dance at the British embassy. On the dance floor, he cut in, saying, "I'm the man you're going to meet tomorrow; would you like to dance?"[28]

While they moved about, they chatted.

"Are you happy?" he asked.

"Oh, Jack, now, what kind of question is that?" she responded. He was flirting, and she seemed to enjoy it.[29] While they were working together on the Lafayette Park plan, an eerie photo of Warnecke and Jackie together shows her wearing the same pink Chanel knockoff suit she would later wear in Dallas.

When Warnecke began working on JFK's permanent gravesite, Jackie gave him his marching orders:

> She wanted me to present a design based on studies of the graves of the different presidents and how they resembled the character of the time. She didn't want some towering monument. It is a simple design. I don't recall her being overly emotional or depressed. She focused on it calmly. She approved the design, but she wanted every member of the family treated as though they were the client, asking me to make a presentation to each of them for their individual approval. Jackie said, "Take your time. Be patient. Don't worry. Keep going." Finally toward the end of the summer, I said, "Come on out and see the model." I remember specifically Jackie loving trees, and how they could protect the grave site. I wanted it all open. So, we put them on side, and we kept the hill open.

I took it for granted, and I'm sure that she knew, that there was a place for her. She knew that the nation revered her, and she was conscious about it. Not that she was looking forward to it! It was not a subject that we would talk about every day.[30]

Having approved the plan, and getting emotionally closer to Warnecke in the process, Jackie plunged into an affair with him—her first serious relationship since her husband's death.

It began when Jackie's mother, Janet Auchincloss, invited him to Hammersmith Farm, her Rhode Island home where Jackie had lived, and, in 1953, celebrated her wedding to John F. Kennedy. Warnecke was asked to inspect the work of a local stone carver who had been selected to carve the inscription on JFK's grave. Jackie was there. Warnecke told biographer Sarah Bradford that after a year of working with Jackie on the grave's design, he realized that they kept looking at each other. Finally, Warnecke made his move: "Why don't you let me drive back to Hyannis Port, let me over from the Secret Service?"

Jackie said yes.

"That's where it started," Warnecke says. "I spent the weekend with her. I can't remember where the children were, I just remember us."

It went on for a year and a half.

When Jackie told Robert Kennedy about the relationship, he wasn't thrilled. Bobby told her—using a phrase he would find himself repeating over the next few years—that it was too soon. His calculus, filtered as usual through a political prism, was that President Kennedy had been gone for only a year. Besides, Bobby, with higher aspirations than the Senate, thought that Jackie would be more valuable if she remained the beautiful, elegant widow. The opinion was fundamentally a selfish one, but Jackie went along. Warnecke would not be seen as her public escort until the autumn of 1965.[31]

November 22 itself fell on a Sunday. Exactly one year before, the eyes of Texas had been upon Jackie as she wore that spectacular

pink-and-raspberry suit and pillbox hat* in Fort Worth and Dallas—
and as evening fell, on Andrews Air Force Base as she accompanied
her husband's coffin off Air Force One. Now, on this day—the first of
thirty anniversaries of November 22, 1963, she would endure—she was
alone, holed up with her children in a fieldstone house on a small island
off Glen Cove, Long Island. Jackie had rented the ten-room home the
month before from the eldest son of the late financier J. P. Morgan.[32]
The home, lonely and in an isolated location, seemed an appropriate
metaphor.

Sleep remained fitful. "I often wake up at night suddenly, and then
I look for Jack next to me…" she told Henry Brandon, a British jour-
nalist who had covered the Kennedy presidency, "and he is not there….
I wonder whether I am going to see him after death!"[33,†]

---

* The hat, torn off by Jackie during the frantic race to Parkland Hospital, is one of the most
important artifacts from the assassination that is missing. I've spoken with two people known to
have come into contact with it that weekend: Clint Hill, who of course jumped into the presidential
limousine on Elm Street, and Mary Gallagher, Jackie's personal secretary. Hill thinks Gallagher has it,
but Gallagher declined to discuss it, saying that after more than half a century, she was tired of talking
about the Kennedys. Another Secret Service agent, Paul Landis—who helped remove a limp President
Kennedy from his car—also declined to discuss it.

† Brandon, with the London *Sunday Times*, had been advised to accompany the Kennedys to
Texas by presidential assistant Fred Holborn—who said there might be trouble. Because of this tip,
Brandon was the only foreign correspondent in Dallas on November 22, 1963. See: Manchester, 38.

Chapter Three

January to June 1965:
Keeper of the Flame

On January 20, Lyndon Johnson was sworn in for his own term as president. No one had ever taken the oath of office twice in a span of just fourteen months, and the thirty-sixth president celebrated with a "Texas-style" inaugural bash. He even rode from the Capitol to the White House in SS100X, the 1961 Lincoln Continental that had carried John F. Kennedy to his death. The car, now painted black instead of midnight blue, had been turned into a fortress on wheels, with a nonremovable bullet-resistant bubble top and heavy armor plating. The days of presidents riding in convertibles were over.*

"Y'all come and see us" was the inaugural theme, and although Jackie was invited as a courtesy, the Johnsons knew by now that they were wasting their time. Jackie wanted nothing to do with the festivities. It was supposed to have been her husband's day, and the sight of the White House, the sight of that car—that awful car—would

_____

* Not only did Lyndon Johnson ride in the Kennedy death car, but so did Presidents Richard Nixon, Gerald Ford, and Jimmy Carter before it was taken out of government service. You can see it today at the Henry Ford museum in Dearborn, Michigan.

have been too much. Even Clint Hill, who had shielded Jackie and her slain husband during the frantic race to Parkland hospital, walked beside the infamous vehicle. When Jackie said she would not—could not—come back to Washington, she meant it. She had even skipped the December groundbreaking for the new John F. Kennedy Center for the Performing Arts. Out of sight, out of mind: that, in essence, was Jackie's philosophy as she strove, day by day, to compartmentalize her painful memories.

NOW SETTLED IN AT 1040 FIFTH AVENUE, she welcomed one of her first visitors that month: Father McSorley. It had been seven months since she had first broached the possibility of suicide with him, and while McSorley knew such thoughts had ebbed, he remained concerned. But as he arrived at 1040, Jackie took him aside, her face somber. She told the reverend of a new worry: John, now four years old, had been hearing stories on TV about his father's death and was asking questions.

"Maybe, sometime, you will get the chance to answer the question that comes to John—'Why did they kill him?'" she suggested. "I don't know what to say. I don't know what's a good answer, and I feel inadequate about saying anything." She began to cry.

McSorley waited quietly until she regained her composure. "Just a word of explanation," she said, "and then moving on to some other subject will be enough.'"

The priest's opportunity came when he took John on a field trip. As their car drove through the Upper West Side, he pointed out the tomb of Ulysses S. Grant to John. He had been a president, too, he told the boy.

"Can we visit him?" John asked.

"No," McSorley replied, "because only his body is there. His spirit went to see God."

"Does everybody here go to meet God where they die?"

"No, only those who are good meet God."

This seemed to satisfy the boy.

"Did General Grant see Daddy?" McSorley said he didn't know.

"If we visit Daddy's grave, can we see him?"

"No, only his body is there, and his body has turned too dust," the reverend said.

John listened patiently, not appearing to understand as McSorley told him about the Catholic faith and the concept of resurrection. Finally, he interrupted:

"How can you go to the bathroom if you don't have a body?"[2]

John's inquisitiveness about death and the afterlife notwithstanding, he was still just a little boy and reveled in being one. New York was pounded with snow that first winter—the city got nearly fifteen inches in January alone—which meant fun and games. As Secret Service agents watched, Caroline and John joined other kids in sledding down Cedar Hill, a graceful slope in Central Park just south of the Metropolitan Museum of Art. Up and down the hill they went, shrieking with glee. Typically, they would come home around four o'clock, shaking the snow off their boots and sitting down to hot chocolate. Their cook—usually Marta Sgubin, sometimes Annemarie Huste, a young German émigré—topped it off with marshmallows and whipped cream; that and cinnamon toast or cookies would tide them over until dinner. Caroline's favorite meal from childhood was creamed chicken with rice and peas; John liked sloppy joes and chipped beef on toast.[3]

Jackie's own tastes were simple as well. Breakfast was little more than tea, toast, and a soft-boiled egg, delivered to her in bed each morning first by her longtime assistant Provi Paredes, and then a nineteen-year-old Irish émigré named Kathy McKeon.[4] Lunch was often cold chicken slices, cottage cheese, and sliced tomatoes. In the country during the summer, she would frequently snack on fresh vegetables, often just picked from the garden.[5]

It was bucolic enough, and conveyed the impression that Jackie herself was showing modest signs of improvement. The passage of the first anniversary of her husband's death, in fact, seemed a demarcation of sorts. Her year of mourning was over. "New clothes in the pale pastels and vibrant rich colors she loves have begun to replace the somber blacks and whites of her mourning wardrobe," one observer wrote in February.⁶ The difference was such that one could almost tell whether a photo was taken before or after that first anniversary.

As First Lady, Jackie often shunned requested social activities, giving others what she called the "PBO"—polite brush-off—or asking Lady Bird Johnson or others to fill in. Much of it frankly bored her. But if Washington was small and parochial—a city of "Southern efficiency and Northern charm," as John F. Kennedy once joked—New York was anything but. Everything that interested her was there; the city unrolled before her like a magic carpet.

She began to dip her toe in the water socially, beginning with small dinner parties and outings to restaurants, museums, galas, and the theater. She obviously never lacked for companionship, and preferred the company of men to women. Although she downgraded most of her old Washington friends, a handful remained in her inner circle, like Defense Secretary Robert McNamara, his assistant secretary, Roswell Gilpatric, and Pierre Salinger. She also enjoyed being with Adlai Stevenson (United Nations ambassador), John Kenneth Galbraith (former ambassador to India), and Schlesinger. That these powerful men found her desirable was a given: who wouldn't want to squire the world's most famous woman about town?

But these men all came from the political world—they were an extension of her husband. Now, in glittering Manhattan, she broadened her circle, surrounding herself with the likes of Leonard Bernstein, the famed composer; director and comedian Mike Nichols; writer Truman Capote; and pop artist Andy Warhol. Writers, directors, composers, and artists—this was a Manhattan crowd, her crowd, dazzling, creative, and fun, and Jackie began to revel in their presence as they did in hers.

In the arc that was Jackie's life, and how she came to be perceived, Warhol merits a closer look. One year older than Jackie, he had burst onto the New York art scene in 1961 and 1962 with his silkscreen images of iconic Americana: dollar bills, Coca-Cola bottles, Campbell's soup cans. But he was also fascinated by the intersection of celebrity and pop culture, and launched a "glamour series" on figures who were so big, they were universally recognizable by their first name alone: Marilyn, Liz, and Elvis. To this list another name would soon be added: Jackie.

On November 22, 1963, Warhol was in his Manhattan studio when word came over the radio that President Kennedy was dead. "Well, let's get to work," he said. From Friday's murder to Monday's burial, there were three days of round-the-clock television coverage. Watching along with the rest of the nation that weekend, Warhol realized that what bothered him wasn't so much that Kennedy was dead, but "the way television and radio were programming everyone to feel so sad. It seemed no matter how hard you tried, you couldn't get away from the thing."[7]

He was right: there was absolutely nothing else. Warhol considered it an assault on the senses. Yet as he watched, he was transfixed, as tens of millions of Americans were, by Jackie. He began clipping photos of her from newspapers and magazines. There was Jackie smiling at Love Field before the motorcade, radiant in her pink suit and pillbox hat. Jackie, with that stunned, blank expression as she stood next to Lyndon Johnson on Air Force One. Jackie, clad in black, eyes swollen, as she emerged onto the North Portico. Jackie, her doe-like eyes peering out from behind her mantilla.

Television that weekend did what it had to do: fill hours upon hours. Much of the coverage was therefore repetitive; viewers were shown the same clips over and over, as events slowly unfolded. Warhol had a different thought: one could also grasp the vast dimension of the tragedy simply by looking at a few carefully curated photos of before-and-after Jackie. Clearly, the photos showed that something dreadful had happened. And yet throughout, Warhol observed, she was glamorous and dignified, seemingly floating above it all.

Warhol took the photos and made some three hundred silkscreen portraits. His minimalist approach was powerful. If Jackie's involuntary transition from beaming political wife to devastated widow began in November 1963, the "Warhol Jackies," as they came to be known, played a role in her rapid elevation to something else, something transcendent: a cultural icon. "Warhol saw cultural changes in America early on," says biographer Richard Polsky. "He saw we were moving to a celebrity culture, and his art helped make Jackie more than a First Lady, it helped make her a celebrity."[8] Jackie did not seek this in 1964 and 1965; it was thrust upon her. Yet she accepted it and, in subsequent years, for what it was worth to her, embraced it.*

AMERICANS WATCHED HER EVERY MOVE with interest, as mourning and sympathy evolved into a near obsession with all things Jackie. Where she went and with whom. Where she ate, shopped, and vacationed. What events she chose to attend. Hungry reporters often begged, pleaded, and sometimes bribed anyone they thought could provide a story: friends, people who worked for her, neighbors in 1040. Her Fifth Avenue building became her fortress; doormen and Secret Service agents kept a close eye on everyone. Of course, whenever Jackie emerged, stepping onto Fifth Avenue and beyond, she was fair game. Her penchant for silence only fueled interest in her; newspapers printed practically whatever scraps of information they could get their hands on, no matter how devoid of news the item actually was.

Much of the reporting on Jackie during this period took on a speculative hue, a reflection of the fact that her loyalists, and there were many, didn't talk, knowing that if they did, they would be cut out of her life immediately. The inability of many reporters to get close to her resulted in news coverage that can best be described as vapid. Even the staid paper of record, the *New York Times*, fell prey to this temptation. Headlines in "the Gray Lady" that year included blockbuster items like:

"Mrs. Kennedy Spends Quiet New Year's Eve in Aspen" (January 1)

"Mrs. Kennedy Rides Chair Lift" (January 1)

---

* While a critical success, the Warhol Jackies were at first a commercial flop. "They did not sell well, they were too depressing," said Polsky. Today, they sell for upward of a million dollars.

"Mrs. Kennedy Ill with Flu" (November 5)

"Mrs. Kennedy Buys Horse" (December 8)[9]

At least these humdrum items were factual. The same could rarely be said of the always-hungry dime-store tabloids, which were quite skilled at taking minor scraps of information and embellishing them to turn them into dramatic, insider-y items. There was no insider access, of course, unless one considers a third party who had never spoken with anyone relevant an "insider."

She serves "hot and cold hors d'oeuvres" at parties, trumpeted *Inside Movie*.

"Her life seems over," proclaimed *Screen Album*. "She is like a garden in which everything has withered," a view which itself had withered.

In one tabloid, *Movie Stars*, Connie Stevens, a blonde starlet, wrote an article called "I Found God in Your School: Connie Speaks to Caroline." She did no such thing. The story mentioned that Stevens had attended Convent of the Sacred Heart, as did Caroline. But the school Stevens attended—years before—was out West, while Caroline's was of course in Manhattan. Upon such flimsiness, many a magazine was sold.[10]

But like a broken watch that's right twice a day, some of these items contained shreds of truth. The February 1965 issue of *Photoplay* provides an example from this period. "Too Soon for Love?" blared the headline on the cover, which featured a wistful-looking Jackie. "How Jackie Faces a Woman's Biggest Problem," was the subtitle. Her problem, the article said presumptuously, was being the single mother of two young children. "The enormous problem of a second father does not diminish," writer Charlotte Dinter says. "It is every widow's dilemma. But for some women, surely, it is easier to resolve."

Every widow's dilemma, yes, but Jackie's was like no other. "If she herself was poor, it would be easier: she would *have* to marry to take care of her family. If she were older, she might not expect to love again, as she had loved before: she might settle for companionship, comfort, affection," Dinter says, but "she is wealthy and young." Dinter then gets to the crux of the matter:

> If she had not loved so unique a man, perhaps she would find it less difficult to give her heart again…. [H]ow can she accept anything less than what she once had, how can she give her children less than what they knew, even so briefly—how can she, and they, call another man husband and father?[11]

The article includes no quotes from anyone who actually knew Jackie, of course, and is purely speculative, but nevertheless conveys some hard truths. It probably would have been harder for Jackie to remarry, given the small pool of available and acceptable men for someone like her. "I can't very well marry a dentist from New Jersey!" she told Truman Capote in 1968.[12]

Reading about herself always amused Jackie; she laughed to friends about how silly the coverage was. She was not amused, however, when it came to stories about Caroline and John. Fearing for their safety, she was offended and alarmed by what she saw as intrusiveness into their lives. Her mother-bear vigilance regarding her cubs, always paramount, had mushroomed since Dallas, and with good reason. They were safer high atop 1040 than on N Street, where merely peering out from behind a curtain would set off flashbulbs and shrieks of delight. But crossing the street into the park, going to school—John had just begun attending Saint David's, an elite private school on East Sixty-Ninth Street—or visiting Serendipity, their favorite ice cream parlor, always exposed them, she thought, to potential danger.* On one occasion, photographers angling for a shot knocked Caroline down, infuriating her mother.

And yet when the world wasn't watching, loneliness and sadness remained ever-present. Yes, she went out, knowing she would be engulfed in the glare of flashbulbs. But what Jackie craved—preferred—was privacy and solitude. Many an evening found her hanging

---

* Had Marilyn Monroe—almost certainly one of John F. Kennedy's lovers—lived, she could have run into Jackie there; the actress was a regular whenever she was in New York.

and rehanging pictures and shuffling the art that adorned 1040's walls. She lost herself for hours rearranging closets, moving shoes and outfits around, often in the middle of the night.[13] It occupied her mind, distracted her from what she was still struggling to overcome. It was all sad, though in relative terms represented progress from 1964 with its endless nightmares, rivers of alcohol, and thoughts of suicide. She was progressing, ever so gradually, to a better place.

Her new home proved therapeutic in that progression. There was Hyannis. And Palm Beach. And Newport. Weekends galloping about the rolling hills of northern New Jersey. Her relentless overseas jaunts. But above all, Jackie had 1040 Fifth Avenue. From the very first place she lived in as in infant in 1929—790 Park Avenue—to 3017 N Street in 1964, Jacqueline Kennedy was associated with twenty-six different addresses before she was even thirty-five years old. But over her final thirty years—three-quarters of her adult life—she would spend the bulk of her time at 1040. It proved to be her favorite destination of all, her haven, her restorative aerie.

Nancy Tuckerman, her lifelong friend and assistant, tells the story of Jackie's very first night there. "The day Jackie moved into her apartment, we spent the day unpacking, emptying cartons, putting books in bookcases. Around 8:00 in the evening, the doorbell rang and Jackie, in her blue jeans and looking quite disheveled, opened the door. There stood two distinguished-looking couples in full evening attire. When they recognized Jackie, they were taken aback. They said they were expected for dinner at Mrs. Whitehouse's. It turned out that the elevator man, unnerved by the thought of Jackie's presence in the building, was unable to associate the name Whitehouse with anyone or anything but her."[14]

The juxtaposition of being in the middle of a teeming, lively city and yet above it all delighted her. The building was also secure. Unlike 3017 N Street, no one could stare at Caroline and John or call out to them. No one could pry the street numbers off the wall. Few even knew what floor Jackie lived on. In addition to her Secret Service agents, there were round-the-clock doormen guarding the front entrance. It wasn't a fortress like the White House, but it was sufficient. It was private, comfortable, and safe. It was heaven.

Taking up the entire fifteenth floor, the sprawling apartment, 5,300 square feet in size, consisted of eight bedrooms (three were tiny rooms for staff), five and a half baths, a library, conservatory, kitchen, dining room, and wine room, and two terraces.

As she had demonstrated with her earlier restoration of the White House, Jackie decorated her new home with exquisite taste and the discriminating eye of a collector that reflected her sweeping knowledge of, and appreciation for, history and art. The first thing visitors would see when stepping into her mirrored entrance hall was an eclectic but typically magnificent display of objects spanning twenty centuries and every region of the globe. There was an eighteenth-century Chinese red lacquered console table. On this sat a marble torso of a Roman god from the second century ("Look, look, it's Daddy's man," John once shouted, eyeing the piece, which had been purchased by his father)[15] and a pair of porcelain miniature garden stools that had been converted into lamps. There was also a French jardiniere that contained an amaryllis in bloom, and in one corner, quince branches in a vase. Hung on the wall were nineteenth-century French watercolors and a spectacular tiger eye maple-framed mirror.

And that was just the entrance hall.

In 1996, Caroline and John wrote in the preface to the huge (593-page) guide to their mother's items that were being auctioned off by Sotheby's: "For our mother, history came alive through objects and paintings, as well as books. Because the things she collected link her with history, and because she cared about them, they represent more than just a record of her life and travels."[16]

Many rooms reflected Jackie's favorite colors—citron (a yellowish-green), raspberry red, blues, and whites, says an interior designer friend, Mark Hampton. "It had the appearance of not being completely decorated. There was something very loose, very Holly Golightly about her style," he says, referring to the Audrey Hepburn character in *Breakfast at Tiffany's*.[17] Complementing this vision—for everything was always displayed with Jackie's typical meticulousness—were flowers, which were everywhere, and books.

Lots of books. Jackie was extraordinarily well read—her reading habit began when she was a young child and endured until her death in 1994*—and owned a vast array of works, displayed in every major room on deep shelves that snaked along walls and stretched from floor to ceiling. A review of just two pages of the Sotheby's catalog shows extensive collections—sometimes scores of books per category—on everything from American and French history to Russia, India, and the Middle East. There are books on Asian poetry; there is ancient Greek and Roman literature; there are biographies of famous women and books on art, architecture, interior design, horsemanship, gardening, botany, and Isabella I, queen of Spain in the latter half of the fifteenth century. The book listings extend far beyond these two pages.

"Her favorite thing was to lie on the couch, reading and smoking," says John Loring, who worked with Jackie during her later years at the publishing house Doubleday. Truman Capote, recalling her prodigious reading habits, says Jackie often devoured a book a day.[18]

For all of the descriptions of Jackie, all the different ways that she has been defined over the decades, her endless quest for knowledge and voracious reading habit reflect one additional, and often under-represented, quality: she was an intellectual and a Renaissance woman. In the 1960s, this was not something that was typically said of women, but how else to describe someone who read endlessly and sought lively conversation and ideas with the Manhattan intelligentsia? That she was all this helps explain her attraction to another famous bibliophile—who preceded her husband in the White House: "I wish I could be married to Thomas Jefferson," she once said. "Now there was a man!

---

* According to the Kennedy library, Jackie had read all the children's books on her bookshelves before she even started school. Her heroes were Mowgli from Rudyard Kipling's *The Jungle Book*, Robin Hood, Little Lord Fauntleroy's grandfather, Scarlett O'Hara from *Gone with the Wind*, and the poet Byron. She read so much that her mother thought she might one day become a writer. Jackie would never write a book herself, of course, but as an editor over the final twenty years of her life, she would shape the books of dozens of authors.

He could do so many things!… Jefferson is the president with whom I have the most affinity."[19], *

All of this—the books, the art, the antiques—may give the impression that her apartment was stuffy, some sort of library or museum. It was not. Among the better descriptions of 1040 is provided, also in the Sotheby's catalog, by Nancy Tuckerman: "It was inviting and comfortable, with a pleasing, lived-in feeling to it."[20] In a world of prying eyes, scrutiny, and later, criticism, it was above all a place to relax and enjoy life.

But what Jackie cared about most was having a place that Caroline and John could enjoy—a place they could call home. After all, Caroline barely remembered the White House, and the two homes on N Street were merely short-term and transitional. John, in the meantime, had no memory of any of these places. The home at 1040, therefore, would be the first true long-term one for both of them. Their mother's philosophy carried over from the White House: "I never want a house where you have to say to the children, 'Don't touch.'"[21]

In fact, 1040 was, as Jackie's former social secretary Tish Baldrige noted, "a magical place for any child to call home."[22] John and Caroline had plenty of toys and games, of course, and kids being kids, they were often scattered about the apartment. And parents being parents, Jackie proudly displayed their artwork in the kitchen (John used finger paints; Caroline made watercolors). Near John's room, a huge collage—four by six feet—hung, composed of dozens of family photos. It was, recalls one of John's friends, "a joyful pastiche—pictures of poignant moments and happy days." But in keeping with Jackie's desire to move on from the past, the photos were all taken after November 22, 1963.[23] In the entire 5,300-square-foot home, in fact, Jackie displayed just one photo of her late husband, in a silver frame on her bedroom dresser.

---

* John F. Kennedy shared his wife's affinity for America's third president. At a 1962 dinner honoring Nobel Prize winners from the Western Hemisphere, Kennedy looked out at the assembled group and said, "I think this is the most extraordinary collection of talent, of human knowledge, that has ever been gathered together at the White House—with the possible exception of when Thomas Jefferson dined alone. Someone once said that Thomas Jefferson was a gentleman of 32 who could calculate an eclipse, survey an estate, tie an artery, plan an edifice, try a cause, break a horse, and dance the minuet."

As First Lady, one of the first things Jackie did was to replace the long rectangular tables used by the Eisenhowers for entertaining with small round ones, which she considered more intimate and conducive for conversation. Her dining room at 1040 consisted of one such table, placed before a window and usually covered with a brownish table cloth featuring leaves and butterflies. There were plush chairs, overstuffed sofas, crimson damask wallpaper, and an off-white marble fireplace topped by a stunning forty-five-by-thirty-seven-inch portrait of a member of the French aristocracy sitting astride his horse.[24] On one wall there was a map of the world, dotted with pins. "See those pins?" John would proudly tell visitors. "My daddy went to all those places!"[25] There also were more quince branches in a vase, and an ebonized baby grand piano that she couldn't play. Were it not, in fact, for the modest round table, a visitor might have confused the space for something other than a dining room.

But the highlight of Jackie's new home was the large living room, which stood between the dining room and the library. All three rooms overlooked Fifth Avenue and had fireplaces that crackled throughout the long New York winters. Jackie displayed gorgeous carpeting in each but left much of the gleaming herringbone floors uncovered. In addition to the wide-ranging display of antiques and art, which hung on wainscoted walls, the living room also had her easel and stool—Jackie had long enjoyed painting and drawing. There were Chinese porcelain trays, stacking containers, and jardinieres, all in blue and white, and towering above the fireplace was a seventy-inch Louis XV-style gilt-wood mirror, "the top rail carved with a shell and scrolling foliage, the lower rail with flowerheads."[26]

Somehow, she was able to combine such refinement with an easy casualness. "It was luxurious," writes Dianne Russell Condon in her 1996 book *Jackie's Treasures*, "but in a low-key, comfortable way, not like a designer showplace." One frequent visitor, an interior designer named Albert Hadley, describes it as "bringing the sense of the country to Fifth Avenue. It wasn't a grand room, the way some of those places can be—it was comfortable. It was a beautiful room, with long windows looking right out over the park."[27]

It was a magnificent vista. When Jackie stood there—or in the library or dining room—she could see all the way across Central Park to the Art Deco and Beaux Arts towers of Central Park West and the Hudson River on the horizon; sunsets were undoubtedly spectacular.* Peering to her left (south), she could also see the Metropolitan Museum of Art two blocks down Fifth, its rear jutting into the park, and just to the right of that, a 106-acre reservoir. Stretching nearly the entire width of the park, the reservoir is forty feet deep, holds over one billion gallons of water, and is ringed by a 1.6-mile running path and a wide dirt path for horses and dog walkers. Over the years Jackie would walk or run countless times around that reservoir, which today is named in her honor.

The living room also had a telescope, and Jackie enjoyed looking at people down below on Fifth Avenue or in the park. Her friend and frequent escort Charles Addams (a famous cartoonist and the creator of the 1960s TV show *The Addams Family*) says Jackie—one of the world's most photographed and scrutinized people in the world—got a kick out of "prying into other people's lives for a change."[28] John loved it, too, though he enjoyed looking at animals in the park, ships navigating the river, or, at night, the moon and the stars. George Plimpton says, "The whole business of peering through a telescope as if you were a captain on the high seas or an astronomer—it was just very exciting."[29]

After her death decades later, it was noted that Jackie hadn't changed the rooms much over the decades. Once she decorated a room, that was pretty much it. That included the most personal room of all, the master bedroom. Between 1964 and 1994, it was freshened up three times, says decorator Keith Irvine, whose work with Jackie dated back to her Georgetown days. Each time, he says, it was "with the same fabric and

---

* Jackie's bedroom, in the southwest corner of her sprawling apartment, also overlooked Fifth Avenue and the park.

everything. And that always impresses me because it shows a great deal of confidence. You've made the decision and it's part of your life."[30]

One tabloid actually got one piece of gossip right: "Jackie's in love with her new surroundings!" gushed *Movie Mirror.* She was indeed.

Yet Jackie understood that while she could leave Washington behind, and stash photos of those years away, the memories were far more difficult to shake. They accompanied her to New York, shadowed her each day, and continued to drag her down time and again. It was so debilitating at times that this most fashion-conscious of women lost interest in her appearance. "She was really in her shell then and Bobby made her give dinner parties," says one frequent guest, Solange Herter, who had been close to Jackie since their glorious junior year at the Sorbonne. "And she wore the same old yellow dress—it was practically unraveling—for every single dinner party she gave…. I don't think she cared about herself in those days, like wearing a pretty dress or a new one."[31]

The memories remained difficult to shake because she stepped up work on her favorite project: the Kennedy library. She traveled around the country, visiting various museums and other facilities, meeting with architects and entertaining ideas. One architect was I. M. Pei. Born a month before JFK in China, he grew up in Hong Kong and Shanghai before moving to the United States in 1935. Earning a bachelor's degree from the Massachusetts Institute of Technology and a master's from Harvard, he eventually started his own firm.

By 1965, he had developed enough of a reputation to land on Jackie's radar. She visited him. "The day Mrs. Kennedy came to my office, I told her: I have no big concert halls to show you, no Lincoln Centers. My work is unglamorous—slum-clearance projects…. [S]he didn't say much, but she kept asking, 'Why? Why? Why?' about what I'd done."[32]

Clearing slums obviously didn't close the sale with Jackie, but Pei's vision did. "I thought I. M.'s temperament was right," she said later. "He was like a wonderful hunting dog when you slip the leash. I don't care that he hasn't done much. I just knew he was the one. I marshaled all the rational reasons to pick I. M., but it was really an emotional decision. He was so full of promise, like Jack; they were born in the same year. I decided it would be fun to take a great leap with him."[33]

The decision reveals much about Jackie. Along with raising her children, preserving John F. Kennedy's legacy was her top priority. She could have chosen any architect in the world, someone safer, more established, more prominent. She could have chosen Warnecke, her new lover—he was designing the permanent grave at Arlington, after all. But Pei? She chose him because it might be fun.*

Jackie's vision for the museum was twofold. Beyond serving as a mere repository for documents and artifacts from President Kennedy's life, she insisted that it should also engage students and encourage something that JFK had dedicated his life to: public service.

"She wanted to help do for other students what she felt part of an undergraduate experience had done for Kennedy—get them interested in politics," recalls Richard Neustadt, a Columbia University professor who served in the Truman administration and as an occasional advisor to President Kennedy. On January 11, Harvard announced that Neustadt would join its faculty and also become the first director of "a new kind of institution in American life within a university setting, which will furnish a meeting place for the scholars and for individuals pursuing careers in practical politics and public service."[34] This would soon become the Harvard Kennedy School's Institute of Politics.

In the aftermath of President Kennedy's assassination, the British government created a scholarship fund for British graduate students to attend Harvard and the Massachusetts Institute of Technology. The Kennedy Memorial Trust, as it was called, was meant to honor JFK's "interest in bringing into fruitful combination the disciplines of traditional humane studies and modern technology and so making their strength effective in the activities of government and in the direction of world affairs."

---

* The library proved to be challenging, including a change in location. Finished in 1979, the nine-story library is of modern design, featuring glass and concrete. Pei later designed an expansion of the site.

But it wasn't enough. Sparked by an idea from David Ormsby-Gore (by then Lord Harlech) and with the input of Queen Elizabeth, it was decided that a parcel of land—one acre—would be donated to the United States in honor of the late president. The location was perfect in its symbolism: Runnymede, just west of London. It was near the very spot where King John had signed arguably the most important document in the annals of western civilization: the Magna Carta, the foundational document for English—and later American—civil liberties.

President Johnson caught wind of this and tracked Jackie down in Florida. "I wanted to suggest that if you cared to, that you and your party take one of the 707s [one of the presidential planes LBJ had at his disposal]. And I think that I might ask Bobby and Teddy if they wanted to go to represent me…. You just let me know and I'll have it all set up for you."

"Oh, that's so nice, but that's wasting taxpayers' money!" Jackie said in her breathless voice.

Johnson disagreed: "It's very important to us, and very important to the country."

"Oh, listen," Jackie replied. "I just don't know what to say."

"You don't say anything."

"That's the nicest thing I've ever heard of."

Jackie was genuinely touched but couldn't tell Johnson what she was really thinking. She feared that flying on one of the presidential planes would dredge up bad memories. But after thinking it over for several days, she decided to accept. She wrote the president: "I did not know if I could steel myself to go on one of those planes again," she admitted. "But please do not let it be Air Force One." She hadn't set foot on 26000—the tail number of the famous plane, whose color scheme and interior she had helped design—since November 22, 1963, and had no intention of doing so now. Just as she avoided even seeing the White House after moving out, she didn't want to see the plane that had carried her husband home from Dallas either.

"Please," she asked Johnson, "let it be the 707 that looks least like Air Force One on the inside."[35]

The ceremony itself was May 14, nearly 750 years to the day that the Magna Carta itself had been signed. Before a crowd of five thousand people, including a large Kennedy contingent, Queen Elizabeth spoke:

"The unprecedented intensity of that wave of grief, mixed with something akin to despair, which swept over our people at the news of President Kennedy's assassination, was a measure of the extent to which we recognized what he had already accomplished, and of the high hopes that rode with him in a future that was not to be," she said, her voice carrying across the bright green meadow.

"With all our hearts my people shared his triumphs, grieved at his reverses, and wept at his death," her majesty added somberly.

Jackie's pen pal Harold Macmillan—prime minister during all but the final month of JFK's presidency—also spoke, calling the death of Kennedy, a man a quarter century his junior, particularly bitter, because he had been "one of those rare personalities who seemed born to bridge the gulf dividing races and creeds and help to build the unity of all mankind." The murder was, he added, not just a public disaster but "to each one of us, a personal, individual, private grief." He was "a good friend, a wonderful friend," Macmillan said. He represented "all the hopes and aspirations of this world that is struggling to emerge phoenix-like from the ashes of the old."

The widow was also escorted before a rectangular memorial to her husband. It read:

THIS ACRE OF ENGLISH GROUND WAS GIVEN
TO THE UNITED STATES OF AMERICA BY
THE PEOPLE OF BRITAIN IN MEMORY OF
JOHN F. KENNEDY
PRESIDENT OF THE UNITED STATES 1961–63
DIED BY AN ASSASSIN'S HAND 22 NOVEMBER 1963
LET EVERY NATION KNOW WHETHER IT WISHES US WELL OR ILL
THAT WE SHALL PAY ANY PRICE BEAR ANY BURDEN MEET ANY HARDSHIP
SUPPORT ANY FRIEND OR OPPOSE ANY FOE IN ORDER TO ASSURE
THE SURVIVAL AND SUCCESS OF LIBERTY

As the British sovereign and her former prime minister offered their tributes, Jackie pressed her lips together firmly, as if fighting back tears. She swallowed hard and stared straight ahead. She was not scheduled to speak and probably couldn't even if she had been; she later issued a statement, which ended with: "To all of you who created this memorial I can only say it is the deepest comfort to me to know that you share with me thoughts that lie too deep for tears."[36]

As the touching ceremony unfolded, John, now four and a half and up to his mother's elbow, took it all in. Not old enough to comprehend his father's death in 1963, he seemed to now. But the most revealing photos of that day are of Caroline. Now seven and a half, looking more like a Kennedy than a Bouvier, she is seen staring blankly ahead, lost in thought, wearing a glum, distant expression. It was a countenance— worn often in the mid-1960s—that reflected the little girl's deep loss.

Unknown to the children, the trip also spelled the end of Maud Shaw's long tenure with the Kennedy family. Fifty-four years old when then Senator and Mrs. Kennedy hired her to take care of Caroline in 1957, the English governess was now sixty-two and wished to retire. Over the prior seven and a half years, she had probably spent more time than anyone else, including Jackie herself, with Caroline; the same could be said of John Jr. after his birth three years later.

On their last day together, Caroline, sensing that something was wrong, followed Shaw around, putting her arm around her, quiet as a mouse. John, meanwhile, asked, "Won't you just come back as far as New York with us?"

"I'll come back later," Shaw promised.

"Will I still be your bestest friend when you get back?" Caroline asked.

"Of course you will. You'll always be my bestest friend. We're blood sisters, aren't we?"

Jackie, watching this tender scene, was touched. "Caroline is so upset about your not coming back," Jackie said. "Can't you come with us even now?"

The nanny, "terribly torn, even at the eleventh hour," shook her head sadly. "The thought of 'my bestest friend' and 'my big boy' making their lives in the future without me hurt me badly—affected me more deeply than I can ever describe," Shaw later wrote. "No words can ever really tell how closely bound I felt toward those two and their parents."[37] She never saw any of them again, though the children continued to send her letters.

All told, Runnymede was a magnificent gesture, one that deeply moved Jackie. And that was the problem. It exposed, again, two desires that were wholly incompatible within her: the need to squelch the grief over her husband's murder, so she could get on with her life, and her desire to glorify his memory. She could do one or the other, it seemed—but not both. While well-meaning and sincere, the ceremony in the English countryside had the unintended effect of gnawing at an open wound. On May 16, Jackie wrote President Johnson to thank him for providing a plane for the trip: "It was such an emotional and difficult day for me," she told him. "So many thoughts of all my loss surged in me again."[38]

Chapter Four

July to December 1965: Phoenix

Jackie's desire to control the past—even as she sought to move beyond it—began to cause friction with authors other than Jim Bishop. A small army of well-meaning Camelot loyalists was busy writing books as well. How she dealt with each would prove revealing.

Three of them—Arthur Schlesinger, longtime speechwriter and advisor Ted Sorensen, and Evelyn Lincoln, the president's personal secretary—had obviously been major administration insiders, and were racing to get their books to market before the second anniversary of the assassination. Also working on books were Paul ("Red") Fay, an old navy buddy of Kennedy's who had served as an usher at Jack and Jackie's 1953 wedding and was later named undersecretary of the navy, and former nanny Maud Shaw. Unlike William Manchester, whose looming blockbuster about Dallas stemmed from a signed contract with the Kennedy family, none of these five authors had any obligation to the widow.

But not wanting to displease Jackie, and also hoping, if not assuming, that Robert Kennedy would run for president one day,

Schlesinger, Sorensen, and Fay deferred to her wishes by allowing her (and Robert) to review their manuscripts before their publishers did. All three men swiftly found out that when it came to editing, Jackie wielded a pencil as skillfully as a surgeon might a scalpel.

In April, Schlesinger sent both Jackie and Robert the first twelve chapters of his history of the Kennedy presidency, *A Thousand Days*. Submissive to Jackie during their taped interviews the year before, he continued to be so now. "Please do not spare my feelings in your criticism," he offered, "for I will be everlastingly grateful for your help in making the book a faithful account of the greatest man I shall ever know." Jackie took him up on his offer, returning the manuscript with numerous edits. She disliked Schlesinger's view that Kennedy had become president "knowing more about domestic than foreign affairs," pointing out that her husband's military service, his book *Why England Slept*, and his Senate work, which included a stint on the Foreign Relations Committee, proved otherwise. She was also sensitive to Schlesinger's description of how Robert had been selected by his brother to be attorney general.

She was also unhappy that Schlesinger had compared Jack to a Roman senator. Schlesinger had described him as cool and stoic, which he no doubt saw as complimentary. But that wasn't what Jack was like, Jackie informed him. Why hadn't Schlesinger described him as she saw him: passionate and engaging—like a Greek?

JFK, after all, had insisted on living life to the fullest, acting as if every day might be the last. That's what he was like, Jackie believed. Her expression of affection for the Greek way is noteworthy.

Most of all, she was upset that Schlesinger wrote about private things—her marriage—and the fact that he gave this material to *Life* magazine, which of course ran it ahead of the book's publication. She let Schlesinger know she was displeased. The author got the message. When *A Thousand Days* came out, such references had vanished. For this literary exorcism, Schlesinger received a warm and grateful letter from Jackie; he was back in the fold.[2]

Ted Sorensen, the bespectacled young Nebraskan who had been by John F. Kennedy's side since January 1953, when JFK first entered the Senate,* had no such trouble, "in part because I showed her the manuscript and she gave me some suggestions," he told biographer Sarah Bradford.³ By "in part," Sorensen meant that he knew from the get-go to avoid anything too sensitive, anything that intruded upon the privacy of Jackie or her children, or diminished her murdered husband's image. The resulting book, *Kennedy*, would sit atop the *New York Times* bestseller list for several weeks in late 1965.

Evelyn Lincoln was another Cornhusker who had been with Kennedy since 1953. She had gone to work for him because she considered him presidential material, and was with him every step of the way, including riding in the Dallas motorcade. As JFK's personal secretary, she knew more secrets about him than just about anybody. It was Lincoln, for example, who, just steps from the Oval Office, fielded calls from the president's lovers, women like Marilyn Monroe and Judith Campbell Exner, who had also shared a bed with Mafia kingpin Sam Giancana. But Lincoln's book *My Twelve Years with John F. Kennedy*, which came out in September 1965, is sanitized of any such salaciousness. Aside from Jackie herself, few were more loyal and more protective of John F. Kennedy's image than Lincoln; when she died in 1995, she took many secrets to her (Arlington) grave.

But Red Fay and Maud Shaw crossed Jackie's line, committing the sin of conveying information that she considered too personal. Fay, who had known JFK longer than anyone—they first met at patrol/torpedo-boat training school in Rhode Island and were stationed on the same navy base in the Solomon Islands (but did not serve on the same boat)—described the "the human side" of his war buddy. The book—*The Pleasure of His Company*—reads today as sincere and moving, an often humorous and courageous account of a deep lifelong friendship. But Fay also wrote

---

* Kennedy once called Sorensen his "intellectual blood bank." See: ABC News broadcast, February 8, 2008.

that Kennedy cursed like the sailor he was. He was macho, a jock. It was revealing and honest. The Kennedys were livid.

Reviewing the manuscript, Robert gutted it, demanding that about a third of it be deleted. Then it was Jackie's turn. "I didn't realize what a locker room relationship you had with Jack," she told him in a long phone call. She demanded that she be referred to as Jacqueline, not Jackie, in the book, and then there was this exchange over how John F. Kennedy Jr. should be referred to:

"John-John should be John," she demanded. "The president never called him John-John."

"Jackie, you've got to be kidding," Fay replied. "He called him 'John-John' all the time."

"He did not call him John-John."

Fay gave in on the names but little else. His refusal to meet all of Jackie's demands infuriated her. Jackie was so angry that she returned a three-thousand-dollar donation that Fay had made to the Kennedy library.[4] *The Pleasure of His Company* is today a wonderful read.*

She also blew her stack at Maud Shaw. When *White House Nannie* was published in late 1965, Jackie was hurt and offended, seeing it as an act of disloyalty and betrayal. The governess, who had gone to work for the Kennedys when Caroline was just eleven days old, did not have any kind of nondisclosure agreement with her employer. But that wasn't the point. Jackie was obsessed with guarding her children's privacy and safety—who could blame her?—and along comes a book about them by the one person who spent more time with them than anyone, including Jackie herself? She was furious.

From the vantage point of nearly six decades, it seems an overreaction on Jackie's part. The book is about as insidery as it gets, but it is benign and touching, a warm and charming homage to two children she treasured and adored, and their parents, for whom she had the

---

* Jackie apparently came around to this point of view as well. According to Fay's daughter Sally Fay Cottingham, Jackie, during a lunch with Fay in the 1970s, even admitted that *The Pleasure of His Company* was "the best book ever written about Jack." "President Kennedy was my godfather and a wonderful one at that," Fay told the author.

greatest affection and respect. President and Mrs. Kennedy obviously felt the same way. In a gold-embossed leather-bound scrapbook Jackie presented to Shaw on their final day together in England, Jackie wrote: "You brought such happiness to all our lives and especially to President Kennedy, because you made his children what they are."[5]

Even so, Jackie now cut her off, instructing Nancy Tuckerman to send a frosty note on November 19 informing Shaw that she was no longer welcome at 1040. But Tuckerman said Jackie would continue to pay Shaw's pension, writing stiffly: "She will live up to the promises made to you even if you have broken the trust she and President Kennedy put in you." Jackie also allowed her kids to correspond with their former nanny. "I miss you very, very, very much," Caroline wrote in one letter.[6]

In cutting off Shaw, Jackie displayed behavior that would be repeated with other once prominent insiders, notably Mary Gallagher in 1969 and Ben Bradlee in 1975. And when one was out, one tended to stay out. To be banished by Jackie was, it seemed, forever.

And yet all of these battles, in retrospect, were just a warm-up for the titanic clash she would soon have with William Manchester. Still conducting interviews and writing up to fourteen or fifteen hours a day, seven days a week—either at home in Connecticut at his office at Wesleyan University or from "a shabby basement room (B-11) of the National Archives, just down the hall from the snack bar and the men's room"—he ground himself down with his singular, zealous, utterly obsessive focus on the events of November 20 to 25, 1963.[7]

"The year 1965 was grueling for me," he later admitted; he raced to finish *The Death of Lancer* (JFK's Secret Service code name had been the basis for the book's original title). On November 26, he broke down and was admitted to a hospital with nervous exhaustion. He was confined for ten days. And yet his troubles were just beginning.[8]

NONE OF THIS KEPT JACKIE from her growing enjoyment with life. Her relationship with John Warnecke deepened; she went out on the town more often. As she dipped her toe into New York's social waters, she was picky. She could afford to be. Even in Manhattan, with its galaxy of A-listers, Jackie stood out. She was without question the most sought after of guests. Any function, any party, any restaurant in which she made an appearance was instantly elevated by her presence.

But ever restrained, ever enigmatic, Jackie held back, carefully parceling out her appearances.

"A lot of the old guard in New York, the Social Register, to her were extremely boring," says Letitia Baldrige, who had been Jackie's social secretary in the White House. "She found the theater and artistic crowds much more stimulating and exciting. Jackie had had to survive with a restricted time frame for so long. She was a very liberal woman."[9]

She may have lived on the Upper East Side, but the boring salons of Fifth and Park Avenues weren't for her. She typically could be found in the theater district, where she took in all sorts of shows, even off-Broadway performances by small repertory houses. The Metropolitan Opera was also a favorite haunt. One evening, she found herself listening to Aristotle Onassis's mistress, Maria Callas, sing in *Tosca*.

Jackie's move to New York just happened to coincide with the expansion of Olympic Airways, Onassis's Athens-based airline. Launched in April 1957, Olympic quickly began churning out profits, flying among major European capitals plus Cairo, Egypt; Tel Aviv, Israel, and Nicosia, Cyprus. But Onassis wanted a piece of the lucrative and fast-growing trans-Atlantic business, too, and in 1965 got a $30 million line of credit from Boeing to buy three 707s. The next year, at Paris's Orly Airport, he snipped a ceremonial ribbon inaugurating the first flight to New York, vaulting Olympic into the big leagues. The Greek tycoon was ferociously competitive, offering his best customers not just the usual in-flight movies and nine-channel stereo, but free champagne and dinners from his favorite Manhattan restaurant, "21," served with golden cutlery by stewardesses who wore uniforms designed by Chanel and Pierre Cardin. Air travel was glamorous in those days, and Onassis, always in search of respectability, was determined not to be outdone.[10]

Olympic's expansion gave Onassis a reason to spend more time in New York; he maintained a suite at the Pierre hotel on Fifth Avenue at Sixty-First Street, about a mile south of Jackie's home. He became a regular guest at parties and dinners, but given Jackie's wide circle of male friends, including her romantic partner Warnecke, nobody thought much of it.

Were Jackie and Onassis involved in the mid-1960s? That he was sexually interested in her cannot be doubted. But it is likely that Jackie's self-proclaimed fondness for all things Greek did not extend in that way to the shipping and airline magnate. Not yet. Onassis, with uncharacteristic patience, bided his time. He had dated and dispensed with her sister, Lee.* He was involved with Callas. He is said to have been a regular client of Fernande Grudet, better known as Madame Claude—the overlord of an exclusive French call girl ring. But he and Jackie were probably nothing more than good friends.

But Jackie—in addition to her romance with Warnecke and her likely intimacy with Bobby Kennedy—may also have been more than good friends around this time with Mike Nichols. If he was indeed Jackie's lover, he was unusual in that he was two years younger than she was and not overly wealthy or powerful, other than being a well-known, accomplished player in the entertainment industry—a departure from her usual penchant for older, powerful, deep-pocketed men. Nichols was, however, charming, solicitous, and a wonderful social companion.

The apparent overlap of multiple lovers lends the impression that Jackie was, at least for a certain time, somewhat promiscuous. Two years after Jackie's death in 1994, one friend, the British writer Antonia Fraser, said that she had "clearly inspired a very romantic feeling in many men," which was certainly true. But the rest of Fraser's comment—"I tend to think that all people sleep together once or twice if

---

* Speaking about Lee, Onassis once told a friend in August 1963, "I am lucky. She's magnificent, isn't she? You know she's Jackie Kennedy's sister, don't you?" The comment is revealing in its suggestion that he was using Lee to stay close to Jackie. See: Taraborelli, *Jackie, Janet and Lee,* 172.

they're the appropriate sexes"—is presumptuous and perhaps says more about Fraser herself than about Jackie."

Regardless of whether Jackie was or was not promiscuous, one observation is clear: two years after Dallas, she was beginning to enjoy life again. This included having any man she wanted—and sometimes did—enabled by more privacy than she had enjoyed in years. She now had the ability to come and go pretty much as she pleased, with the knowledge that the press, far less ravenous and intrusive than it is today, would treat her with kid gloves. Newspapers and magazines wouldn't even run photos of Jackie, a heavy chain smoker, with a cigarette in her mouth. Her image and reputation remained pristine. The image she had crafted in November 1963 remained dominant: she was the proud, elegant, dignified widow of a martyred president, existing on a pedestal. She was untouchable. It wouldn't last.

JACKIE EMERGED FROM HER SHELL, coincidentally or not, as social and cultural mores began to change at an accelerating pace. The first oral contraceptive, Enovid, had been approved by the Food and Drug Administration in 1960; now the Supreme Court (in *Griswold v. Connecticut*) gave married couples the right to use birth control, ruling that its use was a protected privacy. Twenty-six states still banned it for women, but the barriers would gradually erode. A 1962 bestseller by Helen Gurley Brown, *Sex and the Single Girl*, encouraged women to seek financial independence and have sex whether they were married or not; the same themes powered her 1965 launch of *Cosmopolitan* magazine. What influence any of this may have had on Jackie—whose sex life with John F. Kennedy had largely been perfunctory—makes for interesting, though inevitably inconclusive, speculation.

If any one event captures Jackie's emergence, it occurred in late September, when with a perfect bouffant, she stepped into a glistening crepe sheath, white, topped by a sleeveless ermine jacket, also white. The effect was stunning. She was driven to the Asia Society on Park Avenue, where she and twenty-seven friends viewed an art exhibit, and then it was off to Sign of the Dove, a ritzy restaurant in the Turtle Bay neighborhood near the United Nations and Bobby Kennedy's apartment.

Ostensibly, the black-tie evening was to honor John Kenneth Galbraith, the economist and diplomat who had served as ambassador to India during the Kennedy administration. But for all intents and purposes, it was really Jackie's coming-out party. She had booked the entire restaurant for the evening and turned it into a discotheque, featuring life-size photos of the towering (six-foot-seven) Galbraith.[12] Guests ranged from European jet-setters like Giovanni ("Gianni") Agnelli, the head of Fiat, to trendy new acquaintances like Andy Warhol and his twenty-two-year-old muse, Edie Sedgwick, dubbed "Girl of the Year" by *Life* magazine for 1965. Warhol and Sedgwick were, said *Vogue* magazine, coining a new phrase, "the beautiful people."

There was a DJ who started off playing Cole Porter tunes. Then Jackie asked him to play "the fastest music you're got." Off came the white sheath, and the party kicked into high gear with Jackie doing the frug and the Watusi as the music blared. One of her dance partners was "Killer" Joe Piro, a dance instructor who had taught her the moves in the White House. At the time, the First Lady had told him: "All my nieces and nephews do these dances so well. I'd like to do them well too." One partygoer called it "the Galbraith a go-go."[13]

As the party raged, passersby on the street, listening to the ruckus, gathered out front, where Secret Service agents kept them at a distance. "It seemed like there were fifteen thousand people in the street, trying to get a peek at [Jackie]," another guest, attorney William vanden Heuvel, says.

Inside, at 1:45 a.m., a late-night buffet of smoked-salmon foie gras, spaghetti, and French pastries was served. When Jackie ducked out at a quarter to three, taken home by Warnecke, the party was still going full blast. "This is my very *very* special friend," she said, introducing her lover to an acquaintance on the way out.[14]

Jackie

"Jackie went to enormous efforts," Galbraith said later. "It was an evening of pure fun. Time had passed and this was her expression of enjoying herself again."[15]

"There'll never be another Jack," she once told a Washington friend, Joan Braden. But there would be another Jackie, a Jackie who could be happy again. It began on this night.

Jackie's formal look that night was a throwback to her White House years, that thirty-five-month window of glittery state dinners and seemingly effortless refinement. As her disposition improved—the slightest thing could trigger a relapse, however—she slowly regained more control of her life and her emotions. The tattered yellow dress she had thrown on for dinner parties at 1040 vanished; she took more pride in her appearance. As she was two years removed from being dubbed America's "First Lady of Fashion," her couture was no longer restricted by political considerations to American designers. Oleg Cassini was out; Givenchy was in. A fitter she worked with for decades at Bergdorf Goodman, Rose Citron, recalled that "Mrs. Kennedy loved Givenchy—*everything* was Givenchy. When she came in, there were Givenchys lined up in the hallway!"[16, *] There was one thing that Jackie never wore though: Chanel-style suits, like the pink outfit she had put on in Fort Worth on November 22, 1963.

Citron always had fond memories of her star client. "Mrs. Kennedy was a very nice woman. She used to come in after lunch, sometimes [in later years] with Caroline. She was very low-key, unlike some of my clients, and knew what worked for her and what she wanted." One afternoon, Jackie dropped in and Citron asked if she was hungry. Jackie said yes, and the two women sat on little gold chairs in the Bergdorf fitting room and split Citron's tuna fish sandwich.[17]

But Givenchy, that was for formal events, like the opera and fancy galas with other A-list glitterati. With fashion, Jackie's true impact in the mid-1960s was to loosen it up, sending the signal to millions

---

* But Citron, a Holocaust survivor who died in 2006, acknowledged a secret: Jackie often evaded the "buy American" restriction in her White House years by having foreign designs shipped to her directly from Bergdorf.

110

of women that simple informality could be both stylish and functional. The 1960s began with formality: men generally wore hats to the office;* women, jewelry around the house. Clothing, in fact, was a kind of demarcation. "The way you dressed reflected your school, your family, where you grew up, how you voted, even how much money you earned," wrote Jackie biographer Pamela Clarke Keogh. It was a staid atmosphere. By mid-decade, that kind of dressing was on the way out.

Jackie gets much of the credit for this change. By opting for simplicity and casualness for everyday occasions, she helped erase barriers. Says Keogh: "Millions of women copied her style, feeling that if she could dress that way, so could they."[18]

"That way" also meant wearing pants in public, unheard of among Manhattan's elite until Jackie, self-assured and stylish, began appearing in them. Other powerful women immediately copied her—women like Barbara ("Babe") Paley (wife of CBS chairman William S. Paley) and Margaretta ("Happy") Rockefeller (wife of New York governor Nelson Rockefeller)—only to find themselves barred from entering the city's top (and obviously not "with it") restaurants.[19] Paley and Rockefeller were fifteen and three years older than Jackie, respectively, yet felt compelled to follow in her wake. Jackie influenced all.

But wearing pants in public, considered risqué in those days, was nothing compared to Jackie's early adoption of one of the boldest fashion statements ever, something that by the end of the decade would be seemingly ubiquitous for young women throughout the Western world: the miniskirt.

If anyone deserves credit for the mini, it's Mary Quant, a British-born designer who opened a small shop in London's trendy Chelsea neighborhood in 1955 at the age of twenty-one. Always looking for the next big thing, she designed in 1964 a skirt that ran out of fabric above the knee. More precisely, she said, the bottom edge of the skirt must hit

---

* It is often believed that John F. Kennedy killed off the men's hat industry by not wearing hats. This is debatable: sales had been declining for years before Kennedy became president. But his aversion to them certainly didn't help.

roughly halfway up the thigh, falling no more than four inches below the rear. She decided to name her creation after her favorite car—the Mini—and thus the miniskirt was born. It was, she said years later, "a way of rebelling." In swinging London in the mid-sixties, rebelling against what, exactly? It didn't really matter. It was different, it was new, it shocked the older crowd, and that was enough.

In 1965, the mini took off in London, spreading to Western Europe and across the Atlantic. A reporter asked Quant what it meant. "Sex," she said. In August 1969, *Life* magazine would run a cover story featuring a shot of a twenty-something woman walking down the street in one. The article was titled "That Young New York Look."

And yet skirts above the knee were old news to Jackie, who was first spotted in what some considered a mini as early as 1960, at a campaign event in California. "I remember Mrs. Kennedy causing a great stir there because it was one of the few times I think Californians had seen somebody with a hemline above the knee," recalls Joseph Cerrell, the director of that state's Democratic Party (a job he was appointed to at age twenty-four). "Her glamour and her unconventional beauty attracted attention and enticed the news media."[20]

But that was trendy, ahead-of-the-curve California in 1960, and Jackie was a mere senator's wife. When she was First Lady, the hems came right back down. Now they began to inch up again. The "young New York look" that *Life* described in 1969 as if it were fresh and new can be traced partially to her.

JACKIE'S FINANCIAL FEARS were never far below the surface. There was lots of cash coming in: $150,000 each year from a Kennedy trust fund in her name, another fifty thousand dollars Robert provided through other family funds, and fifty thousand dollars from the government to cover her expenses.[21] All told, the quarter of a million dollars she received each year she was on her own amounts, in 2019 terms, to about $1.9 million annually. Her problem was that she insisted on a

Fifth Avenue lifestyle, with all the upkeep on 1040, salaries for her household staff, and private school tuition for Caroline and John—plus all the shopping, entertaining, and constant jet-setting.

She'd had to borrow from Robert to buy her post-White House home on N Street, and 1040 was also beyond her means. Kennedy family largesse made the purchase possible, but in the larger scheme of things, Jackie was not expanding her wealth in any appreciable manner.*

Yet because of the rarefied circles she traveled in, Jackie would always meet the right people—who naturally wanted to meet her as well. One of them was a fellow resident at the Carlyle, an investment banker and venture capitalist named André Meyer. Born in France in 1898, Meyer, who was Jewish, escaped the Nazi occupation during World War II and took his family to New York, where he soon took a job with the asset management firm Lazard Frères. Decades later, he would be called "the most creative financial genius of our time in the investment banking world" by none other than David Rockefeller.[22] Even if they hadn't been neighbors, it was all but inevitable that he and Jackie would cross paths.

The initial connection was actually made by Robert, who approached Meyer and asked for help managing the vast Kennedy family trust, which at the time totaled about a hundred million dollars. Because of his financial prowess, Meyer also joined the board of the John F. Kennedy library, where he served as one of its key fundraisers. It naturally meant that he would have close contact with Jackie. He was one of the few outsiders whom Jackie and Robert trusted.[23]

That Jackie took to Meyer when they did meet was almost preordained. He was just the kind of man she typically gravitated toward: powerful, sophisticated, connected, and well versed in the art of turning one dollar into two. Joe Kennedy was like this, of course, as was Aristotle Onassis; and biographical descriptions of Meyer could easily be applied to the other two: "Interesting, funny, warm, companionable,

---

* Not that Robert or JFK himself possessed any financial acumen, though with the multimillion-dollar trust fund that Joseph P. Kennedy had given each of his children, there was no overriding pressure for them to acquire any. See: Bradford, 313.

interested," per *Washington Post* publisher Katharine Graham[24]—but also "greedy, vindictive, and domineering."[25] That all three were significantly older was also no coincidence: Kennedy Sr., Meyer, and Onassis were forty-one, thirty-one, and twenty-three years Jackie's senior, respectively.

Many a tycoon became so by cutting corners and flouting the spirit, if not the letter, of the law when they were younger. Joe Kennedy was a bootlegger during Prohibition, and an inside trader on Wall Street (though this wasn't illegal in those days); Onassis's swashbuckling business dealings led to multiple scrapes with the U.S. government, including indictments, fines, and at least one arrest. Meyer, regarded by rivals as "the world's greatest schemer," was known for, among other things, needless cruelty and bottomless greed. Although such characteristics were only part of each man's overall personality, they were ultimately indispensable to their towering financial success. Jackie adored them all.*

Jackie and Meyer had much in common. She loved his French background and his love of art—Rembrandts, Renoirs, Picassos, and van Goghs hung on his apartment walls. But the principal attraction was money. Jackie needed it; Meyer knew how to make it. André Meyer had always been attracted to rich, famous, beautiful women, but Jackie—Jackie was in a galaxy all her own. She quickly became one of his superelite "AM" (as in André Meyer) accounts at Lazard.[26]

There was another reason for Jackie's attraction to Meyer. Although she was quite well off, her financial well-being was dependent on the Kennedys, and deep down, Jackie resented it. The family had an office on Park Avenue that was managed by her brother-in-law Stephen Smith, but instead of handling financial matters through him, Jackie dealt with Meyer whenever possible. "I don't ever recall her going to Steve Smith for advice," a friend told Jackie biographer Sarah Bradford. "It was always André."[27] And the financier loved what Meyer biographer

---

* Meyer's ability to manage money wasn't the only reason Jackie liked him: the ruthless banker ingratiated himself to her by spending hours helping John and Caroline with their homework. See: Reich, 22.

Cary Reich describes—accurately—as "the breathless, little-girl lost way in which she would implore Meyer, 'André, what should I do? I don't know what to *do*.'" (emphasis original)[28]

New men, new homes, new fashions, new attitudes. Jackie's life was changing in every way. But some things were constant: her lifelong passion for horseback riding, for example, remained undiminished. Even in hurly-burly Manhattan, she had an outlet, renting horses from the Claremont Riding Academy on West Eighty-Ninth Street and taking them into Central Park, which has a six-mile-long bridle path that circles the reservoir and North Meadow. Despite her proven skill in the saddle, Jackie did as other customers did, riding in a sixty-five-by-seventy-five-foot indoor arena until she was given permission to clop through the busy streets, with all of Manhattan's noise, into the lush confines of the park itself.

Claremont's owner back then was Paul Novograd, who eventually arranged for Jackie to get some special treatment. Instead of requiring her to travel crosstown to get her horse, he arranged for someone to meet her with her horse at Engineer's Gate on Fifth Avenue at Ninetieth Street, just five blocks from her home. Jackie, clad in jodhpurs, a tweed jacket, and a helmet in the middle of a teeming city, would then ride to her heart's delight. She rode several times a week, mostly alone, sometimes with others, and sometimes with Caroline, to the girl's utter delight, after she took lessons from Novograd.

Horseback riding had always been her joy; but it now offered Jackie what she craved: peace and privacy. It was restorative. "Her horse was her counselor, psychologist, and spiritual advisor," Novograd says.[29] Also restorative: she began weekly sessions with a psychiatrist and took up yoga.

To better indulge her passion for riding, Jackie—despite her constant fretting about money—also rented a ten-room house, described in the *New York Times* as a "badly made-over barn" in Bernardsville, New Jersey. She would later rent a two-story, seven-room

Jackie

home dubbed "Windwood" in the small village of Peapack, about six miles further west.*

A land of old money—estates first sprang up during the gilded age of the late nineteenth century—this rarefied stretch of the Garden State had some fifteen thousand acres of rolling green hills where Jackie could gallop about; each Thanksgiving there was a fox hunt. The privacy and expansiveness reminded Jackie of the long weekends she had spent in Virginia's Loudoun County during her White House years, and she soon adopted a similar schedule, arriving on Friday and returning to the city on Monday.

She often rode to the hounds with her new equestrian friends or just meandered down paths or dirt roads covered by canopies of trees. Caroline often rode as well but lacked her mother's skill, "just clinging on for dear life," one observer claims.[30] Jackie stabled her horses at the nearby home of Charles and Peggy McDonnell, who became wonderful friends, and whose eight (eventually nine) children meant an instant slew of playmates for Caroline and John. This included one daughter born a year before Caroline and one born a year after, and a son born three months before John. Weekend gatherings were raucous and fun.

Other neighbors were less enthusiastic about Jackie's arrival, fearing that her fame would bring unwanted attention into their rarefied lives. When Jackie applied for membership in the exclusive (only eighty-five members) Essex Hunt Club, some tried to block her. Fortunately for Jackie, one member of the club was Douglas Dillon, who had been President Kennedy's treasury secretary. Dillon told the club that if Jackie's membership were rejected, he would ban members from riding across his property. Jackie was quickly accepted.[31] The club's newest and most prominent member quickly acclimated and rode often, and almost always in the club's annual Thanksgiving Day hunt.

As for Jackie's house, it was small, at least by her standards. Kathy McKeon remembers having to share a room with John, and she, Jackie,

---

* In 1974, Aristotle Onassis bought the house for Jackie for two hundred thousand dollars. See: Spoto, 259. It would be one of her retreats for the remaining twenty years of her life, and neighbors often saw her in riding pants or—egads—even a sweatsuit, galloping about the property.

and Caroline did the shopping and cooking. Within two years, Jacqueline Kennedy had gone from living in the White House, where her hand-picked French-born chef, René Verdon, created the most sublime dishes at the drop of a hat, to fixing hot dogs, fish sticks, and spaghetti. Jackie would be the first to admit that she wasn't the greatest cook. "She could boil an egg," McKeon recalls, "but it was probably going to end up hard-boiled." But it was all great fun. "We were more inclined to laugh and eat our mistakes than start all over," she writes. It was surely the closest Jackie ever came to experiencing the life of an average suburban American mom.[32]

But Jackie's renewed appetite for life did not extend to the month of November. She dreaded its arrival, and the countdown to its twenty-second day. Social engagements were curtailed, and she found herself being dragged, against her will, down memory lane again.

Truman Capote told his friend Bennett Cerf, the all-powerful chairman of publishing company Random House, a story that Cerf recounted in his unpublished oral history at Columbia University:

> Truman arrived home and there was a girl waiting for him in his house, a girl who had a key to his apartment, and was upstairs painting when he arrived, waiting for him to come home. That girl was Jacqueline Kennedy. It was just about the anniversary of the assassination—two years…after the assassination. She was very low. Who did she turn to? Her great friend Truman Capote. As Phyllis [Cerf's wife] said, "That was one place where she knew she was safe alone." The Secret Service were in the car below. Truman went to the refrigerator and found two bottles of the best champagne on ice. The two of them together killed these two great big bottles of champagne and set up practically all night talking. At about five in the morning, Jackie went down to her car and went home with the Secret Service people.[33]

Chapter Five

January to June 1966:
Jet-Setter

The impression that William Manchester had of Jackie when they first met in April 1964—that he was "in the presence of a great tragic actress"—was apt and was, he emphasized years later, a judgment rooted not in criticism but in praise. On the afternoon of November 22, 1963, she understood, immediately, that she had been thrust without consent into the biggest, most unsparing global spotlight that had ever existed—and had no choice other than to put on the best performance she could. "There was a weekend in American history," Manchester writes, "when we needed to be united in our sadness by the superb example of a bereaved First Lady, and Jacqueline Kennedy—unlike Eleanor Roosevelt, a more extraordinary woman in other ways—provided us with an unforgettable performances as the nation's heroine."[1]

But that was two long years ago, and Jackie was weary of the role. By her own admission, she wasn't cut out for it in the first place: just twelve days after the assassination, she had complained to Philip Hannan, the archbishop of Washington, "I don't like to hear people say that I am poised and maintaining a good appearance. I am not a movie actress."[2]

Yet many Americans expected her to remain as she was then: the grieving, dignified black-clad widow. They had put Jackie on a pedestal and wanted her to stay there; she wished to climb down and get on with her life. Although the expectations of the former were understandable, they were also unreasonable, perhaps even selfish. After all she had been through, Jackie was still only thirty-six years old and entitled to live the rest of her still youngish life as best she could—and as she saw fit.

In this vein, she may have been inspired by someone who actually had been a movie star, one of the biggest ever, whom she had come to know in 1963: the reclusive Greta Garbo. At a small White House dinner party on November 13, 1963, Garbo* and Jackie enjoyed each other's company, and shortly after JFK's assassination, a stunned Garbo dispatched a heartfelt condolence letter—a rare instance of her reaching out to anyone.

Garbo can be considered a template of sorts for what Jackie became after her husband's murder. At the peak of her fame in 1941, the Swedish-born Garbo—strong-willed and enigmatic—fled Hollywood for what she hoped would be the privacy and anonymity of New York. She was just thirty-six, a year older than Jackie when Jackie fled Washington seeking the same things. Garbo settled in a Sutton Place apartment on Manhattan's East Side that rivaled Jackie's for its unique blend of glamour, comfort, and simplicity.

After Jackie moved to 1040, they renewed their acquaintance, and it is not difficult to see why they grew to admire each other. Since Garbo had quit the movie industry, her allure had only grown, fueled in no small part by her unavailability. This intense reclusiveness likely piqued Jackie's interest—the way Jackie's own aloofness piqued others.

---

* The Kennedys invited Garbo to stay overnight; she declined—a missed opportunity, she later suggested: "That could have been done—and then had a visit from the President in the night," she said, laughing. "The President visited a lot of ladies [at night]." She stayed instead at a hotel. Garbo came to the White House in the first place thanks to an invitation from JFK's longtime friend "Lem" Billings, who had first met her years before on the French Riviera. See: "Garbo Forever."

"I have often regretted my speech, never my silence," said a first-century philosopher, Publilius Syrus; it was a sentiment that undoubtedly resonated with both women.[3]

One thing both women had in common was their disdain for reporters. In 1988, Barbara Walters, the legendary television journalist who interviewed seemingly everyone over the course of her long career, was asked who she had failed to nab. At the top of her list: Jackie and Garbo.

Of Garbo it is usually assumed, incorrectly, that her most famous line is "I want to be alone." Yet in one of her very few public utterances, she clarified to *Life* magazine in 1955: "I never said, 'I want to be alone.' I only said, 'I want to be *let* alone!' There is all the difference." There is all the difference indeed, and it describes Jackie well. Jackie did not so much want to be alone (though she enjoyed solitude); she wanted people to lay off and let her live the way she wanted to live—on her terms, not theirs.

Jackie was fascinated by Garbo. One of the few people who actually knew both of them is the writer Richard de Combray: "Garbo, of course, wanted to have two lives, that of the anonymous unobserved woman who is also the great star, so that she required you to look at her when you saw her in the street, but as soon as you acknowledge her, she'd shy away as if you'd done something shocking. Jackie was similar." Before Manhattan's Whitney Museum had its official opening, he escorted Jackie to a private event there and "some construction workers noticed her and she obviously liked that, but when someone she didn't know tapped her on the shoulder, she became almost crazed with fear and anger."[4]

The two women had something else in common as well: Aristotle Onassis. Years before Ari turned his sights on Jackie, he had dated Garbo. Onboard the *Christina*, she stayed in its "Ithaca" cabin, second only in lavishness to that of Onassis; it was the same suite that Jackie, and all of the tycoon's "special women," would stay in over the years.

For all of her sophisticated tastes and erudition, Jackie liked good old-fashioned gossip as much as anybody. In the White House, she and Jack were always trading juicy tidbits that they had vacuumed up throughout the day.

To stay current now, she often dispatched Kathy McKeon to run down to the newsstand and buy an armful of magazines and newspapers. McKeon, who also doubled as a dog walker for Shannon, the black-and-white cocker spaniel given to the then-first family by Irish president Éamon de Valera, would return with an armful of publications—a few of which would invariably have Jackie herself on the cover.

And why not? She was more famous than any Hollywood icon, and by now more than just a former First Lady. Bess Truman, eighty-one, was a former First Lady; so was sixty-nine-year-old Mamie Eisenhower. But even in their heyday, photographers didn't clamor for photos of them; photographers wouldn't hang outside the Truman home in Independence, Missouri, for hours on the off chance that Mrs. Truman would come out. Ditto Gettysburg, Pennsylvania, where the Eisenhowers retreated after their time in the White House. News on their doings—even during their stints in the White House—was never as sought after as even the most mundane Jackie item.

But Jackie, now *that* was a subject. When she entered the White House in 1961, she was only thirty-one—the youngest First Lady since twenty-eight-year-old Frances Folsom married Grover Cleveland in the Blue Room in 1886. She was beautiful, had two photogenic children, and, despite her global fame, managed to remain mysterious. How could the world's most famous woman be, at the same time, so elusive? The beguiling discrepancy only added to her appeal.

The endless covers both frustrated and amused Jackie. Always a lioness when it came to protecting Caroline and John's privacy, she would get incensed when articles about them appeared. But Jackie couldn't complain, knowing that the complaint itself would simply result in more unwanted publicity.

One common subject of the tabloids was her love life. "Jackie Will Elope!" shouted the December 1965 cover of *Movie Mirror*, featuring a photo of her looking radiant. "Read the Love Letter That Changed Her Life!" Without mentioning any particular name, the accompanying article speculated that she had "discussed marriage" with one suitor, "but the look on her face must've told him she could not listen to his words." Yet there were predictions in the article that in retrospect seem rather close to the mark:

> If she married again, she'd probably elope. She would keep all the plans secret except of course, from family and friends. She would wed in a small church somewhere far away…[in a place] with a minimum of public awareness. A boat pulling up to a small dock can unload its passengers quickly and quietly…

The honeymoon could take place in Paris or London, the article added, dropping another hint. But who was this mystery man? Why, it said, a man who traveled abroad frequently and was now in "his fifth year without the wife he had once loved so much." Any amateur sleuth might have deduced that it was Aristotle Onassis, who owned homes in Paris and London, and who had been single for five years following his 1960 divorce from Athina Mary ("Tina") Livanos. The idea of Jackie and Ari's getting married was, as 1966 dawned, outright ludicrous. And yet, there it was, a rather eerie bit of foreshadowing.

MUCH TO HIS RELIEF, William Manchester finished the first draft of his manuscript, now titled *The Death of a President*, in February. Of all the books written about November 22, 1963—some two thousand and counting, it has been estimated—none, to this day, has matched its sweeping raw power and emotionally searing narrative. It is, simply, extraordinary, a book for the ages. On March 8 he wrote Jackie and Robert Kennedy of its completion, telling Robert, "I felt as though I had emerged from a long, dark tunnel."⁵ Jackie wrote back:

> Dear Bill,
>
> I was very touched to receive your letter and am so glad for you that the book is finished. I know and appreciate all you went through in

writing it. After Bob Kennedy and Evan Thomas have gone over the manuscript, I want you to know that I will read it too, whenever they think I should. Thank you, Bill, for all you did.

Affectionately,

Jackie[6]

That Jackie—for more than two years weighed down, haunted, trying so desperately to forget the horror of those fleeting seconds on Elm Street—would want to relive it again in excruciating detail would have surprised anyone who knew how much she wanted to move on. Indeed, shortly after Jackie penned her letter, she told Robert to pass word to Manchester, via Evan Thomas, that she wouldn't—couldn't— read it after all. Neither would Robert. The Kennedys, hoping to inoculate themselves against further agony, decided that two of Robert's closest friends would review the manuscript: John Seigenthaler, the editor of the *Nashville Tennessean* and Edwin Guthman, who had recently left Robert's employ to work at the *Los Angeles Times.*[7]

On March 25, two years to the day after his agreement with Robert Kennedy, Manchester, lugging a seventy-seven-pound suitcase, boarded a Trailways bus bound for New York. It contained five copies of his magnum opus—all 1,201 pages and 380,000 words of it. He gave one copy to his agent, Don Congdon, and one to his editor, Evan Thomas, and dropped off the remaining three at Robert Kennedy's office. As he distributed copies, Manchester felt as though a great burden was being lifted off his shoulders. Little did he know that his troubles were just beginning.[8] For that matter, neither did Jackie.

THE FIRST HALF OF 1966 was a time of personal growth for Jackie. Dallas was now more than two years behind her; the crippling nightmares, while still just below the surface and easily triggered, had subsided. Caroline, now eight, continued at the Convent of the Sacred Heart school on Ninety-First Street, the same school that her grandmother

Rose Kennedy had attended. John, five, had now been at Saint David's School on Eighty-Ninth for a year.

The move to Manhattan had generally paid off. Washington, the president's town, was two hundred miles and seemingly a lifetime away. Yet there were downsides. In a city teeming with boldfaced names, Jackie's fame was second to none. The anonymity she craved—or professed to—was impossible.

For all of their self-proclaimed jadedness and nonchalance about being in the presence of a celebrity, New Yorkers often fell silent when she glided into a restaurant or party. Those seeing her in person for the first time couldn't help but gawk. Men made little attempt to conceal their interest; women eyed her with a blend of fascination and curiosity, occasionally bordering on resentment and envy. Jackie was, after all, more famous than they, perceived as wealthier—which often wasn't true—and a threat, given the allure she held for their men.

These attitudes were neither Jackie's fault nor her problem. She knew that New Yorkers, with their facade of disinterest, were staring. "You were just compelled to watch," Susan Wilson, a classmate from Vassar, once said. Sometimes Jackie, with the deep, dark, almond-shaped eyes that had helped snag a future president more than a decade earlier, stared back. Her gaze and that breathy voice, so rarely heard in public, were formidable weapons. "She was very feminine," Clint Hill said, "and very persuasive." A friend of John's who came to know Jackie in her later years, John Perry Barlow, said: "I don't think I've met a more accomplished flirt…. [I]t was the best I'd ever seen because it was based in genuine interest. She could be talking to five or six guys and have each of them think he was the real object of her focus."[9]

She made the most of New York, exploring the city relentlessly. One day she would head out to Coney Island, at the far end of Brooklyn, to eat hot dogs. The next she could be found in a gallery on Madison Avenue or at the movies. She walked and walked, often with friends, but sometimes (and like Garbo) alone. One of her later escorts, the journalist and bon vivant George Plimpton, told her: "Taking you anyplace is like going out with a national monument."

"Yes," she replied, "but isn't it fun?"

Plimpton remembered a night at the opera: "I don't remember the opera, but I do remember that while we were sitting in a box, the public curiosity about her was absolutely extraordinary. She said she wanted to go to the ladies' room. We walked out from behind a box and this enormous crowd followed her—into the ladies' room!"[10]

The casual look she helped spread in 1965 became the norm. With no need to impress anyone or put on airs, she often appeared in public as she did at home—in casual yet stylish clothes.

In Washington, the "Jackie look"—followed closely on both sides of the Atlantic—typically had consisted of those Cassini gowns or the simpler Townley clothes purchased from Dorcas Harden, a Georgetown hostess whose quiet Washington boutique had been a favorite for years.* But now, ensconced in Manhattan, Jackie's tastes pivoted to the simple: sleeveless A-line dresses for spring and summer, usually made of soft Irish linen or raw silk in light colors—white, pink, and taupe. Unless it was a fancy event like an evening at the opera—when she reverted to shimmering gowns and elbow-length white gloves—dressing up meant a good French suit, with a hem around mid-knee and three-quarter sleeves. Casual wear meant white bell-bottom jeans and a black turtleneck that was never tucked in, pulled down snugly over the hips.

Accessories blended wealth, style, and taste. Long before Manolo Blahnik, Christian Louboutin, and Jimmy Choo sent women's hearts racing with their shoes, there was Hélène Arpels. A former model and designer from Monte Carlo, she opened a small shop in midtown Manhattan just after World War II, and for decades was the "couture cobbler" for the smart set. A customer and friend for decades, Jackie had a massive walk-in closet at 1040 that bulged with her creations. At size 10A, her feet were a tad on the large size, but this wasn't a

---

* One of the biggest influences on Jackie's fashion tastes is largely forgotten today: Claire McCardell, the principal designer of the Townley clothes that Jackie often favored. Prior to her death in 1958, McCardell had been one of the most important clothing designers of the twentieth century—big enough to land on the cover of *Time* magazine in 1955.

problem for Arpels, nor was the fact that—and this seemed to be a state secret—one shoe in every pair she bought had a quarter-inch lift meant to compensate for one leg's being slightly shorter than the other." Ever protective of her former employer and friend, McKeon, decades later, won't say which one. Jackie adored Canfora sandals, made at a shop on Capri, and Keds sneakers, and weekends would find her in riding boots that she had worn in the White House.

As for jewelry, Hélène Arpels happened to be the onetime wife of Louis Arpels of Van Cleef & Arpels. Baubles that hung around Jackie's neck or dangled from her ears or wrists typically came from its Fifth Avenue store—purchased for her by others.* But she also proved to women the world over that good taste, style, and elegance needn't be expensive. Arguably the most famous piece of jewelry Jackie ever wore wasn't even real: a triple-strand faux-pearl necklace with a crystal clasp, designed by Kenneth Jay Lane. One of the iconic photos of the Kennedy era shows John Jr. playing with it while his mother laughs. After Jackie's death, that triple strand, which cost Jackie just a few dollars, was auctioned off in 1996 for $211,500. John Block, an executive at Sotheby's, which handled the auction, said: "People wouldn't have paid one dollar more if they were real pearls. They were buying the dream." He was right.[12]

Usually topping all of this off were dark, oversized sunglasses (in her later years, a friend from Doubleday, the publishing house where she worked, once found a dozen pairs in her desk drawer)[13] and a Hermès scarf. A political wife might not have had the luxury of being so cavalier about her wardrobe—Lady Bird Johnson and Ethel Kennedy, for example, rarely appeared in public in such casual attire—but Jackie, to her delight, could do as she wished.

---

* One of the most touching pieces of jewelry Jackie ever received from John F. Kennedy was given to her after his assassination. In the fall of 1963, JFK visited Van Cleef & Arpels in New York, where he ordered a ring for her—featuring a large (forty-seven-carat) kunzite surrounded by twenty diamonds. The president intended to give it to her for Christmas. After his murder, the ring was delivered to the White House, and Evelyn Lincoln, the late president's personal secretary, gave it to her. See: Gem Select, "Jackie O's Jewelry," story of Jacqueline Kennedy's Kunzite Ring.

Oleg Cassini, Jackie's designer during her White House years, often claimed that his star client never wanted to be a trendsetter in the White House—and certainly didn't want to be one after returning to private life. He called it a misconception, saying: "Jackie basically had her own carefully directed style. She dressed for herself. She wanted to be noticed, not copied."[14] She even expressed displeasure at being seen as a fashion icon. Perusing a draft, in 1992, of Carl Sferrazza Anthony's book *First Ladies*, she read a sentence that said, "If there was one sphere where Jacqueline had great influence, it was fashion." "Much to her annoyance," she wrote in the margin.[15]

It was ridiculous for her to expect that she would not be seen as a trendsetter, given that she was a) arguably the most famous woman in the world, b) young and beautiful, with a model-like form, and c) someone who sought out prominent designers to create bespoke outfits for her to wear. Of course she would be copied. As First Lady, a term she disliked, she had taken, among other things, the sleeveless shift, bouffant hairdo, pearl necklace, and of course the pillbox hat, mainstream. On her own in the mid-sixties, it was different.

Fashionable, desirable, and restless, she traveled at a frantic pace, roaring off from the airport that bore her husband's name in search of sun, sand, and snow. She began the year with Caroline, John, Robert Kennedy, and his family on the ski slopes of Sun Valley, Idaho; they then headed for more powder and several days of après-ski in Gstaad, Switzerland. A short hop to Rome followed, where Jackie insisted that she sought "a quiet few days." Yet exactly the opposite occurred, with events including a high-profile visit with Pope Paul VI, a dinner party with fashion maven Princess Irene Galitzine, a gala dinner at a fifteenth-century palazzo, and a visit to Gianni Agnelli's beach resort. Surprisingly, given her antipathy to guns, she even went on a fox-hunting trip at one point with Dino Pecci-Blunt, a half-American count whom she and Lee had first met during a 1951 trip. Most of this could have been done in a low-key manner had she truly desired, yet once word had gotten out that she was in town, the Roman and international press had their usual field day. So much for peace and quiet.

And so it went with her jet-setting. Photographers were always on hand; locals always wanted a peek. In Argentina over Easter, Jackie was photographed changing into a bathing suit on a private beach. At least one tabloid ran photos of her backside, but newspapers in the United States—who still wouldn't even show her smoking a cigarette—declined. Jackie, for now, remained on her pedestal.

Returning to New York barely long enough to drop off Caroline and John, she crossed the Atlantic again, this time headed for Spain. Rumors of a relationship with yet another man—Antonio Garrigues Walker, who had been ambassador to the United States during the Kennedy administration and was now envoy to the Vatican—were swirling about, and when Jackie landed in Madrid, she was met by hundreds of reporters and photographers. Garrigues, a sixty-two-year-old widower, had just been seen with Jackie in Italy after all, and that was enough for the journalists to think that there was something—possibly even marriage—in the works.

The next day she headed for Seville, where she was mobbed at a charity gala benefitting the Red Cross. Drama was guaranteed, for the ball's official host and hostess were Prince Rainier and Princess Grace of Monaco, the latter of whom had a relationship with Jackie that had once been warm and friendly and then turned ice cold in later years. The reason for this, not surprisingly, was a man they had in common: John F. Kennedy.

Some context is needed to explain how these twentieth-century icons grew frosty toward each other. When JFK was in the hospital in October 1954—he had undergone a dangerous procedure to fuse his spinal disks with a metal plate, and later developed an infection and for a time fell into a coma—Jackie met Kelly at a dinner party and convinced her to visit him in his room. Kelly, by then a major Hollywood star—she was a year away from winning an Academy Award for Best Actress for her role in *The Country Girl*—took things further and, as a prank, dressed up as a nurse. What actually transpired next has been debated ever since.

What Jackie obviously didn't know was that her husband had once dated—and apparently fallen hard for—Kelly. He'd wanted to marry her, but Joseph P. Kennedy, eyeing a big political future for his then-congressman son, ultimately decided that she was "too Hollywood."[16]

Had Jackie—always territorial and who designed a bracelet for Kelly as a thank-you gift—known of the affair between the "nurse" and her "patient" five years earlier, she certainly wouldn't have set up the visit. Gore Vidal, a friend of all three people, says Jackie figured it out two years later when she and Jack were looking at press coverage of Kelly's wedding to Monaco's Prince Rainier. "Jack frowned and said, "*I could have married her!*" Jackie's face, he claims—though one wonders just how he would know—"was tear-stained."[17]

Jackie's dislike of Kelly almost certainly dates from here. When Prince Rainier and Princess Grace visited the White House in 1961, Jackie had the royal visit downgraded to a quick (eighty-minute) lunch. Kelly is said to have been miffed. Eleven days after Kennedy's assassination, Kelly returned to Washington and, tears streaming, stood before his grave. Then, armed with toys for Caroline and John, she tried to pay Jackie a courtesy call at the White House. The widow refused to see her.[18]

Now, in Seville, these two iconic women who had risen to the top—one marrying a prince; the other, a future president—were scheduled to sit at the head table. Even though Kelly was the event's hostess, she showed up forty minutes late. And when Jackie—whose global fame was now unmatched—arrived, the princess scurried into a powder room for an hour. When they finally did appear together at the head table, they sat stone-faced, ignoring each other, separated only by the Duke of Medinaceli. Reporters, noting the apparent and mutual contempt, had a field day. One photo shows them bumping into each other but avoiding eye contact: Kelly is unsmiling and seemingly uncomfortable; Jackie, meanwhile, aware that she had upstaged royalty, wore a demure smile. Naturally, both ladies looked spectacular.

Jackie had learned to enjoy the fame she claimed not to have sought. Donning a crimson jacket trimmed in black and a broad-brimmed black hat, tilting it to the left ("rakish," declared the *New York Times*), she toured the Seville Fair from atop a white horse. "To visit Seville and not ride horseback at the fair is equal to not coming at all," she remarked.

She later took in a bullfight, where the country's top bullfighters (bypassing the nearby Grace) dedicated their soon-to-be-butchered animals to her. When the terrible moments came, when the picadors sliced into the animals, Jackie "grimaced and turned her eyes away." At one point, a matador, covered in blood, turned to face Jackie. She "gasped and put her hand to her face." Despite her apparent shock—one wonders what was running through her mind at that terrible moment—she later called the spectacle "exciting and beautiful."

Back home, her attendance at the slaughter drew some of her first public criticism, with a Humane Society executive even referencing President Kennedy's assassination: "It is a sad and singularly ironic foot-note in our age of modern violence that Mrs. Jacqueline Kennedy, of all people, who has seen the barbarism of the present era at such tragic first hand, should now see fit to condone and even compliment the bullfight..."[19]

She was unfazed by the criticism, says journalist Jay Rutherford, who covered the trip. Jackie "was anxious to avail herself of pleasure and privilege," he says, "and wasn't taking into account the consequences of public evaluation."[20] It seems quaint today, but it has also been noted that Jackie was seen—egads—knocking back a glass of sherry. Looking back on 1966, one can see that the trip furthered the sense that the thirty-six-year-old widow appeared to be making good progress. "She was young, attractive and she clearly wanted to live her life with a certain brio," the *Times* said in her 1994 obituary.

FOR ALL THE HOPSCOTCHING she had done around the globe over the course of her still young life, there was one place Jackie had yet to visit: Hawaii. She could have accompanied President Kennedy there on his brief June 1963 visit, but six months pregnant with Patrick, did not want to make such a long journey. Hearing of its sublime beauty and seeking what the locals called *hau'oli*, or happiness, she was eager to visit now. Walking through the airport in a shimmering white coat and heels—she arguably never looked more stunning than in the mid-1960s—she smiled demurely as fellow travelers pointed and gawked. Caroline and John, in tow, were also dressed up; five-and-a-half-year-old John wore bangs hanging down his forehead, like the Beatles did.

After departing New York, she stopped in San Francisco to pick up her brother-in-law Peter Lawford, two of his children (Caroline and Sydney Lawford were particularly close), and a friend. Nursing a drink as they zoomed over the Pacific, Jackie told fellow first-class passenger Buck Buchwach, the managing editor of the *Honolulu Advertiser*, "I hope I get a real rest in Hawaii."[21] They were met in Honolulu by a throng of some four thousand people and the usual batch of photographers. Jackie's hair blew in the warm trade winds; she brushed it away from her face as a pair of colorful leis were hung around her neck.

The trip, scheduled to last four weeks but extended to seven, was more than just a long vacation. Jackie had been dating John Warnecke for nearly two years now, and the architect, who owned a home near Oahu's famous Diamond Head, was working on the new state capitol in Honolulu. He invited Jackie to join him and, wanting to be with her boyfriend, she accepted.

For appearances' sake, however, it was decided that Jackie couldn't actually stay with Warnecke. The architect arranged for a Hawaiian friend, the socialite Cecily Johnston, to help. "Cecily rented the house for her down the beach from where I was, and that's how she [Jackie] came to Hawaii," he recalled years later. It provided a convenient cover, as Warnecke would admit years later.[22]

Her three-thousand-dollar-a-month redwood-frame house on trendy Kahala Beach was surrounded by tall hedges and trees that

Jackie

shielded it from public view; her Secret Service detail, led by John Walsh, kept an eye on passersby. When Jackie first arrived, waiting in the living room was Warnecke.

Forty-seven-year-old John Warnecke, refined, intelligent, and said to possess impeccable taste, was not a rogue, at least not on the same level that prior key men in Jackie's life—her father, her husband, her father-in-law—were. Yet he was said to be a womanizer, and "there was an element of danger" to him, as one friend noted.[23] Jackie typically found this alluring.

The relationship was serious: they had contemplated marriage. "Maybe I can make you a Catholic," Jackie joked when Warnecke told her that he had never been baptized. But there were too many obstacles. Robert Kennedy, looking out not only for her future but his own, vetoed marriage. "Bobby says it's too soon," she told him.[24]

Then there was the matter of money. Jackie—resentful of being financially dependent on the Kennedy family—knew that Warnecke, for all his architectural prominence and success, was wealthy but not *wealthy*. She knew there were richer men out there, but she loved Warnecke and kept the door open.

Jackie quickly got in the spirit of the islands. At a party at Johnston's house—where the famed singer Don Ho was brought in to entertain—Christopher Lawford pushed his sister in the pool. John pushed in Caroline, and Ho, getting into the act, approached Jackie from behind and pushed her in, too. Jackie, laughing, then got revenge on Ho or, according to another description of the moment, yanked in a Secret Service agent who had offered her a hand.

But it was not all fun and games. Wading into the ocean three days after their arrival, Caroline slashed her left foot on a piece of coral. It took five stitches to patch her up. John had an even bigger scare. During a camping trip on the big island of Hawaii, he tripped and fell backward into a pit of hot coals left over from a campfire. Yelping in pain, he instinctively tried to push himself up with his right arm, only to suffer first- and second-degree burns. A panicked

Jackie and Agent Walsh yanked him to safety and rushed the boy, crying in pain, to the hospital.

She indulged in art classes—Chinese calligraphy and drawing. In one intriguing work using ink and watercolors, she drew a bird in a cage with the door left open, a seeming allegory to the free spirit—"I'd like to be a bird"—she had described in Jim Fosburgh's backyard two summers before.

She appeared in a bikini, unusual for grown women in that era and no doubt a thrill for Warnecke. The lovebirds spent a week or ten days in a small cottage on Kauai, perhaps the most beautiful of all the Hawaiian islands, and Jackie spoke of buying a home, a secluded retreat from the spotlight that she claimed to dislike.

But what of their marriage talk? Bobby's cautionary advice—and Jackie's knowing, deep down, that the architect wasn't loaded—weighed heavily. A decision would have to be made.

Preparing to return to New York in late July, Jackie thanked the Hawaiian press for doing what reporters elsewhere would not have done: leaving her alone: "I had forgotten, and my children have never known what it is to discover a new place, unwatched and unnoticed."[25]

Chapter Six

July 1966 to December 1966:
Steel Beneath Velvet

It was a huge crowd, some five thousand people. They gathered outside as the wedding party arrived, hoping for a glance—not of the bride—of three guests: Jackie, Caroline, and John. They were attending the July 30, 1966, marriage of Jackie's step-sister Janet to Lewis Polk Rutherfurd.[1]

The venue, Saint Mary's Church in Newport, Rhode Island, surely brought memories flooding back for Jackie: it was where she had married John F. Kennedy thirteen years earlier. When she got out of her car, wearing a striking yellow suit, she was met with wild screams from middle-aged women, jumping up and down in a frenzied excitement. "Jack-eee!! Jack-eee!!" they cried, acting like their teenage girls might have acted watching the arrival of the Beatles. A policeman had to push people out of the way so she could make her way inside. Caroline— the flower girl—"was clearly frightened," and John ran as fast as he could for the safety of the church. Arriving last, the twenty-year-old bride barely made it inside. "Help me; somebody help me," she was heard to cry.[2] Some twenty people tried to crash the wedding and were kicked out; others climbed walls to take pictures through windows. Janet "should have been the star of the show," the *Providence Sunday Journal* reported, but "it was her famous relative who stole the show."

This was peak Jackie mania. "No queen or movie star—with the possible exception of Rudolph Valentino—had been greeted with the hysteria that surrounded the thirty-seven-year-old widow," notes biographer Sarah Bradford. But Jackie wasn't royalty; she didn't grace the silver screen. She was a widow whose idolization stemmed from the behavior she displayed in the seventy-two hours after her husband was martyred. She would forever be remembered for that weekend, during which that behavior was nothing less than perfect and majestic. And yet she herself just wanted to forget.

She was now at the utter height of her popularity—and power. Perhaps she thought she could have her way with anything and anyone. This belief would soon collide with the pending publication of *The Death of a President*.

❧

On July 29, Robert Kennedy sent William Manchester a telegram, indicating that after four months of wrangling over sensitive parts of the text, "members of the Kennedy family will place no further obstacle in the way of publication" of the book.[3] While Bobby had not read the manuscript himself—Jackie had not, and certainly could not, either—others, namely, Ethel Kennedy, Arthur Schlesinger, and two former Justice Department aides of Bobby's, Ed Guthman and John Seigenthaler, had. It was smooth sailing for the book's publication.

Or so it seemed. Bids happened to be due at five p.m. that same day for the right to publish excerpts. *Look* offered $405,000; *Life* offered $500,000. *Look* then raised its bid to an astronomical sum: $665,000—nearly $5.2 million in 2019 dollars—which *Life* declined to top. At this point Jackie, who had returned from Hawaii the day before and was marking her thirty-seventh birthday, got involved.[4] She seemed surprised that excerpts from her most tragic hours would be peddled on newsstands alongside gossip rags and chewing gum. Referring to the book, she would soon tell Manchester: "I thought that it would be bound in black and put away on dark library shelves."[5] In his account of the struggle to get *The Death of a President* published, Manchester says he concluded that "[s]he really didn't want any book, that at most she would accept only a dull, obscure volume." It was obviously a naive sentiment. Jackie was also upset, Manchester deduced, that *Look*'s money would go to him and not the Kennedy library.[6]

She told Robert to do something. Essentially rescinding his telegram to Manchester, he sent a blunt message to Manchester's editor at Harper & Row, Evan Thomas: "Mrs. Kennedy and I must give permission for publication of the book and that has not been given."[7]

Jackie's anxiety was such that she summoned Mike Cowles, the editor of *Look*, to Hyannis and, with help from Robert, pressured him into reducing the number of book installments *Look* would serialize from seven to four. And, for all her previous contempt of Jim Bishop and his own book on the assassination, she had Robert send a telegram to editor Thomas that ended with this bombshell: "It just seems to me that rather than struggling with this any longer we should take our chances with Jim Bishop."[8] Yet even while this was going on, Jackie had her secretary Pamela Turnure send Manchester seventy-seven demands for revisions.

This was Jackie at her most irrational: trying to toss one author overboard (while suggesting scores of edits), considering another she didn't even care for, and squeezing a magazine publisher. And even after suggesting that Manchester be dumped, she invited him to Hyannis to discuss the whole thing.

The author, burned out from two years of round-the-clock work and a breakdown of his health, says he was "convinced Jackie and I [could] work this out," and when he and former JFK and now LBJ aide Dick Goodwin's plane touched down in Hyannis, "Jackie was waving to us as we came down the ramp. I remember that she was wearing sunglasses and a green miniskirt; she looked stunning," Manchester wrote. There were some pleasurable moments first: Jackie waterskied while Manchester held on to John in the boat, then the two of them plunged into the chilly sea for a swim.

Back on land and in dry clothes, they got down to business. Manchester soon realized that meeting with Jackie was a waste of time. She was "hostile toward *Look*, bitter about Cowles, and scornful of all books on President Kennedy."[9]

Jackie had promised Manchester and Goodwin that she wouldn't get emotional, and then she got emotional. In a tone Manchester describes as "savage," Jackie promised to fight and, thinking of her exalted public image, warned: "Anybody who is against me will look like a rat unless I run off with Eddie Fisher." Whenever Manchester or Goodwin tried to discuss the book calmly, Jackie responded with "tears, grimaces, and whispery cries of 'Jesus Christ!'" Given her mood at the time, he said, "any open disagreements with her would have purposelessly ruptured the thin membrane of civility."[10]

Imagine her dilemma. Here was a woman whose policy, even in the best of times—the glorious 1,036 days that the Kennedys called the White House home, when they were the most glamorous couple in the world—had been to dispense information with an eyedropper. "Minimum information with maximum politeness," she had instructed aides in 1961. And yet she had spoken with Manchester for hours in the spring of 1964, telling him everything about the most gruesome event imaginable, in excruciating, gory detail: the sight of her husband's shattered head. The back seat wet with blood and brains. The expression on his lifeless face. Struggling to put her wedding ring on his finger. Jackie was particularly unhappy about two deeply private things concerning Caroline and John: the description of how they were informed of their father's passing (Maud Shaw was given the heart-rending task on the evening of November 22) and the contents of letters that they had written to their father, that Jackie placed in the coffin in the East Room on November 24. Now these intimate, shattering moments were to be shared with the world? She was determined to stop it.

It was inevitable that these many months of wrangling over the text would spill out into the press. Jackie was, as a *New York Times* reporter wrote, "raising hell" over the whole project. Her national stature, still unassailable, allowed for this, and the ensuing tension even affected her relationship with Robert. She blamed him for not managing the situation better, even confiding in Manchester that her beloved brother-in-law had been acting "like a little boy who knows he's done wrong."[11]

Robert, ever protective of his sister-in-law and determined to ease her suffering, fell on his sword. "It's really mostly my fault," he said. "I just never wanted to spend the time on that."[12] It was clear that nearly three years after the assassination, the two people who were most shattered by it were still struggling to deal with it—to compartmentalize it, to forget it. When Jackie referred to "dark library shelves," she was also referring to some distant crevice of her mind; she wanted memories of Dallas stuffed away where she wouldn't have to think of them again.

Bending to her wishes, Robert told Harper & Row that not only had the Kennedys not given their permission for the book to be published, but they now wanted it killed outright. As Harper & Row executives were pondering their next move, Manchester flew to Washington to meet with Robert. It did not go well. The author reminded Kennedy that in addition to the book, there was also the side deal with *Look* to serialize it. Manchester mentioned his health problems to Robert, only to have Kennedy explode: "Do you think you've suffered more than Jackie and me?"[13]

But kill both the book and *Look*'s serialization? The toothpaste was out of the tube. Contracts had been signed, money had changed hands. *Look* was now selling its excerpt rights to publishers in forty-two countries. This too got out, with the *New York Times* writing about the *Look* deal and the pushback from the Kennedys. After three years of "Mrs. Kennedy Buys Horse"-type stories, press coverage of Jackie, universally deferential since Dallas, would no longer be automatically fawning.[14]

Jackie's privacy concerns weren't the only issue. Kennedys being Kennedys, there were also concerns about how the book would be received by voters and how they might react. It was a given in 1966 that Robert, despite being in the Senate for less than two years, was beginning to ponder a White House run for 1968. Noted the *Times*: "The senator and his advisors allowed practical politics to determine what the historical record [of the president's assassination] would show. They did not raise the question of truth or falsity…. They wanted a truly authorized history, perhaps not an accurate one, but one that just omitted part of the history."[15] Thus, it seemed, Robert and Jackie were attempting to sanitize the past for the sake of the future.

IT HAS BEEN SAID THAT THE ASSASSINATION of President Kennedy proved, once and for all, how utterly dominant television news had become in American life. When Franklin D. Roosevelt gave his Fire-side Chats three decades earlier, Americans gathered around the radio. Now the national hearth was the TV. Each evening, some sixty million Americans would watch one of the three evening network news broadcasts—"a nightly national seance," as one reporter, Daniel Schorr of CBS, once put it.[16,*]

TV was, quite simply, all-powerful.

Television's ascendancy and Vietnam went hand in hand. For the first time in American history, war was being fought in living rooms across the nation; Americans ate dinner while watching it. The jungles of Vietnam weren't ten thousand miles away—they were six feet away. If in 1960, the small screen forever changed the way political campaigns were waged, just a few years later it was changing the way wars were fought and how they were perceived back home.

As it did for millions of Americans, unrelenting coverage of the war gradually had an impact on Jackie. She grew increasingly disturbed over

---

* The U.S. population has grown some two-thirds since the mid-1960s, yet in 2018, says a Pew Research survey, the combined audience for the nightly news broadcasts of ABC, CBS, and NBC was about 75 percent less than it was in the 1960s—just 15.6 million. And, despite all the noise cable news generates today, its audience is significantly smaller than this. The data show that TV network news used to be ubiquitous but today no longer is.

reports of young men being cut down in their prime. On some level, in some crevice of her mind, it reminded her of what she herself had been through, how her husband also had been sacrificed—seemingly, she believed, for nothing. Here she was, in 1040, her sanctuary in the sky, only to learn that she was not immune from the violent imagery that she tried so desperately to forget.

Exposed to all this violence, and to a widening war that she believed her husband would have avoided—a matter of debate even today—her antiwar feelings intensified. Vietnam was, she said at one point, "more complex than any dark hell that Shakespeare ever looked into."[17] Her views, fueled in no small part by Robert Kennedy's own increasing apprehension, were made clear in a dramatic way to Robert McNamara, the defense secretary who had served her husband and then stayed on to serve Lyndon Johnson. One evening McNamara had flown to New York to have dinner with Jackie at 1040. After dinner, as they sat on a couch in her small library, talk turned to Vietnam. Jackie, McNamara writes, "had grown very depressed by, and very critical of, the war." She became "so tense that she could hardly speak. She suddenly exploded. She turned and began, literally, to beat on my chest, demanding that I 'do something to stop the slaughter!'"[18]

It is no coincidence, argues Jackie biographer Barbara Leaming, that Jackie's visceral reaction to what she was seeing on television occurred at the same time as she began fighting the Manchester manuscript—which, it appeared, she still had not and could not read. "The present sense of helplessness," she writes, "echoes the powerlessness experienced during the original traumatic incident."[19]

In the aggregate it shows that for all her efforts—leaving Washington, traveling globally at a frenetic pace, hitting the town, trying to enjoy herself again—the past was always present, and no matter where she was, there was no escape.

Meanwhile, Manchester, noting Jackie's globetrotting, socializing, and ravishing appearances in miniskirts, made the mistake of assuming that she was fully recovered from Dallas. He was wrong. The sudden violence that had shattered her then had instilled a permanent sense of paranoia and unease in her that had not gone away. Such concerns proved to be justified; events happened that were not only cruel and painful but downright terrifying—not only to her but, much to her horror, to her children.

One Sunday in July, Jackie and Caroline had just departed the Church of Saint Thomas More on East Eighty-Ninth Street, four blocks north of 1040, and were walking west toward Fifth Avenue. Suddenly a woman lunged at Caroline, grabbed her, and began screaming. "Your mother is a wicked woman who has killed three people! And your father is still alive!"

Caroline, terrified, struggled to free herself from the woman's grip. Jackie and a Secret Service agent yanked her away, and the woman was hauled off to nearby Bellevue Hospital for mental observation. It was Jackie's worst nightmare. "I still haven't gotten over that strange woman," she said a year later.[20]

Four months later, on the third anniversary of the assassination itself, no less—November 22, 1966—Jackie was walking John home from school:

> I noticed that a little group of children, some of them from John's class, was following us. Then one of the children said, quite loud, 'Your father's dead...your father's dead!' You know how children are. They've even said it to me when I've run into them at school, as if.... Well this day John listened to them saying it over and over, and he didn't say word. He just came close to me, took my hand, and he squeezed it. As if he were trying to reassure me that things were alright. And so we walked home together, with the children following us.[21]

Such moments were searing to Jackie. The statement she had made to Pierre Salinger on the weekend of the assassination—that all she had now were her kids and that she must protect them as they grew up—was always top of mind. Now, of all things, a group of schoolchildren on the sidewalk had violated that thin sense of security. John was now just three days shy of his sixth birthday—old enough to know that his father was gone, and that this often made his mother cry. She had pledged to protect him, but now he was protecting her. *"He just came close to me, took my hand, and he squeezed it. As if he were trying to reassure me that things were alright."*

November remained ever painful, what she called her "difficult time of year." She retreated once again, turning away the numerous invitations she always got, including what came to be known as "the party of the century": the Black and White Ball thrown at the Plaza hotel on November 28 by her friend Truman Capote.

Capote, the squeaky-voiced, luxuriously snarky writer at the very zenith of his career thanks to *In Cold Blood*, his blockbuster book about the real-life slaughter of a Kansas farm family, had decided to throw a bash in honor of Katharine Graham, the publisher of the *Washington Post*. Capote had curated an ultra-hot guest list, skimming the very cream of Manhattan and Hollywood.

Among "the Chosen"—as the media called those on the guest list—was Jackie's sister Lee, who was forever fawning over the flamboyantly homosexual Capote. But at this very apex of midcentury glamour and celebrity, perhaps the most desired guest of all—Jackie—skipped it. If Capote thought that no one could turn down such a sought-after invitation, one that others were begging and conniving to receive, he was wrong—and also naïve. Did he really imagine that Jackie would attend such a frivolous event just days after the anniversary of her husband's murder?

Even if it hadn't been November, she was in no mood for frivolity anyway. She summoned editor Thomas and his boss, Cass Canfield—the president and chairman of Harper & Row, to 1040. She ripped into Thomas, blaming him for the *Look* serialization "and various other acts of irresponsibility." Decades later Thomas's son, Evan Thomas III, shared an anecdote that reveals just how vengeful Jackie apparently could be. "As they're leaving," he said, "Jackie is hugging Cass—they were old buddies and social equals*—and she leans over Cass's shoulder and whispers to my father, 'I'm going to ruin you.'"[22]

Media attention regarding the dispute remains enormous. One rumor, described by Manchester as an "absurd canard," is that Jackie offered $3 million (which she almost certainly did not have) to kill the book. Jackie, in her final weeks of being largely untouchable, continued to float above it all, but Manchester was hounded by reporters and total strangers at his door wanting to discuss the assassination.

On December 2, Manchester, in London, got a cable from Canfield and Thomas. It appeared to be a capitulation to Jackie. If Manchester didn't agree to yet more demands from her to change the manuscript, Harper & Row would kill the book outright. But four days later, and after *Look*'s Mike Cowles stiffened Canfield's resolve, the two men wrote Jackie separately, informing her that the book and the serialization would go forward whether she liked it or not. Cowles, who made his letter public, told the widow: "I realize that you may not be entirely happy about all the particulars but I feel we have gone the limit to try to be fair and thoughtful of everyone's feelings and yet consistent with accuracy."[23]

Jackie picked up the phone and told her lawyer, Simon Rifkind, to sue.

In 1964, 1965, and now 1966, tabloids had published countless distortions about Jackie. But she had never sued, never asked anyone to stop, for doing so simply would have generated yet more unwanted publicity. But now, not getting her way for the first time, she went to war. Recalling this in the mid-1970s, Manchester says Jackie didn't want to sue in 1966, either. "The only thing Jackie wanted, and the one thing she couldn't have, was no magazine series, no book; just one big blank page for November 22, 1963." History demanded otherwise.[24]

The lawsuit seemed absurd in more than a few ways. The day of the filing, she released a statement to the press calling the book "tasteless

---

* They were more than equals; they had been family. Canfield's son Michael had been married to Jackie's sister Lee between 1953 and 1959, and although the marriage failed, the elder Canfield had maintained his ties to the Kennedys.

and distorted"—and said, "I have never seen Manchester's manuscript." Of course she hadn't: for months she had refused to. She added, "I have not approved it nor have I authorized anyone else to approve it for me." This too was a distortion of the truth. The text had been shown to others as she had requested months before.[25] Trial was set for January 16, 1967.

Jackie was alone here, and out on a limb. Her legal argument seemed less than sturdy and, for the first time, a clear and public rift between her and Robert Kennedy emerged. Robert, sensing political damage, declined to join Jackie—whom he now privately referred to half-heartedly as "my crazy sister-in-law"—as a plaintiff. It was also announced that Jackie would not be joining Robert and his family for a ski vacation in Sun Valley, Idaho, after all.[26]

Watching all of this with great interest was Lyndon Johnson. On December 16, the same day the news about the Sun Valley vacation broke, the president, at Lady Bird's urging, sent Jackie a hand-written letter:

Lady Bird and I have been distressed to read the press accounts of your unhappiness about the Manchester book. Some of these accounts attribute your concern to passages in the book which are critical or defamatory of us. If this is so, I want you to know while we deeply appreciate your characteristic kindness and sensitivity, we hope you will not subject yourself to any discomfort or distress on our account.... [Y]our own tranquility is important to both of us, and ...[w]e are both grateful to you for your constant and unfailing thoughtfulness and friendship.[27], *

Johnson's thoughtfulness needs a bit of context. LBJ knew that one area of contention with the book concerned the portrayal of him by Manchester. More than a few early readers of the manuscript said it was too harsh, and claimed that the new president, eager to take over in the hours after the assassination, was insensitive to Jackie. This was

---

* These magnanimous words were not composed by LBJ, however, but by his good friend, Supreme Court justice Abe Fortas.

not true. What was true, however, was that tension between LBJ and Robert Kennedy, which had always existed, began to deepen that very afternoon, fueled by the supercharged and frightening atmosphere that existed in the immediate aftermath of the murder. The assassination also meant that Lyndon Johnson was no longer a Kennedy subordinate—it was suddenly the other way around—and LBJ seemed eager to put Robert in his place. Johnson's problem was that Robert and Jackie were tied at the hip, meaning the president had to handle RFK carefully, so as not to offend Jackie. But now that a rift between Robert and Jackie had been exposed, Johnson unquestionably sought to exploit it.

Jackie's lawsuit shows, as veteran White House correspondent Paul Healy wrote in the *New York Daily News* on Christmas Day, that "[a]s always, it was Jacqueline doing exactly what she wanted to do." The dispute with Harper & Row (she had quickly settled with *Look*) "reveals to the public for the first time the steel beneath the velvet that sets off her glamorous image." He added, "She can be as tough as the occasion demands."

Having had her way editorially with Theodore White and *Life* days after the assassination and then in the innocuous—or so it seems today—interviews with Arthur Schlesinger in the spring of 1964, Jackie might have presumed that she could also pressure Harper & Row into meeting her demands now—and that she would pay no price for her fight with it and with Manchester. This was not presumptuous: on December 29 a Gallup Poll revealed that Jackie, for the fifth year in a row, was ranked as the most admired women in the world.

And yet public opinion was beginning to turn. On December 20, syndicated columnist Vera Glaser wrote that since 1963, "[t]he nation's heart has gone out to her in love, sympathy and protectiveness," but that Jackie's fight over *The Death of a President* served only to "prolong the nation's trauma." She went further, accusing the widow of being "a professional martyr" who was mourning "beyond a reasonable statute of limitations." She pointed out that thousands of Vietnam War widows who lacked Jackie's wealth and beauty were also struggling while mourning their young husbands whose lives had also been cut short by violence.[28]

Even the *New York Times* lambasted Jackie for fighting Manchester. In an editorial, it said: "History belongs to everyone, not just the participants.... [H]aving made her original decision [in 1964 that a book be written by Manchester], she cannot now escape its consequences."[29] Indeed Jackie could not. Her Gallup streak was about to be snapped for good.

Chapter Seven

January to June 1967:
The Secret Burial

For Jackie, 1967 would bring more personal sadness, including the violent death of a dear friend—and, in a cold, swift sea—nearly her own. The new year began as the old one had ended: with coverage, much of it negative, about her fight to squash *The Death of a President*. When she returned to 1040 on January 8, after a holiday at Bunny Mellon's estate in Antigua, she was greeted by an unwelcome surprise: TV lights and aggressive photographers swarming about. Ignoring the shouted questions, she shielded her eyes as a doorman helped her into the lobby.

It was dreadful. Not only had Manchester recreated, in excruciatingly granular detail, the most horrifying moment of her life, but the resulting battle surrounding its publication had left new scars. It seemed that the press, or at least the tabloids, were no longer going to treat her with the same gentle deference to which she had become accustomed—and perhaps taken for granted.

That very day, one of those tabloids, the *New York World Journal Tribune*, had launched a multipart series about her, splashing the headline

"Jackie Comes Off Her Pedestal" across the front page. The writer, Liz Smith, raked the widow over the coals for her Manchester histrionics, calling it "tasteless, undignified and ultimately pointless." In the same paper, another writer, Lawrence Van Gelder, piled on: "From now on, she would never again appear in the limelight with quite all that queenly dignity intact."

Other critics said she was trampling on press freedoms—Americans had a right to read about the assassination of their president, after all—and for allowing herself to be guided by self-pity. The avalanche of criticism was as harsh as it was correct.

And yet the Kennedys didn't seem to get it. Jackie, wrote Robert in a letter to Katharine Graham, was just "a girl who hadn't committed any great crime but who day after day was pilloried in all kinds of scandalous ways."[1]

The bad headlines kept coming. "Bitter Row on Book," shouted the *New York Post*. "Manchester vs. RFK, Jackie—Words Fly." Mary McGrory, an old Kennedy friend, wrote: "For the first time...Mrs. Kennedy has her back to the wall."[2]

Before her lawsuit against Manchester and Harper & Row proceeded, Jackie showed signs of wanting to settle. She had finally steeled herself to read *The Death of a President*—starting with the sixty thousand words that *Look* was about to run. She asked that only 1,600 words be changed. Her requests, when Manchester reviewed them, were deemed "harmless."[3] He soon learned from a "reliable informant" that Jackie, being the voracious reader that she was, had plowed through the book itself, all 710 pages, rendering a one-word verdict: "Fascinating." It surely could not have been easy for the widow.[4]

In the early hours of January 16, the day the trial was set to begin, a settlement was reached. It was over. Days later, *Look* published the first installment of *The Death of a President*. It was a smash. All four thousand copies given to newsstands in Times Square alone sold out instantly; United Airlines, which bought 1,800 copies for its planes, had nearly all of them stolen by passengers. A Gallup survey found that seventy million people read at least one of *Look*'s four installments;

fifty-four million read all four. Three and a half years after the assassination, Manchester's sweeping work took Americans back like no work had done before—or since. It was a monumental achievement.[5]

And those were just the excerpts.

The book was published on April 7. To provide context, an average nonfiction book would be very lucky indeed to sell one thousand copies over its entire lifetime. *The Death of a President*, over its first four years, sold 1,685,232. It was the bestselling nonfiction book of 1967 and one of the biggest for the entire tumultuous decade. Ironically, Jackie's highly publicized fight to squash it only made it bigger.[6]

It also knocked her off the pedestal she had occupied for more than three years. On January 31, a survey conducted by former JFK pollster Lou Harris showed that a third of Americans now "thought less" of Jackie, and 20 percent thought less of Robert. By a two-to-one margin, they said the public's right to know about the assassination of President Kennedy trumped his widow's right to privacy. The damage had been done.[7]

If Jackie hadn't understood before that her reputation was tarnished, she certainly did now.

Coverage of the book battle seemed to open a Pandora's box from which every detail of Jackie's once sacrosanct private life emerged. One tabloid, the *National Enquirer*, ran a long story detailing what it claimed were all the juicy details of Jackie's new life. "From Mourner to Swinger," the headline said. As usual, sourcing was skimpy, and some facts were anything but, but the broader point was that the post-assassination era was giving way to something new. The president's widow was no longer off limits.

The new aggressiveness about covering Jackie emboldened one local photographer in particular. In May, he got his first image of her at an art gallery on Madison Avenue. He decided to follow her home. "That's the night I found out she lived at 1040 Fifth Avenue—and got some shots of her outside."[8] It was the beginning of an obsession that would last for years, and yield—whether she liked it or not—some of the most iconic pictures of Jackie ever taken. The photographer's name was Ron Galella.

Galella was one of the first true paparazzi—*Newsweek*, a frequent buyer of his work, would dub him a "paparazzo extraordinaire"—and his early photos of Jackie quickly led to requests for more. "Her name started to show up more and more often on the 'request lists' that *Time* and *Newsweek* sent me every week," he recalls; "gradually, Jackie became more and more a part of my life." He found her elusiveness and mystery intriguing, and was drawn to the challenge of capturing her in his lens.[9],*

Galella had found his meal ticket, and the game was on. Already prominent for his photos of stars like Elizabeth Taylor, Richard Burton, and French bombshell Brigitte Bardot, whom he followed one night into a St. Tropez club called the Zoom Zoom, Galella began stalking Jackie.

While his complete obsession with her would reach its zenith in later years, it had its roots in 1967. A typical day involved Galella getting off at the Eighty-Sixth and Lexington subway stop and walking three blocks west and one block south to his "office," which often consisted of bushes or a lamp pole to hide behind until Jackie emerged. The doormen at 1040, protective of their tenants, refused to tell him anything, but Galella soon began bribing doormen in neighboring buildings for any information on Jackie sightings.[10]

Galella would insist that he was just doing his job and that Jackie, when out in public, was fair game. While both points are true, the photographer pushed it to the limit with Jackie, to the point where she got a restraining order against him. Galella's determination to get closer was so over the top that in the early 1970s he even began dating Jackie's maid in an attempt to learn more about Jackie and her whereabouts. Jackie saw them together on the street one day and the maid was fired immediately.

Of course, Galella could not have had Jackie as his "meal ticket" had public interest in her not been so durable and intense. This often

---

* Small world: the term "paparazzi" dates only to 1960, when the Italian movie director Federico Fellini coined it while shooting *La Dolce Vita*, a movie about sixties elites. It is believed the female lead, the Swedish bombshell Anita Ekberg, had been one of John F. Kennedy's lovers.

confused and amused Jackie. She was several years removed from the White House and was (in her eyes at least) just a single mom trying to raise her kids. The sentiment was ludicrous of course, unless one truly thought that being the world-famous widow of a slain president living on Fifth Avenue with maids, butlers, cooks, secretaries, Secret Service, and all the rest was somehow ordinary.

Yet some who knew her best thought that for all the efforts to capture "the real Jackie," the photographers usually missed something. "It was funny," Kathy McKeon pens in her memoir, "how the paparazzi could so easily capture her aura of mystery, yet her more beguiling ordinariness always eluded them."¹¹

That's because the "real" Jackie wasn't so accessible. That Jackie was the 1040 Jackie, unadorned with couture and fancy jewelry, puttering about in a t-shirt or turtleneck and jeans. The real Jackie, who spent hours sprawled out on the couch, a book in one hand and a cigarette in the other. The Jackie who spent hours writing long letters or quick notes to friends. The Jackie who lingered in the kitchen each day with John while Caroline was in school, "sweetly indulging his endless questions and listening with delight to his funny stories."¹²

This was what 1040 provided: privacy on her terms.

ON MARCH 14 CAME A MOMENT Jackie had been dreading: the second burial of her husband's body at Arlington. The gravesite from November 1963, hastily prepared after the assassination, was always meant to be temporary while a permanent site was designed.*

Unlike November 1963, when a global audience had watched JFK be laid to rest, his reburial, along with Patrick's and Arabella's, was private, conducted in the dark of night. Knowing that the sight of those three coffins—all that she had lost—would be too much to bear,

---

* Planning for the site began on November 27, 1963, two days after Kennedy was first laid to rest. Jackie, Robert, and Warnecke visited Arlington and walked around, strolling up to the Lee mansion, the cemetery's highest point, which offers sweeping views of Washington.

Jackie did not attend, leaving Robert and Edward Kennedy, Defense Secretary Robert McNamara, and Richard Cardinal Cushing to serve as somber witnesses.

She did appear, at seven o'clock the next morning, at a brief graveside service, this time with a larger contingent of Kennedys, President Johnson, and the Secret Service in attendance. It was drizzling and chilly, and as she knelt before the graves, holding a bouquet of lilies-of-the-valley, she fought to maintain her composure. At one point, she sighed loudly. Cardinal Cushing wisely kept the service brief. "Be at peace, dear Jack," he said, "with your tiny infants by your side, until we all meet again above the hill and beyond the stars." The cardinal later called it one of the saddest moments of his life. "I don't know how they can stand it," he said.[13]

It was a difficult moment in a difficult year. Jackie, and all Americans, had been stunned in January when three astronauts died during a training exercise for what would have been the first Apollo mission; it looked like the goal established by John F. Kennedy in 1961—"before this decade is out, of landing a man on the moon and returning him safely to the earth"—might not be met.

Things didn't get better. Race riots erupted in Detroit. They were was so bad—the worst urban unrest in the United States since the Civil War, one historian estimated[14]—that the Army's eighty-second and 101st Airborne divisions, which had parachuted into Normandy on D-Day, were sent in by Lyndon Johnson, along with thousands of National Guard troops, to keep order. "The long, hot summer of 1967," it came to be called.

And there was Vietnam. The American presence swelled by an additional one hundred thousand troops in 1967 and by year's end, there would be half a million troops there. The steep escalation sparked growing unrest at home, including an April protest in Central Park of some three hundred thousand people—just one of many protests held across the country. Clearly Jackie's beating on Robert McNamara's chest to end the killing had been for naught. The intensifying conflict on the other side of the globe would soon—to the mixed emotions of Jackie—alter the 1968 presidential campaign.

On May 27, two days before what would have been President Kennedy's fiftieth birthday, Jackie, Caroline, and John Jr. traveled to Newport News, Virginia, for the christening of an aircraft carrier named in his honor. Speaking at the ceremony, President Johnson noted JFK's love of the sea and his World War II service as commander of a patrol torpedo boat—the famous PT-109—in the Solomon Islands.

LBJ's tribute to his predecessor was poignant. "No president understood this nation's historic role and purpose better than John F. Kennedy," he said. "No man knew more deeply the burdens of that role. And no man ever gave more…. [L]et this ship we christen in his name be a testament that his countrymen have not forgotten."

As the president spoke, nine-year-old Caroline Kennedy, sitting next to her mother, appeared to wipe away a tear. Six-year-old John Jr., in a tan suit with short pants, sat patiently—the squirming little boy of 1963 no more. The highlight of the day for him appeared to be when John Glenn, the former astronaut, kneeled down to show him a model airplane.

As for Jackie, she cast a downward gaze, seemingly lost in thought. Happy as she was that her husband was being honored, the ship's christening was also a reunion of Kennedy administration alums. It was a reminder to her of everything she had fled—and everything that had been lost.

There was also a glimpse of the future. Unknown to Jackie, Aristotle Onassis had decided to attend the ship's christening. When it was over, Jackie was chatting with friends, when all of a sudden he emerged from the crowd and walked up to her. According to one account, she stopped in midsentence and spun towards him.

"Oh Ari, I didn't know you were here!" she said, obviously delighted to see her Greek friend. Perhaps deliberately, she avoided using his affectionate nickname—"Telis."[15]

Ari's presence in Newport News that day was significant. His and Jackie's interest in each other, carefully guarded for several years, was now observed by many of her friends for the first time.

Still, it seemed unfathomable that they were anything beyond friends. After all, European gossip columnists, who kept an eye on Aristotle Onassis during the spring of 1967, saw that the tycoon's romance with Maria Callas—the world's most famous opera star—continued unabated. Or at least it appeared that way. In March, as Jackie mourned at Arlington, the *Christina* pulled into Nassau harbor in the Bahamas, where a picture was taken of Ari and Maria gazing out from the deck. Ari, shirtless, had a long towel wrapped around his waist; Maria, beaming, wore a dark swimsuit that accentuated her long legs and hourglass figure. She looked happy behind her dark sunglasses. "Ari and his constant companion," photo captions typically read.

Each was divorced; they had been together for nine years, and it was assumed they would eventually wed. But when asked about it now, Ari's response was telling: "We are good friends," he said. It wasn't what the forty-three-year-old Callas, who was surely a diva if there ever was one, wanted to hear. Privately, Onassis's diplomatic veneer vanished: "Unless our friendship is given deeper significance, there is no spice," he remarked.[16]

In fact, the photo of the two together on the *Christina* was one of their last. The opera singer, like the rest of the world, didn't realize it, but Ari's eye was on—and had been on—someone even more famous than her.

Jackie had slipped in the public eye, but this hardly meant that people no longer admired her, only that the temperature had been turned down a notch. Interest in her remained intense, and this certainly extended to her love life.

As usual, the press, for all its interest in this, was usually playing catch-up. "Jackie to Wed," blared one headline in April 1967, right above separate photos of a beaming, sunglasses-clad Jackie and John

Warnecke. The scribes were wrong, but not by much: her long romance with the architect had just fizzled out.

Money may have been the reason. Robert Kennedy generally had liked Warnecke but didn't sense that he could support Jackie's spendthrift ways. This was ridiculous, Jackie had countered; Warnecke always spent big on her, plying her with gifts and travel. He owned two homes. Jackie didn't think he had Kennedy-type money (few did, after all), but thought he was doing just fine.

Then came the phone call that brought her down to earth. Warnecke recalled the conversation years later:

"There's something I have to tell you," he began.

"What is it, Jack?"

"The thing is…well, Jackie, I'm in a little trouble. I think I'm…I'm six hundred fifty thousand dollars in debt."

"Oh?"

Warnecke had been dreading the conversation, knowing that money wasn't exactly a minor matter with Jackie. But he felt that he should be transparent. He told Jackie that he would have to focus on his business and that they would have to cut back. She sounded "rather distant," Warnecke remembers, and then Jackie said she was sure that he would "figure things out." The architect then expressed his hope that this wouldn't change their relationship. Jackie said no, of course it wouldn't—but of course it did.

"I love you, Jackie," Warnecke ended.

"Goodbye for now, Jack."[17]

Warnecke, lovestruck, certainly should not have expected that Jackie would discount his financial troubles. "Money and power," her mother, Janet Lee Bouvier, had told Jackie and Lee in 1951—those were "the secret to happily ever after."[18] Years later, Janet, by then remarried to a wealthy man herself—Hugh Auchincloss, an heir to John D. Rockefeller's Standard Oil—arranged for Jackie to meet a young New York stockbroker named John Husted. They got engaged in January 1952. It was thought that Husted, handsome and polished, had money, but when it was discovered that he didn't (he made only the

2019 equivalent of about $162,000 per year)—the relationship cooled. Husted didn't set Jackie's heart racing anyway, and besides, by then she had met someone who did: a young playboyish congressman named John F. Kennedy, the eldest son and an heir to one of the greatest fortunes in the United States. "Money and power," Janet had lectured. Jackie remembered.*

WARNECKE WAS OUT OF THE PICTURE, but a new suitor was about to enter. On May 30, Sylvia ("Sissy") Ormsby-Gore, whose husband, David (Lord Harlech), had been ambassador to the United States and a close friend of the Kennedys, was killed in a car crash in England. It was yet another reminder that for Jackie, sudden death was always near. She and Robert flew to the funeral.

As they emerged from the church service on June 4, Jackie, whose eyes appeared puffy, donned her trademark oversized sunglasses. The death of Sissy drew her and David closer, as their shared grief gave way to more intimate feelings. They would soon contemplate marriage.†

"THIS IS NOT THE LAND OF MY BIRTH," John F. Kennedy had said as he departed Ireland after a brief visit in June 1963. "But it is the land for which I hold the greatest affection, and I certainly will come back in the springtime."

He added wistfully, "This is where we all say goodbye."

---

* Years later, Husted told the story of how he was dumped. Jackie simply took off her engagement ring and put it in his pocket, he told Jackie biographer J. Randy Taraborrelli. "She was ice cold, like we never knew each other. I understood that the end had come. I never heard from her again. Not ever." See: Taraborrelli, *Jackie, Janet and Lee,* 35.

† In January 1985, Lord Harlech would die in a car crash as well. Had Jackie married him—and he did, in fact, propose—he, and not Aristotle Onassis, would have made Jackie a widow for the second time.

Jackie, pregnant with Patrick at the time, did not accompany her husband on that trip, nor did Caroline and John. But now, in the springtime of 1967, she took them—now nine and six years old, respectively—for a six-week visit. It was largely a vacation, but Jackie was also determined to pay homage to the Kennedy family's roots and to make sure that her children knew of their father's heritage.

Contrary to conventional wisdom, Jackie herself was more Irish than French. Her mother, Janet Lee, was 100 percent Irish, and her father, despite his Gallic-sounding name—Bouvier—was only one-quarter French, the rest being a blend of Scottish and English. Therefore, Jackie was only one-eighth French.[19,*]

So the journey was a homecoming of sorts for her as well. Although it couldn't match President Kennedy's 1963 visit, Jackie mania was in full swing when she landed at Dublin's Shannon Airport on June 15. Perhaps thinking they were meeting royalty, Caroline curtsied and John bowed as they were greeted by U.S. ambassador William Fay.[†] Joining the Kennedys were Murray and Peggy McDonnell, who lived down the road from Jackie's weekend home in the New Jersey countryside, and their eight kids.

"I'm just happy to be here in the land my husband loved so much with his children," Jackie said, her hair blown out in full bouffant style, "and for them I think it's a little bit like coming home—and I hope we will come back again and again."

She had rented Woodstown House, a massive twenty-room Georgian mansion near Waterford, just west of County Wexford, the ancestral village of President Kennedy. John and Caroline, exposed to their Irish heritage throughout their young lives, were now making their first visit to Éire. As their chartered bus drove though the countryside, they gazed out the window at lush green fields, seeing for the

---

* Nor did the Bouviers come from French aristocracy, as Jackie's grandfather claimed. The one-eighth of Jackie's blood that was French descended from ordinary folk—tailors, farmers, even servants—in southern France. The surname Bouvier, as elegant as it may sound, actually means "cowherd" in French. See: Tina Santi Flaherty, *What Jackie Taught Us,* 11.

† Caroline was taught to curtsy and John to bow by Maud Shaw, their former English nanny. A very British custom, of course, but Jackie appreciated (as did JFK) such refinement in their children.

first time the origin of all the stories, music, and legends that they had until now merely read and heard about. John, in fact, probably knew Ireland's geography better than America's. Among the things he hoped to do in Ireland, he said, was catch a leprechaun.[20]

The seclusion suited Jackie perfectly. Most mornings, she and Peggy either mounted horses and galloped about the damp countryside or went for a walk along a lonely beach. Their kids would play games, picnic, and go on hikes and trips to a nearby beach.

The trip was cathartic. Even before Dallas, Jackie had never been as religiously devout as, say, mother-in-law Rose or sister-in-law Ethel. The loss of her son and husband in the space of just four months had further shaken her faith, causing her to question the purpose, if not the very existence, of God. Yet that faith, while flickering, had never been extinguished, and as she found her footing in 1965 and 1966, it had revived. Ireland, where devotion to the church ran deep, gave her new strength. "The poetry and prayers—such as the sad laments for brave men killed in their prime—gave a poignant voice to her grief," notes Kennedy family biographer Thomas Maier, "and became part of the legacy left to their children."[21]

One evening, she went with a few friends to a nearby fisherman's pub, where surprised regulars serenaded her with a rendition of "The Boys of Wexford." She requested that they also sing one of her husband's favorites, "Danny Boy." By now, some three and a half years after his murder, the last two stanzas had, perhaps, taken on a greater meaning:

> *But when ye come, and all the flowers are dying,*
> *And I am dead, as dead I well may be,*
> *Ye'll come and find the place where I am lying,*
> *And kneel and say an "Ave" there for me;*
> *And I shall hear, though soft you tread above me,*
> *And all my grave will warmer, sweeter be,*
> *For you will bend and tell me that you love me,*
> *And I shall sleep in peace until you come to me!*

The Kennedy curse that had struck so often nearly struck Jackie herself one evening. One afternoon, while her kids and the McDonnells were at a picnic, she went for a swim by herself. She walked half a mile to a channel that she had previously swum across at night—at low tide. But it was high tide now, making the distance greater. She made it half-way before being overtaken by the powerful current; it began to drag her past a small spit of land and out to sea. In a subsequent letter to the Secret Service, she said:

> The water was so cold that one could not hold one's fingers together. I am a very good swimmer and can swim for miles and hours, but the combination of current and cold were something I had never known. There was no one in sight to yell to.
>
> I was becoming exhausted, swallowing water and slipping past the spit of land, when I felt a great porpoise at my side. It was Mr. Walsh [of the Secret Service detail]. He set his shoulder against mine and together we made the spit. Then I sat on the beach coughing up seawater for half an hour while he found a poor itinerant and borrowed a blanket for me.[22, *]

Unbeknownst to Jackie, Walsh had followed her to the cove. If he hadn't, the devastated widow who had once considered taking her life, but couldn't do it, likely would have been swept out to sea—and vanished without a trace.

And so, for the second time in three and a half years, she had escaped death. But little did Jackie, or anyone, know that another event that June—the Six-Day War between Israel and its Arab neighbors—would set forces in motion that would, a year later, claim another member of her family.

---

* This is same John Walsh who had saved John Jr. the year before in Hawaii after he fell into a campfire.

Chapter Eight

July to December 1967: Marriage Proposal

With the sudden death of his wife, David Ormsby-Gore (Lord Harlech) had gotten a taste of what Jackie had been going through for more than three and a half years. Devastated, he even sounded like Jackie did after Dallas: "It is hard to see much point or pleasure in life now," he wrote to Joseph Alsop, an influential newspaper columnist. "But we had a glorious 27 years together and perhaps the happiest years were in Washington."[1]

There are less-than-subtle signs that the Jackie/David bond, forged first in friendship and now in mutual grief, became romantic. At meetings of the Kennedy School of Government at Harvard—Harlech served as a trustee—he and Jackie shared adjoining rooms at the Ritz-Carlton hotel.[2] He also visited her during her long stay in Ireland—"they were like two wounded birds together," said Harlech's eldest daughter, Jane; "[g]hastly things had happened to them"—and at Hyannis Port.[3] At one such get-together on the cape, Jackie told David that she hoped to visit Cambodia—adjacent to war-torn Vietnam—and would he like to join her? Why yes, of course he would.

Jackie unquestionably had deep feelings for David. But she had no lack of suitors, and unbeknownst to him and others, it seemed clear that the one man who wasn't squiring her about the globe—but seeing her quietly in New York and elsewhere—was the man who seemed to intrigue her more than any other: Aristotle Onassis.

Onassis was playing the long game. Until mid-1967, his relationship with Jackie—still likely platonic at this point—had generally remained in the shadows. His courtship of Jackie was kept so deliberately low key that he didn't even tell his teenaged children, Alexander or Christina, that they were seeing each other. Whenever Jackie visited him at his palatial residence in Paris, at 80 Avenue Foch in the sixteenth arrondissement, Onassis would not divulge her name to his servants. They were told to remain in the kitchen while the tycoon served his dinner companion personally.[4]

But Ari's May appearance in Newport News for the christening of the U.S.S. *John F. Kennedy* seemed to signal that their relationship was intensifying, though they still tried to keep it a secret. Taki Theodoracopulos, an American-educated Greek journalist, tells the story of sailing from Greece to Italy with Gianni Agnelli and dropping in on Onassis at his retreat on Skorpios. "We got off the boat," Theodoracopulos told Sarah Bradford in 1977, "and Onassis seemed very inhospitable suddenly. He took us around the island in his car, a little dune buggy...and then, as were coming down to the tiny harbor, we saw a woman leaving. I didn't recognize her, but Gianni said to me 'You know who that was? It was Jackie.'" She took off waterskiing, Theodoracopulos says, and stayed away until he and Agnelli left. "And then that's why Onassis wanted to get rid of us because he was ill at ease."[5]

They began to let their guard down a bit as the year wound down, dining out in high-profile restaurants like "21," the nightclub El Morocco, and the Greek eatery Mykonos. One night at another Greek restaurant in Greenwich Village, Ari smashed dinner plates while a beaming Jackie clapped along to the music. Jackie even took him to Newport to visit her mother. Ari, enchanted by the seaside setting, announced that he wanted to buy a home there. A real estate agent who showed the couple a few mansions claimed, "It was obvious that Mr. Onassis was delighted to be with her, and Mrs. Kennedy appeared to feel the same way about him. I'd guess they were in love."[6]

Still, Jackie was seen with many men, and the notion of there being anything between them wasn't taken seriously. There were even oddsmakers who took bets on whom Jackie might marry (or whether she would marry, period) and Onassis was a fifty-to-one shot.

HAVING TURNED HEADS—and perhaps raised a few eyebrows—with her miniskirts, Jackie continued to evolve her look. She was often seen walking around Manhattan in a black turtleneck; she often bought them at Jax, a shop favored by the trendy and unimpoverished. The owners, Jack and Sally Hanson of Beverly Hills, California, also made tight-fitting pants for her—size ten—and the likes of Elizabeth Taylor and Audrey Hepburn.* Jackie wore white at night, often bell-bottom pantsuits or miniskirts that showcased her toned and tanned legs. The exquisitely cut French suits, pillbox hats, and white gloves—all of which she had worn in the earlier part of the decade, including in Dallas—seemed relics of a forgotten era.

For all the changes she had endured in her life, there had always been one constant: Jackie was a clotheshorse. JFK had complained about her spending; Aristotle Onassis would essentially give her a blank check, only to learn that she had exceeded it. Years later it was noted that the bible of the fashion industry, *Women's Wear Daily*, covered her so extensively that it should have just changed its name to *Jackie's Wear Daily*.

---

* "Jax clothes are actually the result of the fact that I like to look at cute broads," Jack Hanson said at the time. "Most everybody likes that, don't they? I just thought if I could make some snug-fitting pants, the women would love it." See: Dan Jenkins, *Sports Illustrated*, July 10, 1967.

JACKIE'S IDEA TO VISIT CAMBODIA seemed odd. The tiny Southeast Asian country had cut off relations with the United States in May 1965, as Prince Norodom Sihanouk, the country's head of state, tried (in his view) to keep his country neutral while the Vietnam War raged next door. Yet his policies allowed Vietnamese communists to use border areas to launch attacks on U.S. troops. This, in turn, led President Johnson to order the bombing of targets in Cambodia. In short, it was a mess.

Adding to this difficulty: the rift between Sihanouk and the United States was more than merely diplomatic. After President Kennedy's assassination (and the murder, three weeks before that, of South Vietnamese president Ngo Dinh Diem), Sihanouk had rejoiced publicly. Blaming both JFK and Diem for attempting to destabilize Cambodia, Sihanouk organized concerts and gave civil servants time off to celebrate. The Johnson administration, deeply offended, lodged a protest, to which Sihanouk responded by recalling the Cambodian ambassador to the United States. A cutoff in relations soon followed.[7]

Jackie was being asked to turn the other cheek to a world leader who had celebrated her husband's murder. Yet she had a lifelong interest in Asian art and culture, and had long dreamed of seeing Angkor Wat, a huge complex of Hindu and then Buddhist temples dating to the twelfth century. Yes, she decided, she would go. Calling in fashion designer Valentino, she picked her wardrobe carefully. "We chose things together," the Italian designer has bragged.[8]

Because of the politics, she asked Robert McNamara for advice and assistance in arranging the trip. McNamara and Averell Harriman, knowing that a visit by Jackie could help reestablish ties, which the Johnson administration desired, discovered through channels that Sihanouk would be delighted to host the world's most famous woman. The Cambodian leader was also astute enough to sense that Robert Kennedy could soon be president, and saw a visit by his sister-in-law in those terms as well.

Jackie herself was astute enough to understand that she was being used politically. It was ironic, given her antipathy toward politics, which she had never enjoyed and assiduously avoided since her husband's death, that she found herself willing to act as an unofficial envoy on a quasi-diplomatic mission with the goal of defrosting an icy relationship.

On October 18, she set off on the long journey to Phnom Penh. Stopping in Rome for an extended stay, she was joined by Harlech and others before continuing on to the Cambodian capital, where she arrived on November 2.

Jackie and McNamara had informed Sihanouk of her desire to keep her visit private and low key. But the Cambodian leader, intent on getting as much mileage out of Jackie's visit as possible, arranged for her to be greeted by some ten thousand people at the airport. Wearing an above-the-knee cream dress and matching blouse, her hands adorned by her trademark white gloves, Jackie waved demurely and smiled as she endured an extravagant welcome ceremony involving a large chunk of the Cambodian government and diplomatic corps.

Exhausted from the long trip, she was privately irritated by the drawn-out, high-profile welcome. When she and David were finally shown to their rooms, they had a heated argument over whether to attend an elaborate dinner in their honor that evening. Jackie said no, but David, the suave and diplomatic ambassador who had so charmed John F. Kennedy, eventually convinced her to go. Privately, he considered Jackie's behavior petulant and childish.[9]

Yet theirs was a lover's quarrel, and as the steam of their argument eased, the ambassador stunned Jackie by asking her to marry him. Given the tempers that had flared only moments before, the jet lag, and the complete unfamiliarity of their surroundings, it seemed an ill-timed and impulsive gesture. Here was Jackie, thirty-eight years old, in a strange place on the other side of the globe, exhausted, angry, and now fielding a marriage proposal. It was an awkward moment to say the least.

Touched by the proposal, Jackie melted. She knew Ormsby-Gore loved her, and she loved him back—but not enough to consent to marriage. Careful not to hurt him, though this was obviously not possible, she turned him down in general terms, telling him gently that she did not wish to marry or be hurt again. And with that, they went to the gala dinner.

Harlech apparently did not press the issue further that evening, but returned to the subject in the months that followed. He and Jackie saw each other frequently in New York, where David's fifteen-year-old daughter, Alice, was in school. He and Jackie even made another trip together, this time to Greenwood, the Georgia plantation of their mutual friend John Hay Whitney, the former American ambassador to Great Britain. Jackie's response remained gentle and loving yet never wavered: no. She did not want to be hurt again.

Her reasons for turning David down have long been the subject of speculation. In many respects, he met many of Jackie's seeming requirements. He was obviously sophisticated and cultured, sharing her love of history and the arts. Jackie also preferred older men, and David was eleven years her senior—JFK had been twelve.

But David's feelings for Jackie were deeper than Jackie's were for him. The way she saw it, there were too many issues to overcome. For starters, he lived in Oswestry, a small hamlet some 175 miles northwest of London; there was certainly no way that Jackie would ever live there—and what about John and Caroline, at school in Manhattan? Had Jackie been serious, Ormsby-Gore certainly could have lived at 1040—but she was not.

Geography was only one issue. Ormsby-Gore fell short in additional qualities that Jackie typically sought in men: a raw, animal magnetism and enormous self-confidence. A sense that the world was his for the taking—and he had taken it. Her father had it. Joseph P. Kennedy had it. John F. Kennedy had it. The first man to propose to her, John Husted, lacked this, and Jackie did not put David, despite his other fine qualities, into this league either.

And like John Warnecke, whom Jackie had recently dispensed with, Harlech simply wasn't wealthy enough. He had known privately that this would be a problem, particularly given his view that Jackie was rather high maintenance—that is, expensive to keep. And yet, one close friend said after David's 1985 death, that "if Jackie had asked him to marry her he probably wouldn't have been able to resist it."[10]

In short, Jackie knew what she wanted: an older man, not just wealthy but *wealthy*. A confident man, unfamiliar with self-doubt, whose exuberance and zest for life emitted an irresistible, animal magnetism. A man who could give her everything she desired. There were few such men.

Reviewing a *Life* magazine cover story of Jackie's Cambodian visit, it would not be unreasonable for one to say that she never looked more ravishing. For the grand dinner that Sihanouk put on for her, she wore a floor-length Grecian turquoise gown, with her right shoulder bare, and elbow-length white gloves. Her jet-black hair was pulled straight back, and two-inch-long diamond earrings sparkled. The overall effect was dazzling.

When she arrived, stepping out of her car onto a gleaming red carpet, Sihanouk bowed deeply and kissed her outstretched hand. The same man who four years before had so crudely given his countrymen the day off to celebrate the assassination of her husband was now kissing his widow. Jackie beamed.

It was November again—her difficult time. And Sihanouk, who fancied himself a Renaissance man who dabbled as a filmmaker and composer, had one of his compositions played for her: "November Blues," he called it.[11] He also praised President Kennedy effusively and named an avenue after him. Rising to join him in a toast, she responded: "By your commemoration of his name, you have shown that you recognize his dedication to peace and understanding between all peoples."[12] In return she gave him a leather-bound copy of JFK's book *The Strategy of Peace*.

If the Johnson administration had been hoping that Jackie's visit would help mend fences, it was right. In the summer of 1969 (after LBJ left office), the United States and Cambodia reestablished diplomatic relations.

The rest of Jackie's visit went off without a hitch. She and David toured Angkor Wat together, the ambassador's impromptu marriage proposal hanging unspoken in the humid air. Ironically, the sight of them together sparked so much speculation that they were more than just friends that David had to issue a formal statement knocking the rumors down. "I deny it flatly," he said. How he wished it could be otherwise.[13]

Little did he know that Jackie's declaration about not wanting to marry again and risk having her heart broken once more was not quite accurate. There may have been a kernel of truth to it in November 1967; perhaps she wasn't quite ready. But beyond not finding that one man who checked all the boxes for her were some very basic political considerations—namely the presidential ambitions of one Robert Kennedy.

That such matters were to be weighed by a woman searching for a new mate underscored that while Jackie wanted nothing to do with politics, it was impossible to break free. She was, and always would be, the widow of a president. She was, and always would be, a Kennedy. And now, with the war in Vietnam nearing its peak, Robert—upset over the war and more contemptuous than ever of Lyndon Johnson—was weighing a run for his late brother's job.

Robert Kennedy had changed since his brother's assassination. He had grown more sensitive, more introspective. Four years later, he was still grieving. He also had a gnawing feeling that he might have had something to do with the murder. He never stopped wondering whether his efforts to crack down on organized crime—first as chief counsel for the U.S. Senate's Rackets Committee and then as attorney general—might have backfired; he had similar thoughts about Cuban leader Fidel Castro, who had been a target for assassination during the Kennedy years. He even, on the day of his brother's death, reportedly asked CIA director John McCone if the agency had been involved. "And I asked him in a way that he couldn't lie to me," Robert later said, "and they hadn't."[14] For these and other reasons, Robert never bought the central finding of the Warren Commission's report (which he reportedly never bothered to read) that Lee Harvey Oswald, acting alone, had killed John F. Kennedy.

Like Jackie, who just wanted to move on, Robert generally kept such thoughts to himself. As they drank iced tea on the patio at Hickory Hill one day in 1966, Don Hewitt, a CBS News producer, asked: "Do you believe Lee Harvey Oswald by himself killed your brother?" The reply was swift: "What difference does it make? It won't bring him back," and said nothing further. Discussing it would only "reopen the whole tragic business," according to Schlesinger's recollection of a conversation with RFK.[15] Robert's answer to Hewitt spoke for itself: What was the point?

But there was another reason for the silence. The mutual hatred between Kennedy and Lyndon Johnson was so intense that Robert even wondered at one point whether Johnson himself had something to do with Dallas. Both men spent years collecting dirt on each other, and both knew that the other was doing so as well.[*] Both also used friendly newspaper columnists to plant negative stories about the other. But fear of retaliation kept both men from launching a frontal assault on the other.

In between these two bitter rivals stood Jackie. She professed to like Lyndon Johnson and worked to remain on friendly terms with him. And yet Bobby was family; she loved Bobby.

Jackie and LBJ were always careful around each other, speaking respectfully and warmly on the phone, and in letters each wrote to the other. But Jackie knew that Johnson was manipulative—the phone call to her in the presence of White House reporters in December 1963 had not been forgotten, for example—and she suspected that the constant invitations for her to attend events at the executive mansion were just as much an effort to be sociable as they were a presidential attempt to be photographed with the most admired person the country. Johnson was such a manipulator that at one point in 1966, he had an aide find

---

[*] One of Robert's spies was a White House housekeeper who rifled through President Johnson's things, looking for "tidbits of petty corruption" on LBJ. See: Thomas, 335.

out whether the Beatles, touring the U.S., would pose with him at President Kennedy's grave. The band's manager, Brian Epstein, turned down the bizarre request.[16]

Privately, Johnson was upset that Jackie didn't do more for him. He blamed both her and Robert for the movie about President Kennedy that was shown at the 1964 Democratic convention, which he feared would revive Robert's former desire to be vice president. "Jackie and Bobby really are behind the build-up," he reportedly remarked.[17]

Naturally, Johnson was delighted at the public spat between the Kennedys and William Manchester, and how it knocked both Robert and Jackie down. In particular, the president was gleeful about a March poll showing LBJ with a twenty-two-point lead over Robert in a hypothetical match-up for the 1968 Democratic nomination—a thirty-point swing from a similar survey taken in late 1966.

"God, it just murders Bobby and Jackie both," Johnson told an aide, using a less than appropriate choice of words. "It just murders them in this thing."[18]

Kennedys could read polls too, and one takeaway was that Jackie and Robert needed to mend their dented public image. That meant, among other things, dealing with Johnson carefully. Robert was now so worried about angering the president that in speeches he would edit out any direct references to him, using instead the blander "the administration."[19, *]

For Jackie, it meant tamping down the always constant speculation about her love life. The president's widow dating around? Robert, overly cautious, feared there could be political repercussions.

Since 1964, Warnecke and Harlech had been her most visible suitors. A third would soon be seen on her arm: Roswell ("Ros")

---

* Given Johnson's own lukewarm popularity, perhaps the Kennedys should not have been so concerned about angering him. The president's Gallup approval at the beginning of 1967 was between 44 and 47 percent; it fell to 38 percent in September before returning to the mid-40s by the end of the year. In early 1968, it dipped into the 30s again, which finally prompted Robert to enter the race. Johnson, who soon dropped out, had tied his fortunes to Vietnam and, as the war raged and expanded, paid the price.

Gilpatric, who had been deputy defense secretary during the Kennedy administration.

But always, there was Aristotle Onassis. The intrigue between the widow and the tycoon was undeniable, and unlike her other suitors, who in their deference to Jackie had never quite figured her out, Onassis read her like a clock. In the fall of 1967, journalist Peter Evans, at a small cocktail party in Paris's George V hotel, reported a rather insightful observation Ari made about Jackie:

> She's a totally misunderstood woman. Perhaps she even misunderstands herself. She's being held up as a model of propriety, constancy, and so many of those boring American female virtues. She's now utterly devoid of mystery. She needs a small scandal to bring her alive. A peccadillo, an indiscretion. Something should happen to her to win our fresh compassion. The world loves to pity fallen grandeur.[20]

Chapter Nine

January to June 1968:
Again

Bang! The sudden, sharp explosion from the revolver terrified Jackie. It was all very innocent, just part of a February performance of *Don Quixote* that she was attending at the New York City Ballet. But it so startled her that she nearly jumped out of her seat and over the rail of the dress circle.[1]

It was a reminder that more than four years after Dallas, the widow remained jittery and fearful of sudden violence. The horror was always just below the surface; it didn't take much for it to burst out into the open. Looking back, that night at the ballet seems like a sad foreshadowing of what was about to unfold.

That 1968 would be a horrible year wasn't obvious at the time, of course. "World Bids Adieu to a Violent Year," said the front page of the *New York Times* on January 1. The new year began, reporter Murray Schumach wrote, "with revelry and prayer, with hope and apprehension." Had readers only known what horrors awaited—that 1968 would render 1967 placid by comparison—they might have crawled back under the covers.

"It's been quite a lonely life for her,"[2] Rose Kennedy said, describing her widowed daughter-in-law. The grand dame of the Kennedy family knew of which she spoke. Perhaps it didn't seem so to the casual observer, who tracked Jackie's relentless travels, socializing, and seeming enjoyment of life. She was beautiful, wealthy, famous, charming, cultured, and socially connected. She had everything, it seemed— everything, that is, except the one thing she longed for most: a partner. But as she once told Truman Capote, she couldn't marry a dentist from New Jersey. It obviously had to be an older man, wealthy, cultured, and successful—someone who would not be intimidated by her. Someone who could provide the security she required—both financial and physical. These requirements narrowed the field considerably.

Observers, oblivious to Jackie's two rejections, were certain that Harlech was the one, and that the only thing holding Jackie back was her deference to Bobby, as he weighed getting into the presidential race.

"Will Bobby Stop Jackie from Marrying Lord Harlech?" blared the headline in one magazine that March.

"That Jackie and the handsome English lord are in love, few people now doubt," the article says confidently. "In his presence she glows with a relaxed warmth unseen in her for years." It goes on to describe their relationship as clearly "something more than friendship," one that gave Jackie "great happiness" with the man "who has won her heart." David, of course, had failed to do any such thing.[3]

It was always known that he and Jackie had been close, but it wasn't until half a century later that historians learned just how close. In late 2016, Bonhams, one of London's premier auction houses, was given two burgundy-colored boxes. Stenciled on the side, underneath the queen's royal insignia, were the words "Rt. Hon. D. Ormsby-Gore." The keys were missing, so a locksmith called in. When the boxes were opened, a treasure trove was found: nineteen letters from Jackie to David.

"For decades, biographers have speculated on the precise relationship between Jackie Kennedy and David Ormsby-Gore," says Matthew Haley, head of Bonhams Fine Books and Manuscripts, which oversaw the auction of the correspondence between the couple. "It was one of those astonishing moments when you can't quite believe what you're seeing."[4]

Covering the period right after President Kennedy's assassination to 1968, when Jackie rejected David's second marriage proposal, the letters—all but one written by hand in her distinctive, sweeping style—reveal why she could never marry him, and how tormented she was about rebuffing him.

Most of their correspondence had been warm before Sissy Ormsby-Gore's death, but it revealed no traces of intimacy until after. There was a change in tone, as Jackie and David, who each knew the pain of sudden loss, began to interact on a deeper, more intimate level.

"Your last letter was such a cri de coeur of loneliness," she wrote him after Sissy's funeral. "I would do anything to take that anguish from you. You want to patch the wounds & match the loose pairs—but you can't because your life won't turn out that way."

But Jackie didn't really mean "anything," it seems. Her subsequent letters indicate that for all her feelings for David, she associated him with all that she so desperately wanted—needed—to forget: the deep pain of her own loss. On the weekend of the assassination, for example, Robert Kennedy phoned the ambassador and asked him and Sissy to come to the White House to comfort the widow: "Jackie's had another bad night," he said.[5] Later, in a receiving line, she told them in a barely audible whisper something that she had never revealed before: she and Jack had planned to ask Sissy to be Patrick Kennedy's godmother.[6] Jackie loved David, but how could she be with someone whose mere presence reminded her of all that had been lost?

Yet David's letters appear to indicate that Jackie gave it closer consideration than prior Jackie biographers knew. After being rejected for a second time, he wrote a draft letter, which revealed his pain:

All the pathetic plans I had brought with me for visits to Cyrenaica [a region of Libya], holidays near one another and a whole variety of solutions to our marriage problem, including one for a secret marriage this summer—plans which I saw us eagerly discussing, calmly and with complete frankness as we did at the Cape and in Cambodia for the next ten wonderful days—all had become irrelevant trash to be thrown away within a few hours of my landing in New York. As for your photograph I weep when I look at it. Why do such agonizing things have to happen? Where was the need for it? I have tried for hours and hours to understand your explanation and I suppose I do in a way, without agreeing with it; but what I find unbearable and in a way, dearest Jackie, untrue is that you could come to such a categorical conclusion...[7]

Harlech was further wounded that fall, when he learned of Jackie's marriage to Onassis. Naturally, he considered the swarthy Greek unfit for her; but in a November 13 letter, Jackie gave him one final, tender explanation:

We have known so much & shared & lost so much together—Even if it isn't the way you wish now—I hope that bond of love and pain will never be cut.... You are like my beloved brother—and mentor—and the only original spirit I know—as you were to Jack.

Please know—you of all people must know it—that we can never really see into the heart of another.... You know me. And you must know that the man you write of in your letter is not a man that I could marry.[8]

It surely didn't help David that his dream woman thought of him as a brother, or that the letter had been written on stationery from Onassis's ship the *Christina*.

And yet associating with people who reminded her of the past didn't stop her from traveling to one of her favorite destinations—Mexico's Yucatán Peninsula—with Ros Gilpatric. "There she goes again," said Agnes Ash, a *Women's Wear Daily* reporter who tracked jet-set Jackie's travel habits. Ash noted that Jackie's party, which included Secret Service agent John Walsh and a Brazilian couple who lived on Park Avenue, were met in Miami and escorted not to Pan Am's Clipper Club—the club for ordinary VIPs—but to a club-within-a-club for truly special VIPs like Jackie.

Even though Gilpatric was twenty-two years older and married, he and Jackie were likely lovers, and perhaps had been for several years. At least that's what his third (of five) wives, Madelin Thayer Kudner, was convinced of when she cryptically described her husband's relationship with Jackie as "very, very close—let's just say it was a particularly warm, close, long-lasting relationship."[9] She divorced him in 1970.

As was the case with many of the men she dated, Jackie kept her affair with Gilpatric so low key that hardly anyone realized that they were even dating—that is, until the Mexico trip.

"We were very much in love," said Gilpatric. "The trip to Mexico was very romantic, and Jackie surprised me by being so free and open about us." Like the recently jettisoned Lord Harlech, Gilpatric hoped to marry her.[10]

Indeed, writes Ash, who covered their trip, Jackie and Ros looked like lovebirds, with "a lot of public smooching and hand-holding.... [I]t took place in full view of the press. Jackie was all over the place, at one point jumping into a stream, fully dressed. Another time she climbed one of the Mayan pyramids and posed like the Queen of England opening Ascot."[11]

And yet Gilpatric knew that something was wrong. "The strange thing about the Yucatán trip," he said years later, "is that by then I realized we weren't going to work out.[12] Even at the most romantic moments, she kept mentioning Aristotle Onassis's name—what did I think of him? Was he as rich as they said he was? Was he, as some people said, a 'pirate'? She also said she felt he was very protective toward her, and that he cared about the children and their welfare. She was weighing the pros and cons, and it became very clear very fast that Onassis was the man who most intrigued her. Not me, not even Bobby."[13]

As was the case with Harlech, Jackie left a paper trail with Gilpatric. In one letter addressing him as "Ros," she mentioned a "spell that will carry over" after they spent a day together in the country. Another, believed to have been written on November 13—less than a month after she remarried—seems to be a coda to their relationship; she said: "You wrote me a letter that I think about a lot—I am grateful for what you said—I know you understand," adding, "I hope you know all you were and will ever be to me."[14], *

Hawaii with John Warnecke. Cambodia with Lord Harlech. Mexico with Ros Gilpatric. Italy and Spain with Antonio Garrigues Walker. Mike Nichols in Manhattan. Brando. And others. Jackie was linked, often romantically, with a different man practically everywhere she went.

And there was Bobby. Were they lovers? Perhaps. Trusted confidants? Of course. Since the evening of November 22, 1963, when he dashed up the steps to Air Force One and ran toward the tail compartment, sweeping past President Johnson to reach his bloodied sister-in-law—"Hi, Jackie, I'm here," he said. "Oh, Bobby," she whispered[15]—these two shattered individuals had leaned on each other, propped each other up, spent countless hours, days, and months trying to fathom the unfathomable. Intimate or not, they were as close as two human beings could possibly be, on a depth known only to them.

It had always been assumed that Robert Kennedy would one day try to reclaim the White House. But a head-on public collision with Lyndon Johnson? This Robert did not want, fearing it would destroy the party and result in something worse: a Republican, like a suddenly resurgent Richard Nixon, in the Oval Office. No, Robert's cautious reasoning went, it would be best to wait until 1972.

All of this changed on January 30, when a surprise offensive by communist forces across South Vietnam—who even penetrated the heavily guarded American embassy in Saigon—shattered, once and for all, Johnson's claim that the Vietnam War was under control and was all but over. From a military standpoint, North Vietnamese and Vietcong

---

* In 1970, a Wall Street lawyer offered to sell four letters Gilpatric wrote to Jackie between April, 18, 1963, and November 13, 1968, to a Manhattan autograph dealer. Gilpatric says he first learned of this from Maxine Cheshire, a gossip columnist for the *Washington Post*, meaning the letters were stolen. It's unknown how many letters Jackie wrote to Gilpatric in total.

troops were eventually routed, but not before they had achieved a political and psychological victory on another important front: the American television screen.

The Tet Offensive shocked Americans. It couldn't have come at a worse time for Johnson, and the North Vietnamese likely factored the U.S. political calendar into their strategic calculations. In late January, before the offensive, the president was seen as the clear favorite to win reelection. By early March, his Gallup approval had plunged twelve points.

On March 12, Johnson won the New Hampshire primary, but his margin over Minnesota senator Eugene McCarthy—a fierce antiwar candidate—was only seven points. It was seen as a humiliation for Johnson, who barely three years before had been elected by a landslide.

That was enough for Robert. Four days later, standing in the same spot where his brother had declared his candidacy in 1960—the Caucus Room in the Old Senate Office Building—he said he would seek the Democratic nomination, too.

The day after Robert's announcement was March 17—St. Patrick's Day. He flew to New York to march in the city's parade, but first went to 1040 to visit Jackie. Their relationship had been briefly strained by the fight with William Manchester, but that was now in the rearview mirror. Robert was now walking in his martyred brother's shoes, seeking to restore what had been taken away in Dallas. Jackie kissed him on the cheek and wished him well.

But the fight against Johnson that Robert had first avoided and then agreed to take on would prove unnecessary. "It was the thing I feared from the first day of my presidency," Johnson said years later: Robert's "intention to reclaim the throne in memory of his brother."[16] On March 31, the president, weakened politically, made a TV address about the war and concluded with a bombshell: he was dropping out of the race.* The path to a possible Kennedy restoration had suddenly gotten clearer.

---

* Had Johnson run and won again, he probably would have died in office from the stress. He died on January 22, 1973, just two days after his term would have ended.

Although fiercely loyal to her brother-in-law, Jackie had mixed emotions about his entry into the race. She wanted to be supportive of his ambitions. But like during that jumpy moment at the ballet when the prop gun exploded, she was afraid. At a dinner party in New York on April 2, she told Arthur Schlesinger: "Do you know what I think will happen to Bobby?" Schlesinger said no. "The same thing that happened to Jack," she answered. "There is too much hatred in this country, and more people hate Bobby than hated Jack. That's why I don't want him to be president. I've told Bobby this but he isn't fatalistic like me."[17,*]

Jackie's words were barely out of her mouth when the sudden violence she so feared did indeed strike. In Memphis, Doctor Martin Luther King Jr., who had gone to that city to lend support to striking sanitation workers, was assassinated by a white supremacist by the name of James Earl Ray.

Within minutes, America's cities erupted in a spasm of rage and despair. Fires, rioting, and looting hit some 110 cities nationwide, in what is said to be the greatest social unrest in the United States since the Civil War. One reporter, Edward Kosner, summed it up well: "It was Pandora's box flung open—an apocalyptic act that loosed the furies brooding in the shadows of America's sullen ghettos."[18]

The nation's capital was not spared. More than seven hundred fires broke out, and as the rioting worsened, creeping ever closer to the White House itself, President Johnson ordered some four thousand National Guard troops into the city. Machine gun nests sprouted on the White House lawn, turning the mansion into a fortress.

---

* Such fears were hardly unfounded. Robert Kennedy had, as Jackie correctly pointed out, more enemies than her husband ever did. He had long been a target of animosity and hatred, and not just on the part of the corrupt union leaders, mob bosses, and segregationist leaders he had gone after in years past. He was also hated by men who held great power in Washington, like FBI director J. Edgar Hoover and his deputy, Clyde Tolson, who once remarked: "I hope that someone shoots and kills the son of a bitch." As for Hoover himself, it was he who first told Robert that President Kennedy had been shot; Robert later told friends that he thought Hoover had enjoyed telling him the bad news. And Lyndon Johnson's hatred needs little additional elaboration, but one anecdote is telling. Once, when Eugene McCarthy paid a courtesy call on Johnson in the Oval Office, Robert's name come up. Johnson said nothing, but silently drew a finger cross his throat in a slitting motion. See: Shesol, 444.

King's assassination naturally horrified Jackie. Its pure senseless-ness—"[T]hey murdered that man for no reason," she told Kathy McKeon—echoed what she had thought about Jack's killing.[19] The murder in Memphis, the rioting, the ongoing carnage in Vietnam—it all fueled her growing perception that things were not safe, that the world was falling apart. The fear she felt for her children intensified.

And more than anyone, she knew what King's widow, Coretta Scott King, was going through. She wrote her: "When will our country learn that to live by the sword is to perish by the sword? I pray that with the price he paid—his life—he will make room in people's hearts for love, not hate."[20]

She also decided to travel to Atlanta to pay her respects to Mrs. King personally; having had her fill of funerals, however, she wanted to skip the funeral service. But politics intruded. Robert told Jackie that she needed to be seen at the service. McKeon packed "Madam's" bags.

Jackie arrived in Atlanta and went directly to Mrs. King's house. "She came to my home," Mrs. King recalls. "She came to my bed-room...and I thanked her for coming and also for what her family and her husband had meant to me.... I told her that I felt very close to her family for this reason."[21] Jackie told Mrs. King how strong she was and how much she admired her, sentiments that were returned by Mrs. King. A photo showed the two widows, clad head to toe in black, including black leather gloves, clasping hands as they commiserated.*

Jackie was moved by the service for King but knew that the emotions it stirred up wouldn't last. "Of course people feel guilty for a

---

* Jackie's sympathy may have been privately tempered to some degree by what she had learned in preceding years about the private side of the slain civil rights icon. In the early 1960s, convinced that King was somehow under the influence of communists, FBI director J. Edgar Hoover sought and received permission from the attorney general—at the time Robert Kennedy—to tap King's phones and bug hotel rooms he was staying in. Hoover, who reveled in collecting dirt on others, quickly struck gold and eagerly shared it with President Kennedy and Robert. JFK told Jackie of King's orgies, including one allegedly held in the Willard hotel when King was in town for the famous march on Washington in August 1963. President Kennedy, a habitual gossip, shared the juicy tidbit with Jackie, who recalled the conversation months later with Schlesinger. "Oh, but Jack, that's so terrible," Jackie had said. "I mean that man is, you know, such a phony then." JFK, with his own sexual history (which was also in Hoover's files), seemed more indulgent of King's behavior, according to the transcript of the June 2 Jackie/Schlesinger conversation. See: Jacqueline Kennedy (Schlesinger interviews), 260.

moment," she said two weeks later, with not a small dollop of bitterness. "But they hate feeling guilty. They can't stand it for very long. Then they turn."²²

Two months later—in a bland Los Angeles hospital corridor—she weighed in again. "I'll tell you who else understands death—people of the black churches," she told Frank Mankiewicz, Robert's press secretary. "I was looking at those faces, and I realized that they know death. They see it all the time and they're ready for it."²³

She was talking about another person as well, of course: herself.

There was no way that Jackie's presence in Atlanta could have been anything but high profile. Wearing the countenance that Americans were more than familiar with—the stoic face of grief—she marched, clad in black and surrounded by police officers. When it was all over, she sought refuge, and to provide it was none other than Aristotle Onassis.

Easter was just a few days away. Would she like to travel to Palm Beach for the holiday with Caroline and John on his private jet? Of course she would; she jumped at the chance to travel away from prying eyes amid the secure cocoon of one of the world's wealthiest men. The short flight gave Ari the opportunity to show, once again, that in times of trouble he would always be there for her. They spent their Easter vacation at the home of Charles and Jayne Wrightsman but did not appear in public.

Onassis followed up a month later with another invitation, this time to spend several days on the *Christina* cruising around the Caribbean. Jackie eagerly accepted. Whatever dent her fight to suppress the Manchester book had made on her reputation the year before, Jackie's star power remained potent. Peering out the porthole of her stateroom, a fellow passenger and friend of Jackie's, Joan Thring, carefully watched her arrival: "It was early in the morning when Jackie arrived," she says, "but I could tell she knew that everyone was looking at her. She was like an actress who's performing in the center of the stage and has studied her part backward and forward…. [S]he was carrying a small white box and dropped it, but a sailor quickly caught it before it hit the deck. She smiled and nodded in a most royal manner. The sailor actually bowed low as he returned the tiny box. I remembered something General [Charles] de Gaulle [at that time the president of France] said to my ex-husband: 'Jacqueline Bouvier Kennedy is every inch the lady—she was born to the crown.'"

Thring also tells a funny story about Jackie's highbrow fashion habits that was making the rounds in 1968:

> It seems that Jackie had just returned from Paris. Reporters asked her what she had bought there.
>
> *Jackie:* "A Givenchy and a Balenciaga."
>
> *Reporters:* "How nice, may we see them?"
>
> *Jackie:* "Certainly. They're upstairs designing dresses."[24], *

It was here, in the lush, soothing balm of the Caribbean that Ari probably first proposed the idea of marriage. Thring is sure of it. "Ari asked Jackie to marry him," she says, "assuring her that if she agreed she would still have her freedom. Perhaps more important, though, she would also have protection by his army of security men, 75 strong, some with machine guns. For a woman still suffering from PTSD from the murder of her husband, this was vital information. He loved her, he said, at least in his own way—which meant that he, too, would have his freedom, ostensibly to see other women, like [opera star] Maria Callas."

Thring insists that Jackie and Ari were not sexually involved at that point. "She was with me all the time. And she certainly wasn't sleeping in his room…. [T]hey never behaved as if anything was going on. There were no endearments or touching or anything like that…"[25]

At the end of the trip, Jackie wrote a thank-you note that is undated and has rarely been seen. It shows her being tugged in two directions:

---

* The joke, which was widely circulated in early 1968, can be traced to the comedian Mort Sahl.

by her loyalty to Bobby and by her evident affection for "Telis"—as she
called Ari:

> I will die for Bobby if that will ever help—but until then—I want
> to stay in the etat d'aire [state of play] I found on the *Christina*—it
> was imprevu [unexpected] and a surprise—and it made me so happy.
>
> All your cares Dear Ari—to make it so carefree for me—How
> can I thank you for that? I can't.

She ended:

> Thank you dear Ari—for those lovely days—I hope you don't
> miss your ship as much as I do—
>
> Jackie[26]

She didn't sign it "Love, Jackie," just "Jackie." But it was clear that
her feelings for the Greek tycoon, which had been building for years,
were cresting. Still, no one seemed to know how deep those feelings
ran. Here she was, surrounded by war, protests, violence in the street,
and now, another political assassination. And in Onassis, she saw an
escape—"days of sea and sun where I didn't know what was happening,"
and the fulfillment of two existential needs—comfort and security,
which "made me so happy."

In her letter, Jackie also referred to the first time she had been on
the *Christina* back in the 1950s with her husband, that magical evening
when they met Winston Churchill. She remembered how glorious it
was, how enchanting, and how wonderful her host had been. Yet there
was no indication at this point that Onassis's charm and the seductive,
luxurious lifestyle he represented were enough to actually pull her away.
Bobby's candidacy, now entering its second month, was accelerating,
and the prospect of another Kennedy in the White House offered its
own seductions. Jackie was so excited about this that at one point she
got carried away, gushing during a family gathering at Hyannis: "Won't
it be wonderful when we're back the White House?"—to which Ethel
snapped, "What do you mean, *we*?"[27]

Jackie returned to New York on May 28. That very night Robert Kennedy lost the Oregon primary to McCarthy by six percentage points. It was a stinging defeat—the first electoral setback ever for a Kennedy. "I think that if I get beaten in any primary, I am not a very viable candidate," he had said days before.[28] As he was worried about his campaign and the crucial California primary—now just a week away—it probably wasn't the right time for Jackie to tell him about Ari's proposal. Yet she did.

Bobby, seeing things through the lens of his suddenly troubled campaign, exploded. "For god's sake Jackie," he cried. "This could cost me five states!" He asked her to cool the romance.[29]

Jackie's loyalty to Bobby and her deference to his ambitions were probably the only inhibitors to her marrying Aristotle Onassis earlier than she did. Bobby, keeping tabs on the men in Jackie's life, knew that the swarthy Greek tycoon was unlike all the rest, who, one acquaintance said derisively, were "all very married, or very old or very queer." Onassis was none of these things, and for his part knew that he had won Jackie over. The timing wasn't quite right, but Ari, always thinking ahead, knew that Bobby's presidential campaign would be over by November at the latest. He would wait. As it turned out, he wouldn't wait for long.[30]

❧

"MAYOR FORTY HAS JUST SENT ME a message that we've been here too long already…so my thanks to all of you and now it's on to Chicago and let's win there," Robert Kennedy said from behind the podium at a victory party at Los Angeles's Ambassador Hotel. He flashed the victory sign, brushed back his hair, and disappeared with his beaming wife, Ethel, into a nearby kitchen. Leaving that way was safer, his security detail reasoned. It was about 12:15 a.m. in California.

He had won the crucial primary in the Golden State. It was a huge relief, coming just a week after his setback in neighboring Oregon, and his quest for the Democratic nomination seemed back on track.

A continent away, Jackie was sleeping. "I feel wonderful. I'm delighted," she had gushed at a Kennedy victory party earlier that evening. She was driven back to 1040 around midnight Eastern time. She got about four hours of slumber when the phone rang. It was Lee and her husband, Stas, in London.

"How is Bobby?" Stas asked.

"He's won," Jackie replied. "He's got California."

"But how is he?"

"Oh he's fine. He's won."

"But how is he?"

"What do you mean?" Jackie asked, oblivious to the shock that was about to come.[31]

"No!" she screamed upon hearing the news that Bobby had been shot. "It can't have happened. No! It can't have happened!" Scrambling to get to Los Angeles—with the help of Ros Gilpatric, a private jet was supplied by IBM president Thomas Watson—Jackie woke Caroline and John to give them the dreadful news. She brought them into her bedroom.

"Something has happened to Uncle Bobby," she began, "and I have to fly out to California to be with him."

"What happened to Uncle Bobby?" Caroline asked.

"A very bad man shot him," Jackie answered, adding that Bobby was still alive and that doctors were caring for him. Caroline, ten, and John, seven, began to cry.[32]

Before flying to California, Jackie waited for Stas and Lee, who flew over from England after Stas delivered the shocking bulletin. The three of them, joined by Watson, immediately departed for Los Angeles; Gilpatric stayed behind.

Met six hours later by Chuck Spaulding, a longtime friend who had been an usher at her wedding and later worked on Jack's and Bobby's campaigns, Jackie got right to the point.

"How is he doing, Chuck?"

"He's dying, Jackie."

At Good Samaritan Hospital, Jackie encountered the ghastly sight of Bobby, his head wrapped in a gleaming white bandage, kept alive only by a respirator. Told by doctors that there was no hope, no one among the large contingent of family and friends would turn the machine off. "I won't kill Bobby," Ethel Kennedy said. Sparing her grieving sister-in-law the task, Jackie signed the form giving doctors the authority to do so. Robert F. Kennedy died moments later. It was 1:44 a.m., June 6, 1968.[33]

For the third time in less than five years, Jackie had suffered a devastating personal blow. Shattered, she appeared to lose faith in what had been one of her greatest anchors: the Catholic Church. "The Church is at its best at the time of death," she told Frank Mankiewicz. "The rest of the time it's often rather silly little men running around in their black suits. But the Catholic church understands death." And then she added something about death that Mankiewicz found chilling: "As a matter of fact, if it weren't for the children," Jackie said, "we'd welcome it."[34]

It was a revealing comment. It had been four years since Jackie had shared thoughts of suicide with Father McSorley. Now here she was, expressing her preference for death once again. Her struggle may have dissipated to some degree since 1964, but it had never gone away.

Lyndon Johnson dispatched a plane from the presidential fleet to Los Angeles to fly Kennedy's body home. Jackie, incredulous that she would again have to fly across the country with the body of a murdered loved one, at first refused to board, in the mistaken belief that it was the same Air Force jet that had carried her husband's body home from Dallas. It wasn't, but it was similar enough to evoke bad memories for her.* Another plane ride. Another coffin. This time there were three widows on board: Jackie, Ethel, and Coretta Scott King, who had also rushed to California. The three women chatted quietly as the 707 raced

---

* Numerous books written about this say that Air Force One was used to fly RFK home. In fact, the tail marker of the plane was 86972—part of the presidential fleet but not the Boeing 707 used by President Johnson. Jackie knew 26000 well: It was the same Air Force One that had flown her and President Kennedy to Texas on November 21, 1963—and carried the murdered president's body home the next day.

across the troubled and grieving country. "You are forced to think," said CBS reporter George Herman, "of what a burden of tragedy this plane carries, what a burden of death and sadness and sorrow."[35]

Back at 1040, Jackie, her face puffy and eyes swollen, saw Kathy McKeon.

"I'm so very sorry, Madam," McKeon told her softly.

"I know, I know," Jackie said, bitterness in her voice. "Same story all over again."[36]

As was the case in 1963, Jackie couldn't bear to tell her own kids the awful news. Maud Shaw had had the awful task then; now Jackie turned to McKeon, her trusted twenty-three-year-old assistant nanny.

"Will you go talk to John and Caroline?" she asked in a whisper. "Their uncle passed away…. [W]e'll all miss him dearly, He was a second father to my children."

Recalling the conversation half a century later, McKeon noticed how Jackie had been trying to minimize the ugliness by avoiding words that described the brutal reality of what had happened in the hotel pantry: "shot," "murdered," "assassinated." No. Bobby had merely "passed away."

But Caroline and John already knew; McKeon found them both bawling in John's room.

"Your uncle Bobby is up in heaven looking down on you two," she told them. "He'll always take care of you."[37]

Like November 1963, June 1968 was a time of shock and grief. But there was now a third element, that of quiet resignation. The grace and stoic demeanor that Jackie had displayed after Dallas ("She gave an example to the world of how to behave," de Gaulle said) was on display again, but she now looked glazed and distant, seemingly numb to her surroundings. At a private service at Saint Patrick's Cathedral on Fifth Avenue in Manhattan, where Robert's body had been borne, she crumbled, breaking down in sobs before the candlelit bier. Her mother-in-law, Rose Kennedy, in agony herself, wrapped both arms around Jackie. At least Rose and Ethel, more devout, could cling to the sacraments of their faith; Jackie—as her hospital comments to Mankie-wicz indicate—was much less of a believer.

At the public service for Robert—it was Saturday, the eighth of June—Jackie, with Caroline and John by her side, sat in the front row wearing a black lace mantilla. She seemed "in a trance, just completely in shock. It just defied belief that she—that we—would be reliving this nightmare," says longtime Kennedy aide Pierre Salinger.[38] As Jackie exited onto Fifth Avenue after the service, Lady Bird Johnson reached out her hand and called out to Jackie by her name. "She looked at me as if from a great distance, as though I were an apparition," she wrote in her diary.[39] She had seen that look before—on November 22, 1963. Another commentator, NBC's Sander Vanocur, said quietly: "She's seen all this before. Not at this cathedral, but she brought dead Kennedys back from the West before."[40]

Clutching the hands of her children as she had then, Jackie, along with the rest of the Kennedy clan, boarded a funeral train at Penn Station, for what should have been a four-hour trip to Washington. It would take twice as long. As the twenty-one-car train rumbled slowly through cities and towns, some two million people lined the tracks to say goodbye. They were young and old. Black and white. Rich and poor. Democrats and Republicans. Parents held their children aloft for a better view. Some perched on bridges. Many held flags or signs. A group of bridesmaids tossed flowers. There were salutes and hands held over hearts. Mostly there was silence and tears as the train passed, the flag-draped coffin visible in the final car. In Elizabeth, New Jersey, the sad journey turned tragic when two mourners, not seeing another train approaching, were struck and killed.

The president's widow took it all in, occasionally wiping tears from her face. One can only imagine the torment she felt. She had progressed since Dallas, compartmentalizing it, pushing the horrific events further into the recesses of her mind. Now it all came flooding back. She had tried above all to protect Caroline and John since their father's death, and yet here they were, exposed to this. She watched helplessly as Caroline clung to eleven-year-old Courtney Kennedy, the fifth of

Robert and Ethel Kennedy's children. The two girls held each other and wept. Fifty years later, a *Washington Post* photographer who was onboard, Steve Northrup, wrote, "It felt like we were on a train to the end of an era."[41]

When the train finally arrived at Union Station, not quite a stone's throw from the Capitol, where John and Robert Kennedy had risen to power, it was 9:25 p.m. As the coffin was moved to a hearse, Jackie suddenly came face-to-face with another reminder of her tragic past—her former Secret Service agent Clint Hill.

"Hello, Mr. Hill. How have you been?" Her eyes, Hill recalls, "were dark pools of grief. She was composed, but shattered."

"Hello, Mrs. Kennedy. I am so very sorry for your loss."

Her eyes, those wide eyes that had beguiled a future president just fifteen years before, closed for a moment, then opened, "glistening with pain."

"Thank you." If Jackie wanted to purge painful memories from her life, crossing paths with the man who had been present at one family murder—and at the funeral of another—must have been unbearable.[42,*]

And then it was off to Arlington. Again. There, on a warm June night, Robert Francis Kennedy was carried to his rest—the first nighttime interment in the cemetery's history. After Ethel and her kids, Jackie knelt to kiss the coffin. She then took Caroline and John some twenty yards to where her own husband—their father—lay beneath the eternal flame that flickered in the darkness. She placed some daisies from Bobby's service on the grave.

"Oh Jack," John heard his mother whisper. "Oh Bobby…"[43]

In some respects, Robert's murder was even more distressing to the family than Jack's because of what was shown, and what was impossible

---

* It was the last time Jackie would ever speak with Hill—the devoted agent who had been with her through the very best—and worst—of times.

to avoid seeing. In the case of President Kennedy's murder, the infamous "Zapruder film" shot by Dallas businessman Abraham Zapruder had yet to be seen in public, and although various frames from the twenty-six-second home movie had been published, the most gruesome frame—frame 313, which showed President Kennedy's head exploding—had been held back by *Life* magazine, at the request of a traumatized Zapruder himself. Immediately after that final shot, the president slumped over, disappearing from view into the back of his car, never to be seen again. There are no pictures of his limp body being carried into Parkland, no photos from inside the hospital. John F. Kennedy vanished on Elm Street and was never seen again. The Zapruder film was also silent; the sharp explosions from Lee Harvey Oswald's rifle are never heard.

In contrast, Robert Kennedy's murder can be heard, the distant *pop-pop-pop-pop* (eight shots in all, the FBI said). Heartbreaking images show the immediate aftermath: Kennedy lying face up on the floor of the hotel pantry, his face ashen and eyes blank. One hears the panic, the screams, the shouts of "Get the gun!" as Kennedy's assassin, Sirhan Sirhan, is subdued. One sees Juan Romero, a seventeen-year-old busboy, gently cradling Kennedy's bloody head in his hands. "I wanted to protect his head from the cold concrete," he said.* One sees Ethel Kennedy, leaning over her husband, frantically waving at people to back away. It's too much, too ugly, and too public.

Yet compared to Dallas, Robert's murder was not as shocking. The assassination of John F. Kennedy was the most unimaginable thing in the world, and yet it had happened easily and in the blink of an eye. But Robert Kennedy's death, while surprising, was hardly unimaginable: Jackie herself had imagined it, even predicting it to Arthur Schlesinger.

Nor was it some sort of stand-alone event. In the broader scheme of things, it was merely the latest in a string of convulsions. Riots. Vietnam. Rising crime and drug use. King's murder. Anger, distrust,

---

* Romero went to school the next day with Kennedy's blood crusted under his fingernails; he refused to wash it off.

and a gnawing feeling that somehow America had lost its way. It was against this cynical and divisive backdrop that another burst of violence conveyed less power to stun than it once did. To whatever degree America had been innocent prior to November 22, 1963, those days now seemed gone for good, never to return. The brutal assassinations of three of the country's brightest hopes for the future had seen to that. Violence was the American way. Who could argue otherwise?

The day after the funeral, Jackie wrote to the newest Kennedy widow:

> My Ethel—
>
> No one in the world could have ever been like you were yesterday—except maybe Bobby—
> We are going home now—Your phone was busy
> You don't want any more callers you must be so tired—I stayed up till 6:30 last night just thinking—and praying for you—and for you in the months ahead—
> I love you so much—
> You know that anything—Stas will take little Bobby to Africa—I'll take them around the world + to the moon + back—anything to help you + them now and always—
> With my deepest deepest love
>
> Jackie[44]

That day she also told Salinger, according to some Jackie biographers: "I hate this country, I despise America, and I don't want my children to live here anymore. If they are killing Kennedys, then my children are number-one targets…. I want to get out of this country." In Salinger's own memoir, written in 1997, there is no mention of this anecdote whatsoever. But whether it is apocryphal or not, there can be little doubt that it reflected Jackie's sentiment.

She had struggled, for four and a half years and with varying degrees of success, to contain her own horror. To relegate it, as she had hoped to do with *The Death of a President*, to some dark corner, never to be seen again. Now it all came back, exploding like a volcano: the brutality, the utter hopelessness, the vivid nightmares. Even another plane ride with a coffin.

The murders of the two principal men in her life seemed to blend together. "She was in a state of panic and disbelief," writes Onassis biographer Frank Brady, "occasionally lapsing into dialogue that indicated that she was confusing both assassinations, at one point even temporarily believing that she was still First Lady."[45]

Her capacity for suffering was not infinite. It now filled her to the brim; there was room for no more. But unlike that first dark winter after Dallas, she was now isolated and alone, with no one to lean on, at least no one she was as close to as she had been with Bobby. "She always used to have company all the time, and all of a sudden it got very quiet," Kathy McKeon wrote. "She was by herself at night, and I think she was very lonely. She needed somebody to talk to."[46]

All of this—her state of mind, the legitimate fears she harbored for herself and her kids, her loneliness—proved the final opening that Aristotle Onassis needed. Willi Frischauer, who penned separate biographies of Jackie and Ari, sums it up well:

> Anger was replacing sorrow and turning her against the violent society which she held responsible for her own bereavement. If America ever had a claim on her after Jack's death, that claim was now forfeited. If she ever had any doubt or obligation to consider the impact of her action on the political prospects of the Kennedys, they were resolved by the shots that ended Bobby's life. For her, escape was the only way out. Jackie was shedding the Kennedy shackles.... [H]er decision to marry Onassis was made at the grave of Robert F. Kennedy.[47]

Chapter Ten

July to October 1968:
Skorpios

Nineteen sixty-eight. It was the year everything fell apart. It was a horrible year, arguably the worst of the entire post-World War II era. Martin Luther King Jr.'s shocking murder sparked rioting coast to coast. The smoke from all the fires had barely lifted when Robert Kennedy's killing, just two months later, delivered a further jolt. Fighting peaked in Vietnam: 16,899 American troops would die that year, more than forty-six per day. In August, violence erupted at the Democratic National Convention in Chicago. "The whole world is watching," student protestors yelled as they clashed with, and were beaten up, by cops. The U.S. population grew about 11 percent between 1960 and 1968, yet violent crime doubled. If confidence and optimism had greeted the dawn of the 1960s, they had long since evaporated, replaced by cynicism and distrust. "Turn on, tune in, drop out," went a popular counterculture refrain. One of the biggest songs of the year, Simon & Garfunkel's "Mrs. Robinson," spoke to a nation adrift and bereft of heroes.

After all she had been through, and all that was happening around her, Jackie wanted to turn her back on America, and who could blame her? In four and a half terrible years, her husband had been murdered. King had been murdered. Her brother-in-law had been murdered. She feared for her life and for those of her children. And things seemed to be getting worse.

The turbulence that was 1968 masked the fact that Aristotle Onassis was now spending more time in New York. His expanding business interests—his airline, Olympic Airways, had recently begun direct flights from Athens to New York—was one reason, but so was the fact that Jackie was just blocks away from the suite that the mogul maintained at the Pierre. She entertained often and he showed up often, scurrying into 1040 after being chauffeured uptown. The veil on their relationship that had been slowly lifting for months was about to rise further still.

Even so, the press remained well behind the curve, completely missing just how serious things were between Jackie and Ari. The June issue of *Cosmopolitan* magazine, for example, featured a fur-clad Jackie on the cover with the headline "The Men Surrounding Jackie Kennedy—and the One Who's Winning Her." Jackie, the fawning writer Doris Lilly wrote, "has more men in her stable than [the racetrack] Aqueduct has horses. *Enough* of suspense building! Who are the sleek, well-shod stallions who have been chosen by Jackie as escorts, friends and—gasp—maybe a husband?"

The article mentioned twenty-five men, none of whom were named Aristotle Onassis. The biggest photo in the four-page spread shows Jackie, in sunglasses, holding hands with Lord Harlech, who is described as "definitely the front runner" in her life. The article plays up their travels and practically has them exchanging vows: "Maybe, just maybe, she and Lord Harlech are holding off nuptial plans until after the Democratic convention in August," Lilly speculates, adding "It would make a luv-er-ly church wedding."

Time magazine, meanwhile, was closer to the truth, noting that Jackie had many escorts and that Onassis was one of them. Even so, it scoffed that the pair couldn't be very serious, given the "alien culture" that separated them.

In retrospect, this was how Jackie and Ari enabled their romance to blossom under the collective nose of the Western world: by taking full advantage of the perception that they were ultimately incompatible.

Except, of course, they weren't. Jacqueline Kennedy, after all, "globetrotted, rode to hounds, sailed, delighted in tete-a-tetes [sic] with such figures as Pablo Casals, Truman Capote, Rudolf Nureyev, and Margot Fonteyn…. Despite her sophistication, world and national affairs were not her forte. Friends felt that she was truly interested in other things—music and books and art, and particularly her children."[1] In other words, Jackie, at her essence, had more in common with Onassis—aside from riding horses—than she may have ever had with the Kennedys and their zest for the issues and the rough-and-tumble world of politics. She may have married into that in 1953, but it was never really in her blood.

Aristotle Onassis, who could—and did—have any woman he desired, was always restless and hungry for more. "I am always searching for the consummate woman," he once said.[2] For years, only one woman truly fit the bill: Jacqueline Kennedy.

He understood Jackie's frame of mind perfectly—in fact, better than anyone. She was scared and needed security for herself and her kids? His private security force on Skorpios—some seventy-five heavily armed men—was equal to half an Army company. There were snarling guard dogs. His homes in Athens, on Paris's Avenue Foch, and elsewhere were surrounded by iron bars. She needed financial security? With a net worth of some $500 million—about $3.7 billion in 2019 terms—he was one of the wealthiest men in the world. She wanted to travel? With his own airline, yacht, and helicopters, she could travel anywhere she wished privately and securely. None of the other men Jackie had dated could remotely match any of it.

Robert's killing knocked the breath out of Americans. Onassis immediately understood what it probably meant for him: that what last bit of resistance Jackie had about marrying him had been swept away. "It's a tragedy for America," he told an aide, "but for Jackie…she's finally free of the Kennedys." It was a selfish sentiment but, it seems, an accurate one.[3]

Or was it? Onassis fretted that Bobby's death might somehow tether Jackie even more to "the Kennedy ethos and reinforce the unwritten tenet that she must never hurt the family prestige by a disapproved-of remarriage." Notes Onassis biographer Peter Evans: "Dead, Bobby could exert even stronger claims on her loyalties than when he was alive."[4]

Such worries would prove unfounded. Bobby's murder only reinforced Jackie's basic—even frantic—need for greater security and privacy, things Ari could easily provide. Her financial needs remained paramount as well; her insistence on dealing with André Meyer instead of brother-in-law Stephen Smith—the Kennedy family's money man— was also a reminder that Jackie had always resented being financially dependent on her family.

Nevertheless, Onassis stepped up his charm offensive in the summer of 1968. Embarking on several visits to Jackie at Hyannis and Newport, he was determined to acquaint himself with her extended family and to make them feel at ease with him.

With one person in particular, the tycoon had his work cut out for him: Jackie's mother, Janet. The two had first met years before in London, in an embarrassing and awkward manner. Lee was cheating on Stas, having an open and blatant affair with Ari. Janet, visiting London, learned that Lee was visiting her lover at Claridge's hotel. Wishing to see her, she went to his suite, where Ari in a bathrobe opened the door. She demanded to see her daughter.

"And who exactly *is* your daughter, may I ask?"

Told that she was Princess Radziwiłł, Ari replied crisply: "In that case, madame, you've just missed her."[5]

Setting aside the fact that her youngest daughter was having a very public affair, it wasn't exactly the optimal way for Janet to form a good impression of Ari. She had also read of the tycoon's numerous affairs with everyone from—among others—Evita Peron, Maria Callas, and Gloria Swanson (who had also been one of Joseph P. Kennedy's mistresses) to, it was assumed, Greta Garbo and Elizabeth Taylor. Now, in 1968, the tycoon had his sights on Janet's other, even more prominent daughter. What was Janet supposed to think?

She would ultimately remain immune to Ari's charms. But Jackie was sold. One longtime neighbor of Jackie's at Hyannis, Larry Newman, remembers how happy they seemed together, going up the street, "holding hands, dancing doing ballet steps, playing like kids. I would see them eating their lunch—hot fish and cold champagne—and they seemed extremely happy. I said to myself, 'Isn't it tremendous that at last she has found someone to be with?'"[6]

Onassis was often weighed down with presents for Caroline and John; he played with them, listened to them, went on walks with them. John, with his love of airplanes and helicopters, was an easier sell for a man who owned an airline than Caroline was. But John, in ensuing years, would never call him "Dad," only "Mr. Onassis." As for Caroline, she did not dislike the strange-looking man who spoke with an accent. But she was, and would always be, the daughter of John Fitzgerald Kennedy.

During his third visit—Ari crossed the Atlantic every two weeks that summer—he gently told Caroline and John that their mom needed someone to care for her, someone who would always be there for her. As the children listened attentively, he said that he could never replace their father, who was a great man, but that he simply wanted to be their friend and protector as well. He did not mention marriage. Jackie and Ari had obviously discussed this approach ahead of time, and had decided that telling Caroline and John about their intention to marry would be Jackie's responsibility.[7]

They were in love. They wanted to marry. But what about the money? Although seduced by his irresistible charm, their shared interests and all the rest, it is undeniable that Ari's vast wealth appealed to Jackie. Gore Vidal, the writer who knew both of them well, puts it best: "As far as Jackie was concerned," he says, "the only thing better than a rich man was an obscenely rich man."[8]

Even so, others who knew Jackie well were skeptical that her attraction was all about the money. Years later, journalist George Plimpton told journalist Christopher Andersen, "Jackie must have said at least ten times to me, 'Isn't it weird that everybody thinks I married Ari for his money?'" Plimpton added: "I knew Jackie really really well. She confided in me. If she had married Ari for the money, she would have talked about it. Sure, the money was part of Ari's attraction, but only a part. She really loved him."[9]

New York and Washington began buzzing about the possibility that Jackie and Ari might be more than just friends. But even at this late date, the notion of their actually tying the knot still seemed too far-out to believe. Truman Capote, as plugged in as anyone, told Kennedy friend Katharine Graham—the swan who had been the guest of honor at his Black and White Ball two years earlier—that the wedding was on. The *Washington Post* publisher, traveling in South America, cabled Ben Bradlee. He cabled back: "You're great, Brenda [he often teased Graham that she was the comic strip heroine Brenda Starr, a glamorous newspaper reporter], but I chickened. Source confirmed but everyone else reached—and we reached scores—most skeptical and I decided 'it was too thin a reed to stake the paper's reputation.'"[10]

Even at this late date, the public had little to no inkling that Jackie and Ari were a serious item. The August cover of *Modern Screen* features a giant headline: "What Will Happen to Jackie and Her Children Now?" yet the article doesn't even mention Onassis."[11]

At that moment, Jackie was taking matters into her own hands. Few Americans seemed to notice that in early August, she and Edward ("Teddy") Kennedy quietly flew to Athens. Jackie stayed in the Greek capital to do some shopping, while Teddy—the only brother-in-law she had left—went on to Skorpios with a tougher assignment: negotiate a prenuptial agreement with Ari.

Like his older brothers, Edward Kennedy was known for many things, but financial acumen was not one of them. Now he was sitting across the table from one of the world's sharpest business minds, a self-made man who had risen, often ruthlessly, from the humblest of beginnings to become one of the wealthiest men in the world. Kennedy was outmatched from the beginning.

Onassis biographer Willi Frischauer writes that Kennedy's opening gambit was to try to talk Ari out of the marriage, citing religious differences and their age gap (Kennedy seemed to be under the impression that Ari was sixty-nine, when he was in fact sixty-two). And forgetting his own fondness for Lord Harlech, Kennedy also hinted that Americans might be hostile to the idea of Jackie's marrying a foreigner.[12]

None of this worked, of course; Jackie and Ari had already decided what they wanted. Kennedy could only say, "We love Jackie."

"So do I," Onassis responded, "and I want her to have a secure and happy future."

Kennedy said that if the marriage occurred, Jackie would give up not only the $150,000 she got each year from the Kennedy family trust, but her widow's pension of ten thousand dollars and her Secret Service protection. Given Onassis's mountain of wealth—which exceeded that of the Kennedy family—and the extensive security he could offer Jackie, both men knew as they spoke that the senator was playing a weak hand.

It was agreed that Jackie would get $3 million, plus another $1 million each for Caroline and John, upfront. Ari would cover Jackie's expenses—a concession he would soon regret—for the length of the marriage. If he died, she would get $150,000 annually, the same figure she was giving up from the Kennedy trust fund.

Later, Onassis reportedly asked an assistant, Lynn Alpha Smith, about the $3 million Jackie would get. Smith replied that in the grand scheme of things it wasn't much—in fact, that was about the price of a supertanker. From that point on, Jackie acquired a new nickname: "Supertanker." "It's Supertanker on the line," Smith would tell her boss whenever Jackie called. It made the tycoon laugh, Smith later claimed.[13]

Those and other details agreed upon, an agreement was typed up and sent to André Meyer in New York, who happened to be a friend of Ari's. The legendary investment banker, perhaps letting his personal affection for Jackie—his former Carlyle neighbor—intrude, cabled

Onassis that details of the proposed "merger" were unacceptable. His counter offer: $20 million upfront for the bride.

Outraged, Onassis flew to New York in September to confront Meyer, and after hours of haggling, agreed to terms that were closer to Ari's original terms than Meyer's: the same $3 million upfront for Jackie, but also interest on the trusts that were being given to both Caroline and John. Jackie would also get the same $150,000 annually if Onassis died.

In return for all this, Jackie agreed to waive her rights under a Greek law known as *nomimos mira*, by which a man typically gives at least 12.5 percent of his wealth to his wife and 37.5 percent to his children. Jackie was never involved in these direct talks.[14]

What happened to the $20 million in cash that Meyer had demanded? The agreement with Onassis stipulated:

> The sum of twenty million indicated in the meeting, as a capital, apart from the fact that in the final analysis would be futile, due to gift, income and other taxes that it necessarily would entail, apart from being detrimental to the feelings of either party, it might easily lead to the thought of an acquisition instead of a marriage.[15]

In other words, taxes would eat up much of the twenty million dollars and, perhaps most important, no one should get the impression that Jacqueline Kennedy was for sale—though she was, of course, for $3 million plus interest on another $2 million. All of this was written up in precise contractual terms, however—with Jackie referred to throughout as the "person-in-question"—that conveyed the sense that a grand transaction was about to be consummated.

News reports later said that the Jackie/Ari agreement dealt with intimate matters, like where they would live and how many times per year they would have sex. This is not so; the agreement was restricted to financial matters. And where *would* they live? The answer was evident: everywhere.

While all this played out, the world continued to spin. In August alone, two more events erupted that reinforced Jackie's belief that the world was dangerous and unstable. Late that month, Soviet troops crushed an uprising in communist Czechoslovakia. She wrote to her spurned suitor, Lord Harlech, who had brought her to tears with a speech on the crisis. An excerpt from her letter: "One's private despair is so trivial now—because wherever you look there is nothing to not despair over—I keep thinking of what Jack used to say—'that every man can make a difference & that every man should try.'"[16]

"Wherever you look there is nothing to not despair over."

Days later, she looked to Chicago, where violence erupted at the Democratic National Convention. Protestors and police clashed in the streets, while inside the convention hall itself, cops roughed up several television journalists. "I think we've got a bunch of thugs here," an angry Walter Cronkite, the CBS anchorman, said after one of his reporters, Dan Rather, was punched and knocked to the ground. It was far worse outside, where four days of clashes left hundreds of protesters and cops injured.

As SUMMER YIELDED TO FALL, the press was beginning to catch on to the Jackie/Ari relationship. *Modern Screen,* ostensibly a Hollywood movie magazine, now discussed Onassis openly, with a long write-up covering his immense wealth and pondering what still seemed unthinkable: "…the world was wondering whether Jackie had actually embarked with [her brother-in-law] Ted's blessing, on a new romance with that strange, wealthy enigmatic man to whom she had just said an affectionate goodbye: Aristotle Socrates Onassis!" And a few paragraphs later: "Does he have a chance? Is Jackie, her life suddenly so bleak and barren once more, hoping that happiness may yet be found with him?'"[17]

As speculation mounted, Onassis knocked it down with self-mocking statement: "Jackie likes tall, thin men," he said at one point, adding, "I do not think I fit the description.'"[18] Meanwhile, photos of Jackie with other men helped throw people off. She was seen with her usual escorts, men like Plimpton and a new one, Michael ("Mike") Forrestal, the forty-year old son of President Truman's secretary of defense. "He's grand company," Jackie said.

But the deception was wearing thin. A gossip columnist for the *New York Daily News* who went by the name Suzy (her real name was Aileen Mehle), reported that "Jackie Kennedy spent last weekend at Hyannisport. So did Aristotle Onassis. They flew together, you see. Ari took some crazy presents for Caroline and John…"[19]

It was during one such weekend that Onassis suggested that the wedding should take place on Skorpios. He suggested a date: Sunday, October 20. Jackie agreed. At some point, he presented her with a spectacular engagement ring: a forty-carat marquise-cut Lesotho III diamond ring from Harry Winston. She wore it rarely, keeping it in a bank vault.*

Ari began to enjoy the attention, and stoked the fire by issuing a statement. "Jackie is a little bird that needs its freedom as well as its security and she gets them both from me," he said. "She can do exactly as she pleases—visit international fashion shows and travel and go out with friends to the theater or anyplace. And I, of course, will do exactly as I please. I never question her and she never questions me."[20] It certainly sounded like they were a couple.

But actually marry? Doris Lilly, a *New York Post* gossip columnist, was booed when she made that prediction on *The Merv Griffin Show*, and afterward was confronted on the street by angry audience members who didn't want to hear it. It summed up what the vast majority of Americans thought: that Jackie marrying *him* was preposterous.[21]

Lilly was right, of course. Jackie's heart was set; the financial details had been worked out. But Jackie still felt the need to win the blessing of key people in her life. One was Richard Cardinal Cushing, the venerable archbishop of Boston who had officiated at Jackie's 1953 marriage to John F. Kennedy, baptized their children, and presided over the martyred president's funeral. She wrote to him and then paid a visit, where the cardinal said Jackie should be free to marry whomever she chose.

---

* After Jackie's death, the ring was auctioned off by Sotheby's for $2.59 million.

He told her that marrying outside of one's faith was possible; his own sister, for example, had married a Jewish man—who turned out to be one of the finest men he knew.[22] The real issue, as the cardinal saw it, was the fact that Onassis was divorced. But even here, he counseled, Jackie would not necessarily face excommunication.

She needn't have looked further than her own family to get a taste of the opposition, anger, and hurt she was causing with all the talk about marrying Onassis. One of her fiercest opponents was her own mother. Just sixty years old, a force of nature in her own right, Janet Auchincloss was one of the few people who could get to Jackie and give her the unvarnished truth. In this case the truth was that Janet found Onassis vulgar and despicable; she was horrified at the prospect of Jackie's marrying him.

But nothing the mother said could dissuade the daughter; Janet grew increasingly distraught. At one point, she snapped at Jackie, informing her bluntly that if she wanted to marry Ari, she would have to do so alone. Janet then called her husband, Hugh ("Hughdie"), who was in Washington:

"You speak to her," she barked. "I don't care what it takes, but talk her out of this marriage!"[23]

Normally loathe to intervene in any kind of drama concerning his wife and stepdaughter, Hugh agreed with Janet and made the call to 1040.

"You know, Jackie, Mummy and I don't feel that you have really thought this thing with Ari through."

"Oh, Uncle Hughdie," Jackie replied. "I've made up my mind."[24]

But not everyone in the family was opposed. One supporter, surprisingly, turned out to be Rose Kennedy, the late president's mother. Although stunned at first, and worried about the age gap, religious differences, and whether Ari could ever be accepted as a stepfather by Caroline and John, the family matriarch decided that it was okay with her.

Rose had known Onassis for years, running into him at parties and restaurants on both sides the Atlantic. "He was quietly companionable, easy to talk with, intelligent with a sense of humor and a fund of good anecdotes to tell. I liked him," she said.

More important, she thought he would be good for her daughter-in-law:

> With contemplation, it seemed to me that Jackie deserved a full life, a happy future. Jack had been gone five years, thus she had plenty time to think things over. She was not a person who would jump rashly into anything as important as this, so she must have her own very good reasons. I decided I ought to put my doubts aside and give Jackie all the emotional support I could in what I realized, was bound to be a time of stress for her in the weeks and months ahead. When she called I told her to make her plans as she chose to do, and to go ahead with them with my loving good wishes.[25]

It was this endorsement, that of the slain president's mother, that meant the most to Jackie. "She of all people encouraged me. Who said 'He's a good man' and 'Don't worry, dear.' She's been extraordinarily generous. I was marred to her son and I have his children, but she was the one who was saying, if this is what you think is best, go ahead."[26]

The public, finally, had caught on. But there was still no official confirmation. So many rumors were swirling about in public that Jackie agreed that a statement to the press would put an end to it. Her mother, still upset but grudgingly accepting of what she could not control, got on the phone with Nancy Tuckerman to hash it out.

"Mrs. Hugh D. Auchincloss has asked me to tell you that her daughter, Mrs. John F. Kennedy, is planning to marry Mr. Aristotle Onassis sometime next week. No place or date has been set for the moment." This last line wasn't accurate.[27]

The news rocketed around the world. One headline, summing up all the others, asked simply: "Jackie: Why?"

And it rocketed *out* of this world. When told about the Jackie/Ari wedding, the astronauts of Apollo 7, orbiting the earth as they laid the groundwork for the first trip to the moon, said simply: "Oh, my."[28]

Lyndon Johnson had no advance notice of the pending nuptials, reading the news as it came across on the wire tickers he kept in the Oval Office. Turning to aide Joseph Califano Jr., he said, "Well, by God, that'll sure take its toll on the Camelot myth."[29]

It HAD BEEN NEARLY FIVE YEARS since John F. Kennedy's murder. Since November 22, 1963, Jackie had moved three times, traveled the world endlessly, at times almost frantically, trying perhaps to distance herself from that day. Conflicting desires—to burnish her husband's legacy while shutting out his final moments—had proven impossible to realize. She had weighed suicide, drowned herself in alcohol, endured years of nightmares, and experienced fresh tragedies that kept bringing the horror of Dallas to the surface time and again. All while trying to raise two children as quietly and in as normal a manner as possible, with the world watching, gossiping about her every move, attaching expectations to her about how she should behave—expectations that were hopelessly high on their part and completely unwanted on hers. In the end, she summed it up simply: "You don't know how lonely I've been," she told Nancy Tuckerman.[30] She was still just thirty-nine years old.

The date and place were set; arrangements were made. Kathy McKeon and Jackie packed six trunks and suitcases. At six p.m. on October 17, a Thursday, the bride departed 1040 under a blizzard of flashbulbs. Driven to the airport that bore her first husband's name, she boarded a Boeing 707 that was owned by her soon-to-be second husband. Some ninety-three Olympic Airways passengers who had been scheduled to take the same flight were quickly removed to make way for the eleven-member wedding party. The bumped passengers were put on a flight that left an hour and fifteen minutes later.

At 8:02, Jackie's plane was wheels up, taking her to her new life. Landing the next morning at Andravida, a Greek military base, her party transferred to Ari's seaplane for the short hop to Skorpios. After arriving, the guests were shown to their quarters either on the island or, for the most special guests of all, staterooms on the *Christina*. Jackie was shown to the sumptuous "Ithaca" stateroom, where she had stayed during prior visits. In two days, she would move into the most opulent quarters of all: Ari's spectacular three-room suite on the ship's upper deck.

But now that the wedding's location and time were known, hundreds of uninvited guests were also making their way to the small island. It became the subject of a British Broadcasting Corporation documentary—*Aristotle Onassis: The Golden Greek*—which showed a flotilla of boats crammed with frantic reporters and photographers.

"The world's press came to Skorpios," the narrator said. "And kept coming." Tipped off that Jackie was on *Christina*, they demanded photos.

"I was alone standing on the deck of *Christina*," one man, who wasn't identified, says. "And the first person who appeared? The bride herself! So I said, 'Mrs. Jackie, doesn't this remind you of the Spanish Armada?'"

In the documentary, "Mrs. Jackie" is then seen, in her trim white Jax slacks, sandals, black top and, of course, sunglasses. Caroline, a month shy of her eleventh birthday and suddenly up to her mom's shoulders, is by her side, wearing red shorts, her hair in pigtails. John, still looking like a junior member of the Beatles with his bangs, is also there. He, too, is a month shy of a birthday, his eighth.

"Mrs. Jacqueline Kennedy, America's fairy-tale princess," the narrator continues, "is about to become Jackie O, wife of the shipping tycoon Aristotle Onassis."

It may have been the first-known use of the name that would define and cling to Jackie for the rest of her life: "Jackie O."

Rain fell as her wedding day, Sunday, October 20, dawned—in Greek lore, a good omen for a successful marriage. The air was heavy with the scent of bougainvillea and jasmine, along with that of the fig, olive, and cypress trees that dotted the island. It would have been peaceful, private, and bucolic, as Jackie and Ari had intended, were it not for the ever-persistent press.

Reporters and photographers, using the nearby island of Lefkas as a staging area, had rented whatever could float or fly. Between Onassis's security force, which he had beefed up to two hundred men, the *Christina*'s crew, and the Greek Navy, the intruders were fended off with speedboats and helicopters. But one press helicopter managed to get too close to the island before being intercepted by two larger helicopters, which blared warnings via electric megaphones.

Eventually, at least one boat packed with journalists outmaneuvered the defenders and made its way to within yards of a narrow, sandy beach. The invaders jumped out, plunging into waist-deep water in suits and ties and black dress shoes. As they scrambled ashore, a few photos were taken of the frantic scene. When they appeared in *Life* a few days later, their blurriness brought to mind—albeit in a far less treacherous way—the handful of snaps also taken for *Life* nearly a quarter century before by Robert Capa on Omaha Beach. The journalists established "a beachhead" before making their way inland.[31] Scuffles broke out on the quay.

At this point the bride and groom, used to press intrusions, issued a statement:

> We know you understand that even though people may be well-known, they still hold in their hearts the emotions of a simple person for the moments that are the most important of those we know on earth—birth, marriage and death. We wish our wedding to be a private moment in the little chapel among the cypresses of Skorpios with only members of the family present, five of them little children. If you will give us these moments, we will gladly give you all the cooperation possible for you to take the pictures you need.[32]

The couple agreed to admit a pool of eight journalists to the proceedings. This seemed to placate the photographers, with the exception of one American who had known Jackie dating back to her Washington years. He sent a note: "Yes, but you undoubtedly will tell us what pictures to take!"*

The situation apparently under control, preparations resumed. The groom, sixty-two and marrying for the second time, appeared. He wore a dark blue double-breasted business suit. In the prior days, as he rushed about the island checking on final arrangements, he had been "as excited as a little boy," an officer on the *Christina* says. Now, he waited calmly.[33]

Finally, the thirty-nine-year-old bride came into view. She wore a lace-trimmed beige chiffon dress, a Valentino that she had worn earlier that year to a friend's wedding, and an enormous ivory-colored ribbon in her hair. Some two inches taller than her five-foot-five fiancé, she wore flat-heeled shoes in an attempt to equalize their heights. She was, as usual, radiant.

But something seemed different about Jacqueline Kennedy now. As the light rain fell, she conveyed a sense that some unseen burden was being lifted from her shoulders. The burden, perhaps, of living as others thought she should. Of leading a life that they, and not she, deemed suitable.

"You know how it is," she would say years later in a rare interview. "When you look back on your life, you hardly recognize the person you once were. Like a snake shedding skins."[34]

She was shedding one this day.

Jackie made her way to the chapel, and when she arrived, the bride and groom, each wearing a spray of orange blossoms, kissed each other on the cheek.[35]

The intimate whitewashed chapel, Panayitsa ("Little Virgin"), could accommodate only about twenty-five people. Standing atop a knoll, surrounded by a grove of elegant cypresses, it had been derelict and forgotten just months earlier; but Ari, anticipating a wedding, had had it restored. On Jackie's side, in addition to Caroline and John—who held

---

* The unnamed American explained to the others: "She never permitted us to photograph her with a cigarette in her mouth or even holding one. Although she's a heavy smoker, there are darn few pictures showing her puffing away!" See: David and Robbins, 80.

candles, seeming at times nervous, subdued, and somewhat confused, as the ceremony was in mostly in Greek—were her reluctant mother and her stepfather, Hugh, plus sisters-in-law Jean Smith and Patricia Lawford, Lee and Stas Radziwill, and the Radziwills' two children, Anthony and Christina. As had been done just fifteen years earlier—it seemed like a lifetime had passed—Jackie was given away by Hugh. Onassis's family included his two children, Christina and Alexander; his sister, Artemis; a half-sister, a niece, and her husband. Various business associates comprised the rest of the guests.

Outside, a Secret Service agent, protecting the widow of a slain president for the final time, kept onlookers at bay; he was seen wearing an emblem of the increasingly distant Kennedy era: a PT-109 tie clasp.

The ceremony itself was performed by Archimandrite Polykarpos Athanasiou, who swooped in on one of Olympic's helicopters in his *riassa*—a flowing black robe with very wide sleeves—and chimney-pot hat, also black. As is the custom in the Greek Orthodox church, he sported a long, thick beard, which was black and untrimmed. It seemed a rebuke to Ari's request that he look "not too much like Rasputin," the Russian mystic who befriended the family of Russian Tsar Nicholas II.[36]

Artemis Onassis placed two thin crowns of leather and white orange blossoms (a symbol of purity and fertility) over their heads and exchanged them three times. Holding a gold-encased New Testament, the archimandrite invited Jackie and then Ari to kiss it. "The servant of God, Aristotle," he intoned solemnly in English, "is betrothed to the servant of God, Jacqueline, in the name of the Father, the Son, and the Holy Ghost, amen."

An exchange of rings was next. Jackie put both rings on Ari; he then put both on her. She then put Ari's ring back on him. Jackie, other guests said, teared up and nearly cried.

The archimandrite, resuming his chanting, then led Jackie and Ari slowly around the altar three times, doing the dance of Isaiah. In the background, a small chorus sang Byzantine hymns. Guests threw flower petals at them.[37]

They were now husband and wife. Mr. and Mrs. Aristotle Socrates Onassis. The world's most famous couple embraced and then made their way out of the tiny chapel, where cheers immediately erupted. They were pelted with bougainvillea petals and tulips that had been flown in from Holland, along with rice and sugared almonds, a Greek custom meant to ensure happiness. The rain picked up. From atop the knoll, one could see the *Christina* in the harbor below, its lights twinkling and crew running about in preparation for a blowout wedding reception.

The small contingent of photographers and reporters took pictures and raised their voices to be heard. One got Ari's attention.

"How are you feeling?"

"I feel very well, my boy," the beaming groom said.

The reporter turned to John. "And how about you? How are you feeling?"

John, whose head had been down, looked up and quickly turned away.

And Jackie? The bride gave a three-word answer:

"We are happy..."[38]

Acknowledgments

How lucky am I that I get to write books? It is a joyous process, starting with nothing more than an idea and a blank screen, and then creating after months—or years—something that hopefully others will enjoy.

Most of the principals from the 1963–1968 period of Jacqueline Kennedy's life are gone, but some are still with us and have helped me. One in particular stands out: Clint Hill—the Secret Service agent who was with Jackie every step of the way in Dallas. Many years ago, Mr. Hill took me on a tour of Dealey Plaza—site of President Kennedy's assassination. I know how difficult that was for him, and I am grateful that he went out of his way to do it. In the ensuing years, he has been equally generous with his time and memories. Thank you, Mr. Hill—a gentleman and patriot. The books he has written with his partner Lisa McCubbin about those years are all terrific.

There are lots of Jackie aficionados out there and I've heard from a lot of them. Thanks in particular to Jane Wypiszynski—a bottomless font of knowledge—who is qualified to write a Jackie book herself.

Thanks to Jack Perry, my literary agent, advisor, and friend. Who knew that lunch in a Japanese restaurant in Manhattan would lead to a book deal? Thanks also to Anthony Ziccardi, publisher of Post Hill Press, for taking the project on, and Post Hill's managing editor Madeline Sturgeon and publicist Devon Brown for their terrific work.

Thanks also to Monica Lee Bellais.

But most of all, as always, there is Kathryn, my ever lovely wife, who gives me the latitude to work, and Julia, my ever precocious daughter, who is beginning to show an interest in writing herself. Like I said: How lucky am I?

Bibliography

Books

Abbott, James A. and Rice, Elaine M., *Designing Camelot: The Kennedy White House Restoration* (New York: Van Nostrand Reinhold, 1998)

Adler, Bill (editor), *America's First Ladies* (New York: HarperCollins, 2009)

Adler, Bill (editor), *The Eloquent Jacqueline Onassis: A Portrait in Her Own Words* (Lanham, Md.: Taylor Trade, 2002)

Andersen, Christopher, *Jackie After Jack* (New York: William Morrow and Company, Inc., 1998)

_____, *Sweet Caroline* (New York: William Morrow Gallery Books, 2003)

_____, *The Good Son* (New York: Gallery Books, 2014)

_____, *These Few Precious Days* (New York: Gallery Books, 2013)

Anthony, Carl Sferrazza, *America's First Families* (New York: Simon & Schuster, 2000)

_____, *As We Remember Her* (New York: HarperCollins, 1997)

Baldrige, Letitia, *A Lady, First* (New York: Viking, 2001)

Beschloss, Michael, *Presidential Courage* (New York: Simon & Schuster, 2007)

_____, *Reaching for Glory* (New York: Simon & Schuster, 2001)

_____, *Taking Charge* (New York: Simon & Schuster, 1997)

Blaine, Gerald with Lisa McCubbin, *The Kennedy Detail* (New York: Gallery Books, 2010)

Bishop, Jim, *The Day Kennedy Was Shot* (New York: Greenwich House, 1968)

Bohrer, John R., *The Revolution of Robert Kennedy: From Power to Protest After JFK* (New York: Bloomsbury Press, 2017)

Boller Jr., Paul F., *Presidential Wives* (New York: Oxford University Press, 1988)

Bradford, Sarah, *America's Queen* (New York: Viking, 2000)

Bradlee, Ben, *Conversations with Kennedy* (New York: W.W Norton, 1975)

_____, *A Good Life* (New York: Simon & Schuster, 1995)

Brady, Frank, *Onassis* (Englewood Cliffs, NJ: Prentice-Hall, Inc., 1977)

Brando, Marlon, *Songs My Mother Never Taught Me* (New York: Random House, 1994)

Brandon, Henry, *Special Relationships: A Foreign Correspondent's Memoirs from Roosevelt to Reagan,* (New York: Atheneum, 1988)

Bugliosi, Vincent, *Four Days in November* (New York: W.W Norton, 2007)

_____, *Reclaiming History* (New York: W.W Norton, 2007)

Califano, Joseph A. Jr., *The Triumph & Tragedy of Lyndon Johnson* (New York: Touchstone 1991)

Callcchio, Denise LeFrak and Eunie David, *High Rise, Low Down* (Fort Lee NJ: Barricade Books, 2007)

Caro, Robert, *The Years of Lyndon Johnson—Means of Ascent* (New York: Alfred A. Knopf, 1990)

_____, *The Years of Lyndon Johnson — The Passage of Power* (New York: Alfred A. Knopf, 2012)

Cassini, Oleg, *A Thousand Days of Magic* (New York: Rizzoli International Publications, Inc., 1995)

_____, *In My Own Fashion* (New York: Simon & Schuster, 1987)

Chandler, David P., *The Tragedy of Cambodian History: Politics, War and Revolution since 1945* (New Haven: Yale University Press, 1991)

Clarke, Thurston, *JFK's Last Hundred Days* (New York: Penguin Press, 2013)

Colacello, Bob, *Holy Terror: Andy Warhol Close Up* (New York: Random House, 1990)

Collier, Peter and David Horowitz, *The Kennedys: An American Drama* (San Francisco: Encounter Books, 1984)

Condon, Dianne Russell, *Jackie's Treasures* (New York: Clarkson Potter, 1996)

Connolly, Neil, *In the Kennedy Kitchen* (New York: DK Publishing, 2007)

Dallas, Rita, *The Kennedy Case* (Putnam, 1973)

Dallek, Robert, *An Unfinished Life: John F. Kennedy, 1917–1963* (New York: Little, Brown and Company, 2003)

_____, *Flawed Giant: Lyndon Johnson and His Times, 1961–1973* (New York: Oxford University Press, 1998)

David, Lester and Jhan Robbins, *Jackie & Ari* (New York: Pocket Books, 1976)

Davis, Deborah, *Party of the Century* (Hoboken, NJ: John Wiley & Sons, Inc., 2006)

Edwards, Anne, *Maria Callas: An Intimate Biography* (New York: St. Martin's Press, 2001)

Evans, Peter, *Ari: The Life and Times of Aristotle Socrates Onassis* (New York: Summit Books, 1986)

_____, *Nemesis* (New York: HarperCollins, 2004)

Fay Paul B., Jr., *The Pleasure of his Company* (New York: Harper & Row, 1966)

Fetzer, James H., *Assassination Science: Experts Speak Out on the Death of JFK* (Ann Arbor: University of Michigan Press, 1998)

Fitzpatrick, Ellen, *Letters to Jackie* (New York: HarperCollins, 2010)

Flaherty, Tina Santi, *What Jackie Taught Us* (New York: Perigree, 2004)

Foner, Eric, *Reconstruction: America's Unfinished Revolution, 1863–1877* (New York: Harper & Row, 1988)

Frischauer, Willi, *Jackie* (London: Sphere, 1977)

_____, *Onassis* (New York: Avon, 1968)

Galella, Ron, *Jacqueline* (New York: Sheed and Ward, Inc., 1974)

Gallagher, Mary, *My Life with Jacqueline Kennedy* (New York: David McKay Company, Inc., 1969)

Gillion, Stephen, *The Kennedy Assassination--24 Hours After* (New York: Basic Books, 2010)

Gitlin, Todd, *The Sixties: Years of Hope, Days of Rage* (Toronto: Bantam Books, 1987)

Goodwin, Doris Kearns, *Lyndon Johnson and the American Dream* (New York: St. Martin's Griffin, 1976)

_____, *The Fitzgeralds and the Kennedys: An American Saga* (New York: Simon & Schuster, 1987)

Gordon, Meryl, *Bunny Mellon* (New York: Grand Central Publishing, 2017)

Gould, Jonathan, *Can't Buy Me Love: The Beatles, Britain, and America* (New York: Harmony Books, 2007)

Graham, Katharine, *Personal History* (New York: Vintage Books, 1998)

Guthman, Edwin, *We Band of Brothers,* (New York: Harper & Row, 1971)

Guthrie, Lee, *The Price of the Pedestal* (New York: Drake Publishers, 1978)

Halberstam, David, *The Best and the Brightest* (New York: Ballantine Books, 1969)

_____, *The Powers That Be* (Champaign: University of Illinois Press, 2000)

Hall, Gordon Lagley with Ann Pinchot, *Jacqueline Kennedy* (New York: Signet, 1966)

Hamilton, Edith, *The Greek Way* (New York: W.W. Norton & Company, 1930)

Hannan, Archbishop Philip, *The Archbishop Wore Combat Boots*, (Huntington, Indiana: One Sunday Visitor, 2010)

Harding, Robert T. with A.L. Holmes, *Jacqueline Kennedy,* (New York: Encyclopedia Enterprises, Inc., 1966)

Harris, Bill, *The First Ladies Fact Book* (New York: Black Dog and Leventhal Publishers, Inc., 2005)

Heymann, C. David, *American Legacy* (New York: Atria Books, 2007)

_____, *Bobby and Jackie* (New York: Atria Books, 2009)

_____, *A Woman Called Jackie* (New York: Carol Communications, 1989)

_____, *RFK* (New York: Penguin Putnam, Inc., 1998)

Hill, Clint with Lisa McCubbin, *Five Days in November* (New York: Gallery Books, 2013)

_____, *Five Presidents* (New York: Gallery Books, 2016)

_____, *Mrs. Kennedy and Me* (New York: Gallery Books, 2012)

Hilty, James W., *Robert Kennedy Brother Protector* (Philadelphia: Temple University Press, 1997)

Hunt, Amber with David Batcher, *Kennedy Wives: Triumph and Tragedy in America's Most Public Family* (Guilford, CT: Lyons Press, 2015)

Ioannidis, Paul J., *Destiny Prevails* (New York: Significance Press, 2015)

Johnson, Lady Bird, *A White House Diary* (New York: Holt, Rinehart and Winston, 1970)

Kaiser, Charles, *1968 in America* (New York: Grove Press, 1988)

Kantor, Michael and Maslon, Laurence, *Broadway: The American Musical* (Bluefinch Press, New York, 2004)

Kennedy, Caroline, *The Best-Loved Poems of Jacqueline Kennedy Onassis* (New York: Hyperion, 2001)

Kennedy, Jacqueline, *Historic Conversations on Life with John F. Kennedy—Interviews with Arthur M. Schlesinger, Jr., 1964* (New York: Hyperion, 2011)

Kennedy, Rose Fitzgerald, *Times to Remember* (New York: Doubleday, 1975)

Keogh, Pamela Clarke, *Jackie Style* (New York: HarperCollins, 2001)

Klein, Edward, *Just Jackie* (New York: Ballantine Books, 1998)

Kramer, Freda, *Jackie* (New York: Grosset & Dunlap, Inc., 1975)

Lawliss, Charles with the Bettmann Archive, *Jacqueline Kennedy Onassis* (North Dighton, Iowa: JG Press, 1994)

Leaming, Barbara, *Jacqueline Bouvier Kennedy Onassis* (New York: Thomas Dunne Books, 2014)

Leigh, Wendy, *True Grace: The Life and Times of an American Princess* (New York: Thomas Dunne Books, 2007)

Life Magazine, *Remembering Jackie* (New York: Warner Books, 1994)

Lincoln, Evelyn, *My Twelve Years with John F. Kennedy* (David McKay Co., 2000)

Maier, Thomas, *The Kennedys* (New York: Basic Books, 2003)

Manchester, William, *Controversy* (New York: Little, Brown and Company, 1976)

_____, *Death of a President* (New York: Harper & Row, 1967)

Matthews Chris, *A Raging Spirit* (New York: Simon & Schuster, 2017)

McKeon, Kathy, *Jackie's Girl* (New York: Gallery Books, 2017)

McLaughlin, Malcolm, *The Long Hot Summer of 1967: Urban Rebellion in America* (Palgrave Macmillan, 2014)

McNamara, Robert S., *In Retrospect* (New York: Times Books, 1995)

Monkman, Betty, *The White House* (Washington: White House Historical Association, 2000)

Moon, Vicky, *The Private Passion of Jackie Kennedy Onassis* (New York: Harper Design, 2004)

Mulvaney, Jay, *Diana & Jackie* (New York: St. Martin's Press, 2002)

Newman, Bruce, *Don't Come Back Until You Find It* (New York: Beaufort Books, 2006)

Nickles, Liz and Savita Iyer, *Brandstorm* (New York: Palgrave Macmillan, 2012)

Peters, Charles, *Lyndon B. Johnson* (New York: Times Books, 2010)

Polsky, Richard, *I Bought Andy Warhol* (New York and London: Bloomsbury Publishing, 2003)

Porter, Darwin, *Brando Unzipped* (New York: Blood Moon Productions, 2006)

Posner, Gerald, *Case Closed* (New York: Random House, 1993)

Post, Gunilla Von, *Love, Jack* (New York: Crown, 1997)

Pottker, Jan, *Janet and Jackie* (New York: St. Martin's Press, 2001)

Reich, Cary, *Financier, The Biography of Andre Meyer* (New York: John Wiley & Sons, 1983)

Russell, Jan Jarboe, *Lady Bird: A Biography of Mrs. Johnson* (New York: Scribner, 1999)

Sabato, Larry, *The Kennedy Half-Century* (New York: Bloomsbury, 2013)

Schlesinger, Arthur, *Journals 1952–2000* (New York: Penguin, 2007)

_____, *Robert Kennedy and His Times*, (New York: First Mariner Books, 1978)

Sgubin, Marta, *Cooking for Madam* (New York: Scribner, 1998)

Shaw, Maud, *White House Nannie* (New York: Signet Books, 1965)

Shesol, Jeff, *Mutual Contempt* (New York: W.W. Norton & Company, 1997)

Simon, Carly, *Touched by the Sun* (New York: Farrar, Straus and Giroux, 2019)

Smith, Jeffrey K., *Bad Blood: Lyndon B. Johnson, Robert F. Kennedy, and the Tumultuous 1960s* (Bloomington, Indiana: Author House, 2010)

Smith, Sally Bedell, *Grace and Power* (New York: Random House 2004)

Sotheby's, *The Estate of Jacqueline Kennedy Onassis* (New York: Sotheby's, 1996)

Spoto, Donald, *Jacqueline Bouvier Onassis: A Life* (New York: St. Martin's Press, 2000)

Swanson, James, *End of Days* (New York: William Morrow, 2013)

Taraborrelli, J. Randy, *After Camelot: A Personal History of the Kennedy Family, 1968 to the Present)* (New York: Rose Books, 2000)

_____, *Jackie, Ethel, Joan* (New York: Rose Books, 2000)

_____, *Jackie, Janet and Lee*, (New York: St. Martin's Press, 2018)

Teitelman, Robert, *Bloodsport: When Ruthless Dealmakers, Shrewd Ideologues, and Brawling Lawyers Toppled the Corporate Establishment* (New York: PublicAffairs, 2016)

Thayer, Mary Van Rensselaer, *Jacqueline Bouvier Kennedy* (Garden City, NY: Doubleday & Company, Inc., 1961)

Thomas, Evan, *Robert Kennedy* (New York: Simon & Schuster, 2000)

Tracy, Kathleen, *The Everything Jacqueline Kennedy Onassis Book: A Portrait of an American Icon,* (Avon, MA: Adams Media, 2008)

Tye, Larry, *Bobby Kennedy: The Making of a Liberal Icon* (New York: Random House, 2016)

Bibliography

Unger, Irwin and Debbie Unger (editors), *The Times Were A "Changin'"* (New York: Three Rivers Press, 1998)

Vidal, Gore, *Palimpsest* (New York: Random House, 1995)

Warhol, Andy with Pat Hacket, *Popism* (Orlando: Harcourt Books, 1980)

West, J.B., *Upstairs at the White House: My Life with the First Ladies* (New York: Coward, McCann & Geoghegan, Inc., 1973)

West, Naomi and Catherine Wilson, *Jackie Handbook* (MQ Publications)

Whitcomb, John and Claire Whitcomb, *Real Life at the White House* (New York: Routledge, 2000)

White, Mark, *Kennedy* (London: Bloomsbury Academic, 2013)

White, Theodore, *In Search of History* (New York: Warner Books, 1978)

Interviews

Cottingham, Sally Fay (daughter of Paul "Red" Fay)

Gallagher, Mary (assistant to Jacqueline Kennedy)

Haley, Matthew (Bonham's Auction House)

Hill, Clint (retired Secret Service agent)

Holloway, Donald (Ford Museum)

Polsky, Richard (Andy Warhol appraiser)

Newspaper/Magazine Articles

Alexander, Ron, "The Evening Hours," *New York Times*, February 10, 1984

Anthony, Carl Sferrazza, "Love, Jackie," *American Heritage*, September 1994, Volume 45, Issue 5

_____, "This Was Jackie Kennedy's Incredible Mark in History," *Reader's Digest*, June 2001

Bainbridge, John, "Garbo Ignores Others' Opinions," *Life*, January 24, 1955

Barron, James, "Jim Bishop, a Columnist, Dies; Author of 21 Books," Associated Press, July 28, 1987 (as published in *The New York Times*)

Bilyeau, Nancy, "Jackie Kennedy's Third Act," *Town and Country*, August 18, 2017

219

Blasberg, Derek, "Ron Galella on the Paparazzi's Golden Era and Why Marlon Brando Broke His Jaw," *Vanity Fair*, November 19, 2015

Brown, Emma, "John Carl Warnecke Dies at 91, Designed Kennedy Gravesite," *Washington Post*, April 23, 2010

Clarke, Thurston, "A Death in the Family," *Vanity Fair*, July 1, 2013

————, "'It Will Not Be Lyndon': Why JFK Wanted to Drop LBJ for Reelection," *Daily Beast*, November 11, 2013

Collins, Amy Fine, "It Had to Be Kenneth," *Vanity Fair*, May 14, 2013

Contrera, Jessica, "'How Could You?' The Day Jackie Kennedy Became Jackie Onassis," *Washington Post*, October 20, 2018

Corliss, Richard, "That Old Feeling: Paar Excellence," *Time*, January 30, 2004

Cotliar, Sharon, "The Private Jackie," *People*, October 10, 2011

Craighill, Peyton M., "Poll: 64 Percent Believe Broader Plot Killed Kennedy," *Washington Post*, November 20, 2013

Dallek, Robert, "How Not to End Another President's War," *The New York Times*, March 12, 2009

Dinter, Charlotte, "Too Soon for Love?" *Photoplay*, February 1965

Erlanger, Steven, "Letters from Jacqueline Kennedy to the Man She Didn't Marry," *The New York Times*, February 8, 2017

Georgetown Voice Staff, "The Kennedys' Jesuit," January 15, 2004

Grice, Elizabeth, "Aristotle Onassis's Yacht Was a Floating Xanadu That Seduced Them All," *The Telegraph*, July 5, 2013

Healy, Paul, "Jackie's Actions in Book Row Show 'Steel Beneath Velvet,'" *The Shreveport Times*, December 25, 1966

Horyn, Cathy, "Jacqueline Kennedy's Smart Pink Suit, Preserved in Memory and Kept Out of View," *The New York Times*, November 14, 2013

"Jackie in Cambodia," *Life*, November 17, 1967

Jenkins, Dan, "Life with the Jax Pack," *Sports Illustrated*, July 10, 1967

"Johnson and Jackie in '64," *Ladies Home Companion*, Volume II, Number 6, May 1964

Jones, Marion, "What Will Happen to Jackie and Her Children Now?" *Modern Screen*, Aug. 1968

Kaese, Diane S. and Michael F. Lynch, "Marble in (and Around) the City: Its Origins and Use in Historic New York Buildings," *Common Bond*, Autumn 2008

Kashner, Sam, "A Clash of Camelots," *Vanity Fair*, August 2009

Kelly, John, "Next Up in the 'Blame Nixon?' Game: Jackie Kennedy's Plaques," *Washington Post*, March 21, 2010

Kennedy, Carol, "Jackie Near Tears as Queen Dedicates Kennedy Memorial," *Saskatoon Star-Phoenix*, May 15, 1965

Kennedy, Jacqueline, "It Is Nearly a Year Since He Has Been Gone," *Look*, November 17, 1964

_____, "How He Really Was," *Life*, May 29, 1964

"Kennedys to Hold Annual Turkey Dinner," *Gettysburg Times*, November 27, 1963 (wire story)

Kirkpatrick, Nick and Katie Mettler, "Reflecting on RFK's 200-Mile Funeral Train," *Washington Post*, June 1, 2018

Kosner, Edward, "Take Everything You Need, Baby," *Newsweek*, April 15, 1968

Kytell, Stacy, "Will Bobby Stop Jackie From Marrying Lord Harlech?" *Modern Screen*, March 1968

Leaming, Barbara, "The Winter of Her Despair," *Vanity Fair*, October 2014

Lilly, Doris, "The Men Surrounding Jacqueline Kennedy." *Cosmopolitan*, June 1968

Lopez, Steve, "The Busboy Who Cradled a Dying RFK Has Finally Stepped Out of the Past," *Los Angeles Times*, August 29, 2015

Lowell Sun, "Bullfight Too Much for Jackie," April 22, 1966

Maiorano, Ronald, "Mrs. Kennedy Rents Secluded L.I. Weekend Home," *The New York Times*, October 22, 1964

Margolick, David, "Robert F. Kennedy's Final Flight: The Storied Journey of the Ride from California to New York," *Washington Post*, June 3, 2018

Malnic, Eric, "Alan Jay Lerner, Lyricist of 'My Fair Lady,' Dies at 67," *Los Angeles Times,* June 15, 1986

McFadden, Robert D., "Death of a First Lady; Jacqueline Kennedy Onassis Dies of Cancer at 64," *The New York Times,* May 20, 1994

McNeil Liz, "Jackie Kennedy: New Details of Her Heartbreak," *People,* November 13, 2013

"Oleg Cassini Remembered," *British Vogue,* March 20, 2006

O'Neil, Paul, "Jackie's Wedding," *Life,* November 1, 1968

Parsons, Michael, "Jackie Kennedy and the Costello Family," *The Irish Times,* June 2, 2014

"Patrick Kennedy, Sister Buried Near Slain Father at Arlington," *Rome News Tribune,* December 5, 1963

Robert, Linda, "The Part Ted Kennedy Played in Jackie's New Romance!" *Modern Screen,* November 1968

Rogers, Patrick and Christina Butan, "Read the Wrenching Letter Jackie Kennedy Wrote to RFK's Wife Ethel after His Death 50 Years Ago," *People*, June 5, 2018

Rowell, David, "45 Years after Death, Recalling Robert Kennedy's Funeral Train," *Washington Post,* June 6, 2013

Sawer, Patrick, "Letters Reveal Why Jackie Kennedy Turned Down British Aristocrat to Marry Greek Shipping Tycoon Aristotle Onassis Instead," *The Telegraph,* February 9, 2017

Shuster, Alvin, "'Very Happy' Mrs. Kennedy and Onassis Married," *The New York Times*, October 21, 1968

Seely, Katherine, "John F. Kennedy Jr., Heir to a Formidable Dynasty," *The New York Times*, July 19, 1999

Selter, Emily, "Up for Auction: Six Portraits of Jackie Kennedy Painted by Warhol after JFK's Assassination," *Town and Country,* November 10, 2016

"Seven Days in April," *Newsweek,* April 15, 1968

Schumach, Murray, "World Bids Adieu to a Violent Year," *The New York Times*, January 1, 1968

Stanfill, Francesca, "The Private Jackie," *Vanity Fair*, November 21, 1995

Swanson, James L., "The JFK Christmas Card That Was Never Sent," *Smithsonian*, January 2014

"The Warren Commission's Report," *The New York Times*, September 28, 1964

Weaver, Matthew, "Jackie Kennedy Rejected British Suitor's Marriage Proposal, Letters Reveal," *The Guardian*, February 10, 2017

Worthington, Christina, "They Spent a Fortune on Beads, but Took Home the American Dream," *The Independent*, April 30, 1996

Television Programs/Film/Video

Award ceremony for Rufus Youngblood and Clint Hill. (U.S. Government film, December 3, 1963)

Secret Lives: Jackie. Directed by Charles Furneaux. UK: Barraclough Carey Productions, 1995

"Secret Service Agent #9," *60 Minutes*, CBS News, December 7, 1975

Other

ABC News broadcast, February 8, 2008

American Public Media, "The President is Calling – Transcript of December 7, 1963, LBJ call to Jackie"

Bennett Cerf transcript, Columbia University Libraries Oral History Research Office, session 15, 704

CarlAnthonyonline, "Jackie Kennedy's Last White House Days and What She Found in JFK's Desk"

CBS News coverage, November 23, 1963

Frank Mankiewicz, Oral History Interview—RFK #5, John F. Kennedy Library, October 2, 1969

Gallup Survey: The Most Admired Men and Women, 1948–1998

Gem Select, "Jackie O's Jewelry," story of Jacqueline Kennedy's Kunzite Ring

Jackie's oral history conducted by Joe B. Frantz for the LBJ Library, January 11, 1974, Tape 1 of 2

Jackie

John F. Kennedy Presidential Library, Runnymede Files, Digital Identifier: JBKOPP-SF075-007-p0001

McSorley, Richard, "Kennedy Letters to McSorley Released," Hoya.com, November 18, 2003

NASA.gov, "Apollo Flight Journal – Apollo 7 – Day 7 (preliminary)"

Nixon Foundation

TheVietnamWar.info, "1965-1973, United States Year by Year in Vietnam"

TJ & John, "Garbo Forever," GarboForever.com, 2005

University of California Santa Barbara, The American Presidency Project

"Unseen Jackie Kennedy Letters to the British Aristocrat Revealed for First Time at Bonhams Harlech Sale," Bonhams.com (press release, March 29, 2017)

U.S. Capitol, Architect of the Capitol, "The Catafalque"

Endnotes

Prologue

1   Edward Klein, *Just Jackie*, 159
2   Frank Brady, *Onassis*, 160
3   Ibid.
4   Peter Evans, Ari: *The Life and Times of Aristotle Socrates Onassis*, 164
5   Brady, 162
6   Clint Hill with Lisa McCubbin, *Mrs. Kennedy and Me*, 72
7   Hill with McCubbin, 77
8   Barbara Leaming, *Jacqueline Bouvier Kennedy Onassis*, 121
9   Hill with McCubbin, 250
10 Ibid., 255
11 Elizabeth Grice, "Aristotle Onassis's Yacht Was a Floating Xanadu That Seduced Them All"
12 Ben Bradlee, *Conversations with Kennedy*, 219
13 Brady, 164
14 Sarah Bradford, *America's Queen*, 255
15 Brady, 164
16 Bradford, 255
17 Brady, 166
18 Bradlee, 219
19 William Manchester, *The Death of a President*, 9
20 Bradlee, 219
21 Manchester, *The Death of a President*, 10
22 Michael Beschloss, *Presidential Courage*, 278
23 Brady, 167
24 Manchester, *The Death of a President*, 555
25 Brady, 167

Chapter One: The Long, Dark Winter

1   Lady Bird Johnson, *A White House Diary*, 11
2   Ibid.
3   Ibid.
4   Ibid., 12
5   Theodore White, *In Search of History*, 520
6   Ibid., 516
7   Manchester, *The Death of a President*, 347
8   Leaming, 144
9   White, 520
10 Ibid.
11 Ibid., 523
12 Ibid., 524
13 J. Randy Taraborrelli, *After Camelot: A Personal History of the Kennedy Family, 1968 to the Present*, xviii
14 Liz Nickles and Savita Iyer, *Brandstorm*, 90
15 Thurston Clarke, *JFK's Last Hundred Days*, 361
16 Beschloss, *Reaching for Glory*, 12
17 Bradford, 286
18 Ibid.

Jackie

19 Hill with McCubbin, 327

20 Manchester, *The Death of a President*, 642

21 "Patrick Kennedy, Sister Buried Near Slain Father at Arlington"

22 Leaming, 152

23 Donald Spoto, *Jacqueline Bouvier Onassis: A Life*, 207

24 Manchester, *The Death of a President*, p. 417

25 Robert Caro, *The Years of Lyndon Johnson—The Passage of Power,* 500

26 Spoto, 41

27 John Whitcomb and Claire Whitcomb, *Real Life at the White House*, 348

28 Paul F. Boller Jr., *Presidential Wives*, 363

29 Ibid.

30 Betty Monkman, *The White House*, 234

31 Ibid.

32 Ibid.

33 Ibid., 238

34 Bradford, 287

35 Maud Shaw, *White House Nannie*, 101

36 Clint Hill interview

37 American Public Media, "The President is Calling – transcript of December 7, 1963, LBJ call to Jackie"

38 Hill with McCubbin, 330

39 Bill Adler, *The Eloquent Jacqueline Onassis: A Portrait in Her Own Words*, 109

40 Bradlee, *A Good Life*, 262

41 Leaming,166

42 Mary Gallagher, *My Life with Jacqueline Kennedy*, 339

43 Ibid., 340

44 "Secret Lives" documentary

45 Manchester, *The Death of a President*, 644

46 CBS News coverage, November 23, 1963

47 Christopher Andersen, *The Good Son*, 57

48 Gallagher, 365

49 Leaming, 155

50 Arthur Schlesinger, *Robert Kennedy and His Times*, 613

51 Clint Hill interview

52 Beschloss, 18

53 J. Randy Taraborrelli, *Jackie, Ethel, Joan*, 265

54 Andersen, *The Good Son*, 56

55 Pamela Clarke Keogh, *Jackie Style*, 146

56 Shaw, 103

57 Taraborrelli, *Jackie, Ethel, Joan*, 274

58 Ibid.

59 James Barron, "Jim Bishop, a Columnist, Dies; Author of 21 Books"

60 Sam Kashner, "A Clash of Camelots"

61 Ibid.

62 Manchester, *Controversy*, 6

63 Ibid., 3

64 Shaw, 105

65 Ibid., 107

66 Ibid., 109

67 Ibid.

68 Taraborrelli, *Jackie, Ethel, Joan*, 273

69 Bill Harris, *The First Ladies Fact Book*, 562

70 Leaming, 158

71 Ibid., 160

72 Evan Thomas, *Robert Kennedy*, 285

73 C. David Heymann, *Bobby and Jackie: A Love Story*, 77

74 Thomas, 285

75 Andersen, *Jackie After Jack*, 111

76 Taraborrelli, *Jackie, Ethel, Joan*, 278

77 United Press International Report, January 28, 1964

78 Clint Hill interview

79 Jacqueline Kennedy, *Historic Conversations on Life with John F. Kennedy*, xxiv

80 Ibid., xii

81 Chris Matthews, *A Raging Spirit*, 201

82 Leaming, 161

83 Leaming, "The Winter of Her Despair," *Vanity Fair*, October 2014

84 Jacqueline Kennedy, *Historic Conversations on Life with John F. Kennedy*, xv

85 Thomas, 285
86 Ibid.
87 Edith Hamilton, *The Greek Way*, 146
88 Ibid., 144
89 Ibid.
90 Hamilton, 145
91 Manchester, *Controversy*, 11
92 Ibid.
93 Leaming, 166
94 Ibid., 167
95 Richard McSorley, "Kennedy Letters to McSorley Released"
96 Leaming, 166
97 Manchester, *Controversy*, 12
98 Ibid.
99 Leaming, 169
100 Ibid.
101 Ibid.
102 Bradford, 300
103 Ibid., 295
104 Jacqueline Kennedy, *Historic Conversations on Life with John F. Kennedy*, xx
105 Ibid., 281

Chapter Two: Farewell to All That
1 Adler, 103
2 Carl Sferrazza Anthony, *As We Remember Her*, 218
3 Leaming, 174
4 Robert Dallek, *Flawed Giant: Lyndon Johnson and His Times*, 135
5 Thomas, 295
6 Charles Peters, *Lyndon B. Johnson*, 95
7 *The New York Times*, July 7, 1964, p. 1
8 Gallagher, 380
9 Leaming, 177
10 Andersen, *The Good Son*, 61
11 Leaming, 182
12 Schlesinger, 665
13 Manchester, *Controversy*, 13
14 Bishop, xvi
15 Ibid.
16 "The Warren Commission's Report," *The New York Times*, September 28, 1964

17 Bradford, 302
18 Anthony Lewis, *The New York Times*, September 28, 1964
19 Manchester, *The Death of a President*, 407
20 Bradford, 285
21 Leaming, 188
22 Doris Kearns Goodwin, *Lyndon Johnson and the American Dream*, 170
23 Robert Caro, *The Years of Lyndon Johnson—Means of Ascent*, xxxi
24 Jackie's oral history conducted by Joe B. Frantz for the LBJ Library, January 11, 1974, Tape 1 of 2
25 Jacqueline Kennedy, "It Is Nearly a Year Since He Has Been Gone"
26 Ibid.
27 Ibid.
28 Bradford, 238
29 J. Randy Taraborrelli, *Jackie, Janet and Lee*, 145
30 Anthony, *As We Remember Her*, 220
31 Bradford, 305
32 Ronald Maiorano, "Mrs. Kennedy Rents Secluded L.I. Weekend Home"
33 Henry Brandon, *Special Relationship: A Foreign Correspondents's Memoirs from Roosevelt to Reagan*, 201

Chapter Three: Keeper of the Flame
1 Thomas Maier, *The Kennedys*, 479
2 Ibid.
3 Marta Sgubin, *Cooking for Madam*, 26
4 Kathy McKeon, *Jackie's Girl*, 25
5 Sgubin, 159
6 Charlotte Dinter, "Too Soon for Love?" 87
7 Emily Selter, "Up for Auction: Six Portraits of Jackie Kennedy Painted By Warhol After JFK's Assassination"
8 Spoto, 230
9 Ibid., 231
10 Ibid., 231
11 Dinter
12 Adler, 129

13 McKeon, 144
14 Pamela Clarke Keogh, *Jackie Style*, 148
15 Andersen, *The Good Son*, 79
16 Sotheby's: *The Estate of Jacqueline Kennedy Onassis*, 12
17 Keogh, 152
18 Ibid., 149
19 Anthony, 141
20 Sotheby's, 24
21 Adler, 49
22 Andersen, *The Good Son*, 78
23 Ibid., 80
24 Sotheby's, 168
25 Andersen, *The Good Son*, 79
26 Sotheby's, 211
27 Keogh, 151
28 Andersen, *The Good Son*, 78
29 Ibid., 79
30 Keogh, 151
31 Ibid., 155
32 Ibid., 153
33 Ibid., 154
34 Anthony, 216
35 Leaming, 193
36 John F. Kennedy Presidential Library, Runnymede Files, Digital Identifier: JBKOPP-SF075-007-p0001
37 Shaw, 126
38 Carl Sferrazza Anthony, "Love Jackie," *American Heritage*, September 1994, Volume 45, Issue 5

Chapter Four: Phoenix
1 Bradford, 309
2 Ibid., 310
3 Ibid., 309
4 Ibid., 308
5 Shaw, 9
6 Bradford, 307
7 Manchester, *Look*, Jan. 24, 1967, 65
8 Manchester, *Controversy*, 14
9 Anthony, 228
10 Brady, 128
11 Bradford, 306
12 Keogh, 159

13 Ibid.
14 Klein, 128
15 Keogh, 160
16 Ibid., 155
17 Ibid., 156
18 Ibid.
19 Ibid., 158
20 Anthony, 111
21 Bradford, 288
22 Cary Reich, *Financier, The Biography of André Meyer*, 18
23 Bradford, 313
24 Reich, 83
25 Robert Teitelman, *Bloodsport: When Ruthless Dealmakers, Shrewd Ideologues, and Brawling Lawyers Toppled the Corporate Establishment*, 47
26 Reich, 351
27 Bradford, 313
28 Heymann, *Bobby and Jackie: A Love Story*, 84
29 Vicky Moon, *The Private Passion of Jackie Kennedy Onassis*, 162
30 Bradford, 312
31 Ibid.
32 McKeon, 161
33 Bennett Cerf transcript, Columbia University Libraries Oral History Research Office, session 15, 704

Chapter Five: Jet-Setter
1 Manchester, Controversy, 11
2 Archbishop Philip Hannan, *The Archbishop Wore Combat Boots*, 26
3 Keogh, 17
4 Bradford, 378
5 Leaming, 207
6 Manchester, Controversy, 14
7 Ibid., 15
8 Ibid.
9 *People*, October 10, 2011, 60
10 Anthony, 231
11 McKeon, 25

12 Christina Worthington, "They Spent a Fortune on Beads, but Took Home the American Dream"
13 Keogh, 166
14 Amber Hunt and David Batcher, *Kennedy Wives: Triumph and Tragedy in America's Most Public Family*, 172
15 Keogh, 18
16 Wendy Leigh, *True Grace: The Life and Times of an American Princess*, 29
17 Gore Vidal, *Palimpsest*, 374
18 Leigh, 32
19 Lowell Sun, "Bullfight Too Much for Jackie," April 22, 1966, 6
20 Naomi West and Catherine Wilson, *Jackie Handbook*, 276
21 Klein, 127
22 Bradford, 315
23 Klein, 130
24 Bradford, 314
25 Adler, 224

Chapter Six: Steel Beneath Velvet
1 Bradford, 316
2 Ibid.
3 Manchester, *Controversy*, 25
4 Ibid., 27
5 Ibid., 29
6 Ibid.
7 Ibid., 30
8 Ibid., 33
9 Ibid., 39
10 Ibid.
11 Ibid., 32
12 Leaming 204
13 Schlesinger, 762
14 Manchester, *Controversy*, 30
15 Ibid., 43
16 David Halberstam, *The Powers That Be*, 407
17 Leaming, 209
18 Robert S. McNamara, *In Retrospect*, 257
19 Leaming, 211
20 Christopher Andersen, *Sweet Caroline*, 128

21 Adler, 90
22 Kashner
23 Manchester, *Controversy*, 58
24 Ibid., 60
25 Ibid., 63
26 Leaming, 213
27 Larry Sabato, *The Kennedy Half-Century*, 287
28 Leaming, 217
29 Manchester, *Controversy*, 66

Chapter Seven: The Secret Burial
1 Leaming, 218
2 Ibid.
3 Manchester, *Controversy*, 69
4 Ibid., 70
5 Ibid., 72
6 Ibid.
7 Ibid.
8 Derek Blasberg, "Ron Galella on the Paparazzi's Golden Era and Why Marlon Brando Broke His Jaw"
9 Keogh, 185
10 Ibid., 183
11 McKeon, 59
12 Ibid., 60
13 Maier, 483
14 Eric Foner, *Reconstruction: America's Unfinished Revolution, 1863–1877*, 32
15 Brady, 168
16 Willi Frischauer, *Onassis*, 256
17 Taraborrelli, *Jackie, Janet and Lee*, 263
18 Ibid., 31
19 Tina Santi Flaherty, *What Jackie Taught Us*, 12
20 McKeon
21 Maier, 483
22 C. David Heymann, *A Woman Called Jackie*, 471-2

Chapter Eight: Marriage Proposal
1 Bradford, 324
2 Ibid.
3 Leaming, 228

4 Lester David and Jhan Robbins, *Jackie & Ari*, 70

5 Bradford, 326

6 David and Robbins, 70

7 David P. Chandler, *The Tragedy of Cambodian History: Politics, War and Revolutions since 1945*, 136-7

8 Keogh, 159

9 Leaming, 233

10 Bradford, 325

11 "Jackie in Cambodia," *Life*, November 17, 1967, 98

12 Anthony, 233

13 Andersen, *The Good Son*, 111

14 Vincent Bugliosi, *Reclaiming History*, 1190

15 Thomas, 333

16 Jonathan Gould, *Can't Buy Me Love: The Beatles, Britain, and America*, 250

17 Jeff Shesol, *Mutual Contempt*, 215

18 Ibid., 331

19 Thomas, 332

20 Brady, 165

Chapter Nine: Again

1 Leaming, 234

2 Spoto, 255

3 Stacey Kytell, "Will Bobby Stop Jackie from Marrying Lord Harlech?" *Modern Screen*, March 1968, 44

4 "Unseen Jackie Kennedy Letters to the British Aristocrat Revealed for First Time at Bonhams Harlech Sale" (press release, March 29, 2017)

5 Manchester, *The Death of a President*, 515

6 Ibid., 464.

7 Matthew Weaver, "Jackie Kennedy Rejected British Suitor's Marriage Proposal, Letters Reveal," *The Guardian*, February 10, 2017

8 Steven Erlanger, "Letters From Jacqueline Kennedy to the Man She Didn't Marry"

9 Spoto, 258

10 Andersen, *Jackie After Jack*, 163

11 Heymann, *A Woman Called Jackie*, 477

12 Ibid.

13 Andersen, *The Good Son*, 111

14 Spoto, 234

15 Manchester, *The Death of a President*, 387

16 Caro, *The Years of Lyndon Johnson: The Passage of Power*, xiii

17 Schlesinger, *Journals*, 286

18 Kosner, *Newsweek*, April 15, 1968, 31

19 McKeon, 192

20 Leaming, 237

21 Keogh, 163

22 Schlesinger, 878

23 Frank Mankiewicz, *Oral History Interview – RFK #5*, John F. Kennedy Library, October 2, 1969

24 David and Robbins, 71

25 Bradford, 330

26 Paul J. Ioannidis, *Destiny Prevails*, 186

27 Larry Tye, *Bobby Kennedy: The Making of a Liberal Icon*, 426

28 Charles Kaiser, *1968 in America*, 186

29 Andersen, *The Good Son*, 113

30 Peter Collier and David Horowitz, *The Kennedys: An American Drama*, 331

31 Leaming, 240

32 Andersen, *The Good Son*, 119

33 Ibid.

34 Keogh, 163

35 David Margolick, "Robert F. Kennedy's Final Flight: The Storied Journey of the Ride from California to New York"

36 McKeon, 185

37 Ibid.

38 Andersen, *The Good Son*, 120

39 Lady Bird Johnson, *A White House Diary*, 684

40 Margolick

41 Nick Kirkpatrick and Katie Mettler, "Reflecting on RFK's 200-Mile Funeral Train"

42 Clint Hill with Lisa McCubbin, *Five Presidents*, 294; author interview

43   Andersen, *The Good Son*, 122
44   Patrick Rogers and Christina Butan, "Read the Wrenching Letter Jackie Kennedy Wrote to RFK's Wife Ethel after His Death 50 Years Ago"
45   Brady, 173
46   Jessica Contrera, "'How Could You?' The Day Jackie Kennedy Became Jackie Onassis"
47   Frischauer, 206

Chapter Ten: Skorpios
1   Frischauer, 268
2   Brady, 172
3   Ibid.
4   Peter Evans, *Nemesis*, 217
5   Ibid., 218
6   Heymann, *A Woman Called Jackie*, 486
7   David and Robbins, 73
8   Andersen, *The Good Son*, 117
9   Ibid., 141
10 Katharine Graham, *Personal History*, 412
11 Marion Jones, "What Will Happen to Jackie and Her Children Now?" *Modern Screen*, August 1968
12 Frischauer, 268
13 Taraborrelli, *Jackie, Ethel & Joan*, 366
14 Evans, 222
15 Heymann, *A Woman Called Jackie*, 491
16 Patrick Sawer, "Letters Reveal Why Jackie Kennedy Turned Down British Aristocrat to Marry Greek Shipping Tycoon Aristotle Onassis Instead," *The Telegraph*, February 9, 2017
17 *Modern Screen*, November 1968, 44
18 Frischauer, 272
19 Ibid., 270
20 Robert D. McFadden, "Death of a First Lady; Jacqueline Kennedy Onassis Dies of Cancer at 64"
21 Andersen, *The Good Son*, 131
22 Frischauer, 266
23 Jan Pottker, *Janet and Jackie*, 265
24 Ibid.
25 Anthony, 241
26 Ibid., 242
27 Pottker, 268
28 "Apollo Flight Journal – Apollo 7 – Day 7"
29 Joseph A. Califano Jr., *The Triumph & Tragedy of Lyndon Johnson*, 295
30 Boller, 369
31 Paul O'Neil, "Jackie's Wedding," 21
32 Adler, *America's First Ladies*, 197
33 Frischauer, 271
34 Francesca Stanfill, "The Private Jackie," *Vanity Fair*, November 21, 1995
35 Brady,180
36 Andersen, *Jackie After Jack*, 203
37 Brady, 181
38 Alvin Shuster, "'Very Happy' Mrs. Kennedy and Onassis Married," 1